Parables of Geoff

Stories and Anecdotes of Geoffrey John Wallace

I0186491

Geoff in the Navy (approx. 1944)

Geoff Notes: *If you put two bottle of water in front of the average man, it will be too much for him to drink. He will complain about being bloated and that he could not possibly drink it all.*

But if you put two bottles of beer in front of him, no problem. Down it goes! Do you ever wonder why?

The Moving Finger writes; and, having writ,
Moves on: nor all thy Piety nor Wit
Shall lure it back to cancel half a Line,
Nor all thy Tears wash out a Word of it.

Parables of Geoff
Stories and Anecdotes of Geoffrey John Wallace

Parables of Geoff

Stories and Anecdotes of Geoffrey John Wallace

Into each life a little rain must fall. It is fair to say that the Wallace family of Duncan, his wife Annette, and the children, Robert, Reginald, Colin and Geoff had somewhat of a torrent fall upon their heads.

The father survived the trenches of World War One, allowing him to father four boys. All four boys then go to war, all four survive World War Two, despite two of them being taken prisoner, with Reginald doing the almost impossible by surviving the Japanese and seeing the mushroom cloud over Hiroshima.

This is the tale of one of the sons, Geoffrey John Wallace, born 10 Dec 1925, deceased 14 August 2016.

The Kids, Girraween Grove circa 1975
From Left: Julie, Trish, Mick, Sue and Greg

Geoff around the time of entering the navy.
Approx: 1942-43
Note: Full head of hair!

"My crown is in my heart, not on my head; not decked with diamonds and Indian stones, nor to be seen: my crown is called content, a crown it is that seldom kings enjoy."
William Shakespeare

The Pre-War Junkers G.31 trimotor that was extensively used to move around vegetables for Geoff in New Guinea. Based at Goroka and flown by Barry Gibbes. The plane that built New Guinea.

Flying in the Highlands of New Guinea was a perilous business at the best of times, but on this particular storm-swept night, flying by landmarks you could barely see, Geoff Wallace was concerned. Yes, he had the best pilot in all New Guinea, Bobby Gibbes, the legendary founder of Gibbes Sepik Airways. But the plane was old, the weather foul, and visibility was next to nothing.

"Do you think we will make it?" Geoff asks Bobby.

Bobby turns, looks at him, and says, *"Geoff, if I only THOUGHT we would make it, I would turn around right now."*

Geoff looked at me, and commented, "He was one of the best pilots in the world, but I honestly thought I would never see home that night, or ever, it was that bad.

"But then, using some intuition, your mother put on a light at Kamaliki. It shone out on the blue patio like a beacon. It was solely by that marker that we could find the airstrip."

INDEX

Geoff at age fifty-five

Geoff on being taken by his father: *I must have been about ten or so when we left Townsville for Sydney by coastal steamer, which were common in those days. They were about 10,000 tons and had names such as Manunda, Manoora, Kanimbla. I remember the trip well, the Whitsundays, and spouting whales.*

Email to Geoff's grandson, Benjamin
(In India with the author on his Fifteenth Birthday, Nov 2006)

G'day Ben

I wish you a very happy birthday on Mondee and trust you will not be offended by the money I shall enclose with this email.

How are you doing? Are you able to understand the language? I suppose it sounds like one giant Call Centre.

I do hope that you are enjoying it all. It's a good sort of a trip for a young fella.

Keep your eye open for a wealthy widow for me. If you find one, please ask her to send me a photo of her bank account.

Much love ... Grandad

(Dad had attached to his email a photo of a hand holding money as the 'enclosed money")

The HURT Versus the HEART

A sigh is a powerful thing. It releases many hardships from within the heart and helps us look over the many hurdles and we have had to cross in order to survive. I write this book with a sigh in my heart and a growing understanding of the deep hurt and pain my father suffered his whole life long.

But he never passed it along. He was brutalised as a child, but he never struck out towards any of his own. He was starved as a child, but he made sure his family were well fed, even when he was no longer living with us. He had nothing as a child, but he made sure his children had everything they needed, including a private school education.

Worst of all, a thing I discovered only yesterday, Geoff's own mother had effectively "sold" Geoff off as a bargaining chip to get her insane husband out of her life. He never told anyone and I only found this out in a letter to his brother, a thing they both knew. His own mother handed him over to "that psychopathic bastard', as he referred to his father.

Geoffrey John Wallace lived an entire life holding this extraordinary hurt in his heart, but he never imposed this upon another. He was the man who stopped the pain, he held it in, and he suffered because of it. Anxiety, stress and nervousness were his constant companions, yet he always had a smile and a story to tell to make the day lighter and more meaningful.

Geoff: Letter to Reg. *"I got to know Mum very well over the five years she was in Hopetoun ... She confided to me that she had lived a life of wretched guilt for all those long years since she handed me over to DHW at age (about) ten.*

"She finally learned how to give and receive affection. And yet I had never, ever, held anything against her. My firm belief back then, and now, had always been that anyone who had an opportunity to get away from that psychopathic bastard, for whatever reason or at whose expense, should cut and run."

We all have hurt in our hearts, to some degree. We all make decisions based on whether we step out with courage, or retreat into fear. These choices are wrapped around how we deal with the hurt within us. The life we choose is based on how we resolve this conflict. In many ways, the point of this book is to show that BECAUSE of this pain, not in spite of it, we can grow to be better people and learn to be kinder to others.

As a result of writing this book I learned more about my father and what he was trying to say. When he was no longer here to talk I was able to hear what he wanted to say. Isn't that odd? I trust in these pages, you too will learn something about this quiet, unassuming man.

Grandma Annette

This is the story of Geoffrey John Wallace. He was a humble man, one who started with nothing, became very rich, spent it, and ended up quite poor. It's a journey worth reading and the first step in this voyage starts with understanding a little of where he came from, and by this I mean understanding his mother and father.

Grandma Wallace (Annetta Svenson, nee: Annette Wallace) was a very unemotional woman. Swedish, seemingly made of iron, she was what you might call a tough old bird. At eighty-six she was still growing her own vegetables and walking up the forty-five degree slope where her house was in Pitt Street, Red Hill. But it was only every second day at that point. She never really smiled and her laugh, if you ever heard it, was a half-hearted "he he" and that was it.

Once, when Mum brought all six kids around to visit Grandma, she remarked casually, without any hint of sarcasm or unkindness, "Oh, and you brought all the piggies," referring to we children. I don't think she was ever much a fan of kids, even her own.

She was not unpleasant towards others, it was just her nature to be brutal and honest. It was not cynicism, bitterness or acrimony that drove her, it was more that she saw no great need for pleasantry. Her interest in the world appeared to be minimal, more-so as she grew older and her memory faded. Half the time when you visited she thought you were a plumber, or whatever, and she would shut the door on you! One day, I caught her in bright spirits. She smiled and invited me in for a cup of tea. We were not really talking about much, when the thought struck me: *Was she worried, living here in advanced years on her own?*

"Do you have any concerns about passing on, Grandma?" I asked.

"That's a strange question," she answered.

"I don't mean to pry and please don't feel obliged to answer. I was just wondering if you were concerned, living here on your own, and all that." I said.

"Not at all. I look forward to it." she said, simply.

"To what?"

"Dying." She could see some further explanation was called for. "I had a vision, or a visitation is more accurate. At nineteen I was taken from my body to see relatives that had passed on. They greeted me warmly and showed me about, including where I would live when I left this Earth. I felt so comfortable and so happy. I knew that THIS was my true home, the other-worlds."

After a minute or two, she carried on. "This was when I joined the Spiritualist Church. I felt it was a good way to stay in touch with those on the other side and, together with the other members in the area, we started up the local CWA. (Country Women's Association) We raised money, got a hall built where, after church on Sunday, we would do the Séances."

I was surprised. She STARTED a local CWA with a group of friends, and built a hall, all because they wanted to have Séances? I was floored, not just because I had never heard of this, but because who ever suspected that in the early 1900's people were so committed to spirituality? "The CWA was a front for the Spiritualist Church?" I asked.

"Well, I suppose, when you put it like that. It was very important to not tell others outside the circle, people did not understand these things. You could hardly tell the local priest you are in the Spiritualist Church, could you? The CWA allowed us to meet openly without too many questions." She answered.

There are very few things that stop me in my tracks, but this was one of them. "Did anyone else in the family go along with you?"

"Oh no. You cannot teach those who are deaf how to hear. It was always something we kept to ourselves." She gathered her thoughts, "So no, to answer your question, I have never had any fear of death. I look forward to it, in fact. It is a better place."

At the time, my immediate thought after she said these words were that getting married to the occasionally insane and often violent Duncan Harry Wallace meant you really needed to have no fear of death.

We spent the next hour or so of my visit chatting about nothing. Grandma Annette was never one to talk much, but she had seemed happy to confide her 'secret' to me. Not that it was really a secret, it was more that no one had every bothered to ask. It also gave me a clue where Geoff got his seeking nature from, as it certainly was not from his father.

Later, I quietly asked other members of the extended family if they knew anything about Grandma being in the Spiritualist Church. Not one of them knew, not even Geoff! Which was odd, I thought, because he was actively looking into all these sort of things at that time. In fact, I suspect most believed I was pulling their legs, it seemed so improbable.

She never mentioned anything like that again and probably forgot that she had told me. But as I was leaving she said something very clear, yet obtuse. "You can live long enough, you know." This was never really explained and I suspect she was saying that the days were no longer rewarding for her, that every new morning was just a repetition of the last.

The Nursing Home

Annette had turned one hundred years and Geoff had made sure his mother got her telegram from the Queen. It is not automatic, as some people think. You have to write and request the telegram, and provide evidence of a Commonwealth citizen about to turn a century to receive this. Geoff knew this would tickle her, so he organised it.

He showed me the paperwork that needed filling in, the applications that needed to be made. I got to understand WHY that telegram was important: It meant someone cared. (However, to see the Lettergram, both from Her Majesty and the Prime Minister of Australia, they were just a short congratulatory. No letterhead, just a standard type of telegram.)

Shortly before this event came the call from the Nursing Home. A bed was vacant and a decision had to be made inside a week. This was a Government offer, based on her not being able to afford private care. If Annette took up the option, she could only do so on the basis of having her house sold and the monies from this being distributed to her heirs.

She was not keen about losing her independence, but she could no longer make the difficult trek up the hill and looking after herself was becoming too much. So the house was sold, the sons received equal shares and she moved into a bed in Hopetoun, a Brisbane nursing home. Geoff did everything to facilitate this: He acted as trustee, sold the house, distributed the money, and continued to look after his mother's needs.

"I do not regret one minute," Geoff said to me many years after she had passed on. "It was sometimes a real task, driving up to Brisbane to say hello, drop off supplies, and then return home. There were times I just didn't want to do it. I was in pain and it was a full day's effort. But if I hadn't, no one would have been there for her. I am very glad I did, however, because now I am old I understand the helplessness you feel.

"Someone coming to say hello, it means everything. You are stuck there, unable to leave or do anything. There is no one interesting to talk to, because they are all half-dead, and then you see THEIR relatives visiting, bringing flowers. Being all alone at that age is a terrible thing. I am very, very glad I went out of my way."

Grandma Wallace lived to age one hundred and four and for most of those years she appeared to be quite dour. You would describe her as being unemotional. Yet, two years before she passed on, she softened. She began to smile warmly when she saw you, laugh, and even hug you. I suspect it was because she realised she would soon be back in the only place she knew true happiness, the other-side.

And maybe it was the port and sherry her son, Geoff, delivered to her every week that helped her transition. At one hundred and two, Annette essentially became a bit of a heavy drinker. Geoff dropped in a flagon of sherry or port every week and it was always gone by his next visit. At first, the nursing staff took it away, but Geoff intervened and told them not to. If getting drunk made her happy, let her drink.

It was better than loading her up with painkillers and it was obvious that she was in better, dare I say, spirits.

I called in to see her shortly before she passed on. In truth, she was already on the 'other side' but she recognised me and smiled. I got a warm hug, full of love. I was surprised as I had never experienced this from Grandma. She must have known she was going home.

Annette Wallace (nee Svenson)
Image taken shortly before she passed on

Note: I had long wondered about what happened, how Geoff had been taken by Duncan, and only as I was preparing to send this book off to printing did I stumble across a letter from Geoff to Reg: *14 June 2004.* In this he wrote what he never told anyone. (I presume to protect his mother's name)

His own mother had used him as a bargaining chip to get rid of her husband. I can imagine she had little choice, Duncan may well have killed the whole family if she had said no, but even so, she knew what hell her youngest was being sent to. She suffered terrible, life-long guilt as a result.

The Funeral of Annette

W hen she finally passed on, Geoff received a call from his brother, Bob. He rang to apologise, he was too old to make it to the funeral, but what should he send? Perhaps flowers? Brother Bob used to call to speak to Annette, but had not bothered to send so much as a Christmas card to his mother since receiving his portion of the property settlement, some five years earlier.

"You know something," Geoff responded. "Mum probably would have preferred them while she was alive."

Bob hung up the phone, calling Geoff a dog. Yet who could argue the truth of it? She 'would' have preferred them when she was alive. Annette liked flowers and always picked the ones from her own garden to brighten up her house. But the truth was, Bob never called by, never rang to say hello, and did nothing for his mother.

His world was the only interest in his life. He ended his life at age eighty-six (as I recall) by suicide. No one mourned his passing. Geoff did, however, send flowers to his funeral.

Annette had four sons: Bob, Colin, Reg and Geoff. She also raised Bob's illegitimate one as her own. Reg and Colin suffered as Prisoners of War during WW2. Colin was great fun, but essentially mad. Reg was the one closest to Geoff and they remained friends, not just brothers, all their lives.

You may wonder at how a man can be so uncaring of his own mother? To understand the callous selfishness of a son like Bob, you only had to look at the father, Duncan Harry Wallace.

Geoff on his Father, Duncan Harry Wallace

I f only DHW had used his talents for good instead of evil, as Maxwell Smart would say. He had a talent for investigating subjects and thoroughly mastering them. Reg has inherited this. Reg had DHW's notebooks (may still have them) when he was studying to be a health inspector. DHW used to be a functionary in the Fiji police force. There existed a photo (Reg may have it) of DHW in uniform standing alongside a Fijian native policeman in sulu and sandals. He may have been the Chief. He was also a prize fighter at one stage somewhere (that's where he developed his talents for hitting me).

I was a quiet kid. He just needed someone to take out his frustrations on, and I was there. He used to fly into an uncontrollable rage.

The Bridge

Duncan Harry Wallace (Often called DHW by his sons) was a health inspector. To all external appearances, a decent chap. In social circumstances he was polite, well spoken and appeared to be interested in listening to what you had to say. But at home, out of the public gaze, he was a very different person.

He has been described as domineering, bigoted and prejudiced by those in his intimate circle, but it would seem he wasn't always this way. The worst traits of his nature emerged after he returned from World War One, where he had survived the trenches. The really curious thing, he volunteered to go. He didn't have to, as he had already served in the British Army in India and in Hong Kong, but he put his hand up to join the Australian Expeditionary force.

Clearly, however, after some time in the trenches he wanted out. A letter was recently found, written in Annette's handwriting, begging the War Department to release Duncan Harry from active duty, as she was unable to cope raising the children. Now, Grandma would never have written such a letter, it was simply not her nature, nor was it in the style she normally wrote. My brother and myself suspect that it was Duncan Harry asking her to write in, and he gave her what to say, specifically.

He wanted out of the pointless blood bath, but for HIM to ask would be cowardice. Regardless of Annette's best effort to extricate him from the gore and stupidity of the trenches, the request was refused. He survived, however, he came back a very different man that the one who left. Perhaps it was the war, perhaps he believed that he showed cowardice wanting to get out of it, we do not know. What IS known is that he came back from Europe a brutal man.

From all accounts, it was after his return that the violent streak first emerged. One of the significant stories in the tale of Duncan Harry is the one about the bridge. He saw a dark skinned man crossing a bridge, and went out of his way to upset the fellow. This is one story that is known to be correct as the matter went to court and the records can be read.

It was a Moroccan man who was crossing the single person bridge. The creek-crossing bridges in the early days of the 20th Century were narrow arrangements. Essentially, a three foot wide wire suspension bridge with a railing and wooden boards to walk on. They were designed for just one person to use them at a time. Now, there was the Moroccan on the bridge, possibly a camel trader, as he spoke English. By all accounts he was simply walking over the creek, minding his own business when Duncan intervened.

"This is a white man's bridge darky, step aside and let the white man pass." Duncan said.

He saw the Moroccan was almost to the end and he purposefully stepped onto the bridge to stop him. It was only a matter of a few yards and the man was off the crossing and on his way, but Duncan apparently wanted to prove some point.

"But please, just step back two steps, and I am out of your way, Sir!" The Moroccan exclaimed.

"This is a white man's country and here black men stand out of the way and let the white man pass. So get back to the other side!" Duncan insisted.

The man stood his ground. This was foolishness and as a result, Duncan (who was a trained boxer) landed a haymaker on the guy, knocking him to the ground. The court record has the following. "And so Sir, you were almost at the end of the bridge and the defendant stepped on, barring your way, is this correct?"

"Yes."

"He asked you to go back to the other side, so he could cross, correct?"

"Yes."

"But you refused, saying it was only a few yards and you were on your way, correct?"

"Yes."

"And Mr. Wallace then hit you, is this correct?"

"Yes."

"Can you please tell the court what you did then?"

"What I do! I go arse over kettle, whadda else you think I do!"

By report, the court broke down in laughter. It is one of those priceless moments.

Apparently, Duncan also laughed after he knocked the man down, and just walked away. It was all about humiliating the person, as he didn't even want to cross the bridge! The Moroccan simply presented an opportunity for trouble, which equalled good fun for Duncan Harry Wallace.

Keep in mind, we know this tale because Duncan himself used to retell it! He had absolutely no regret, and considered the entire matter extremely funny. Once when he retold this story a person asked him, "Do you think you are racially prejudiced?"

To this Duncan answered, earnestly, "I am NOT racially prejudiced. I just hate bongs (Islanders) wops (Italians and Greeks) and Abos! (Australian Aborigines)" Was he joking? I don't think so.

He worked as a health inspector and in the course of his duties he constantly had to enforce orders over aboriginal and islander housing. The health inspector had the power to coerce people to be more hygienic. If some person or persons in public housing failed to meet their expectations of hygiene, they would be evicted. Native people did not like Health Inspectors and would often tip chamber pots over tem when they came looking about their houses. As a result, there was a natural conflict between the local aborigines, the islanders and the Duncan Harry Wallace's of this world. It is not hard to imagine that he genuinely DID hate these races.

Geoff was convinced his father hated him. Given that he used to call his kids "curs" and "dogs" while pointing loaded shotguns at them, well, you could understand why a child would come to believe this. There are any number of stories where Duncan takes offence at some odd thing, with the result being one of the children escaping from the car, or the house, in fear of their life. They would often walk home just outside of shotgun range, while Duncan kept shouting at them.

Is this child abuse? Of course it is. The man was pathological and yet, as a health inspector, he was lauded and respected by his peers. One of my favourite stories in regards this surrounds the award he got for improving hygiene and general behaviour in Broken Hill.

Greg Writes: *There is a bit of interest in family history so you may have some anecdotes or some heirlooms/relics/photos of ancestors to show or just recall some history. Duncan and Annette Wallace, what part of Australia did they live and move to (Townsville), what were their parents names, where did they live (India), what wars did they fight in, how many people did they kill and so on.*

Geoff Responds: *I don't have any heirlooms, relics, or many photos, just some scars received from my doting father, Duncan Harry Wallace. He was born in Bangalore on his birthday. His father was involved in building dams across the country, either as an engineer or concrete mixer, or something else. I have a picture of his female relatives somewhere. I'll see if I can find it. He served in the British army and did a march from Now-sheera to Ferozapor (phonetic spelling). He taught me some Tamil, wherever he learnt it from.*

He had a unique, quick and successful way of teaching. If you got it wrong, you received a swift fist to the head.

The Man who Cleaned Up Broken Hill

T he following is a tale Geoff regaled me with on occasions. Keep in mind, it cannot be proven, but apparently Duncan was regarded as the "*The Man who Cleaned Up Broken Hill*". Broken Hill was a mining town and in preparation for this story, I drove through the place. There, on the outskirts of town, were some of the original mining huts. These were the old company houses and back then they were just tin sheds. People have lined

A typical Broken Hill Mining Hut of the 1930's. This is what the Wallace family would have moved to

them now and installed insulation, but in those days these places would have been freezing cold in winter, and cooking hot in summer.

This was exactly the sort of place Duncan and his growing family would have been installed in. Even if not for the violence, I do not doubt Annette was happy to escape this hell hole after a couple of years, but this is the next story. By report, when Duncan first arrived, the miners would pee and crap wherever they damn well pleased. This was simply not good enough. Not in HIS town.

Broken Hill was a dangerous place. Even the police would not venture out to break up the many fights that happened up and down the dusty streets. These were hard men, miners who had short lives and lived them to the fullest without care of consequence. They were not to be taken lightly and would as soon cut your throat as say 'good morning' to you.

Little is known about the father during this period, other than he enforced sanitary regulations and became known as a man you did not argue with. How did he do this? By report, Duncan used to carry two shotguns on his daily rounds, both at quarter charge. One was loaded with saltpetre for shot, the other with lead pellet. Saltpetre was for the white guys peeing and crapping in the streets, lead shot was for any one who wasn't white.

Duncan had a job to do and by God he was going to do it right! Shotguns in hand, he subdued the town in just eighteen months and was awarded for it. This is a hard thing for people to imagine in the modern world. A gun-toting health inspector bringing hygiene to an outback town sounds more like a Mel Brooks script. It is worthy of a Clint Eastwood western, though I suspect it will be a movie that will never be made. The hero health inspector is just not the stuff legends are made of.

The Broken Hill story has two stages, the first where Annette leaves and takes the children to Sydney and then, some six year later she comes back and discovers Duncan is even worse. This was when she moved the kids and herself to family lands at the Black River, near Townsville, QLD.

The background to this story comes directly from the trenches of World War One. Duncan, unlike so many others, survived the squalor, violence, death and cruelty of that insanity. But what came back was not the same man that left. We know and understand how shell shock, post traumatic stress, or whatever you wish to call it, affects the personality, but at that time it was just seen as weakness. One thing is certain, since the end of WW1 a cloud of unbridled anger descended over Duncan. It was clear that the man had fallen into some sort of abyss.

We all know the stereotype: A man doesn't show he is hurt, he stands tall, shouts at the devil, and carries on. Well, to the outside world, Duncan did exactly this, but to the family, he was a monster. Children regularly walked many miles home with him shouting names, while pointing a loaded shotgun at them. He would be calling them a cur, a dog that deserved to be put down. The rest of the children and Annette were forced to sit in the car as it idled along, listening to his threats of death.

"You said nothing. You certainly didn't speak up to defend the offending child, or else YOU were the one who was in for it," Geoff explained.

To be fair: He never actually shot any of the children, but Geoff confided in me one day that his greatest fear was not that he would be killed by his father. This he fully expected, what he was afraid of was that the man would get away with it. He mentioned this to me many times. Curious logic, isn't it? Dying was one thing, but dying for no purpose and having your murderer walk away scot-free was far worse.

There is so much in this curious fear. A deep sense of fairness was being conflicted at the most basic level of reason. Duncan was pushing buttons in his child that were to have long-lasting ramifications.

Broken Hill proved to the world that Duncan was not a man who was going to go quietly into the night for anyone. (Keep in mind: This was well before the family ended up on the Snake River, near Townsville, where the greatest excesses of violence happened.)

Then it all changed. At age Two, Geoff started having convulsions. Medical advice suggested it may have been the toxins in the air of Broken Hill that caused this. This was the reason Annette gave to leave her husband there, while she took the boys down to Merrylands, Sydney, near to where her sister lived. The whole family, bar Duncan, up and left Broken Hill and went to a back-blocks of Sydney. Geoff later said to me he suspected the real truth was that he was allergic to his father.

I gathered no one was unhappy with the new arrangements, apart from, perhaps, Duncan.

No-one at the time really understood what happened to the father but, as mentioned in the previous chapter, shortly after Geoff's passing, my brother, Greg, discovered a letter to the War Department. This is when the pieces started to fall into place. It appears Duncan had written to Annette after he experienced the reality of what the trenches were and she in turn wrote to the war department asking that he be returned, with the reason being that she was not able to cope with raising the children. This letter, if it had been seen as coming from Duncan, as it indirectly had, would be grounds for cowardice and he would have been shot.

I cannot help but feel that in the background he had a deep, dark fear: *the fear of being called a coward.* Everything he did was to prove to the world he was not. If we think about it, so much of what we do that appears unkind, or stupid, derives from some sort of fear we hide in our hearts.

The man had been brutalised by World War One. He had seen men die, he had killed men and watched as they tried to kill him. Anything and everything he did after that was, by comparison, light-weight stuff. After all, he never actually SHOT any of the kids, he just disciplined them. And they needed to toughen up anyway! You were not a real man unless you stood tall and stared down death and in Duncan's life there had been an awful lot of death to stare down.

The scenario is not complicated. The war ends: You come back to society with all its polite shoulds and should nots and you see it for what it is, a myth. It is a story you tell to keep the children in line. Against this sort of backdrop, Duncan may well have believed that merely pointing guns at them was a more honest way to teach them to behave.

Geoff Notes: *His name was Duncan Harry Wallace and was called Duncan or DHW, not Harry. He was born at Bangalore on 7 March 1878. He was 12 years older than my mother whose birthday was 31 July 1890. She was born at Townsville.*

Duncan was an avid gun buff. He got me a shotgun at about age 12 and I had a natural aptitude for shooting. I shot about 6 flying quail straight at my first attempt. I remember his surprise. He looked like the judges at Susan Boyle's first public appearance. Then, as a kid, I used to win at trapshooting against the adults.

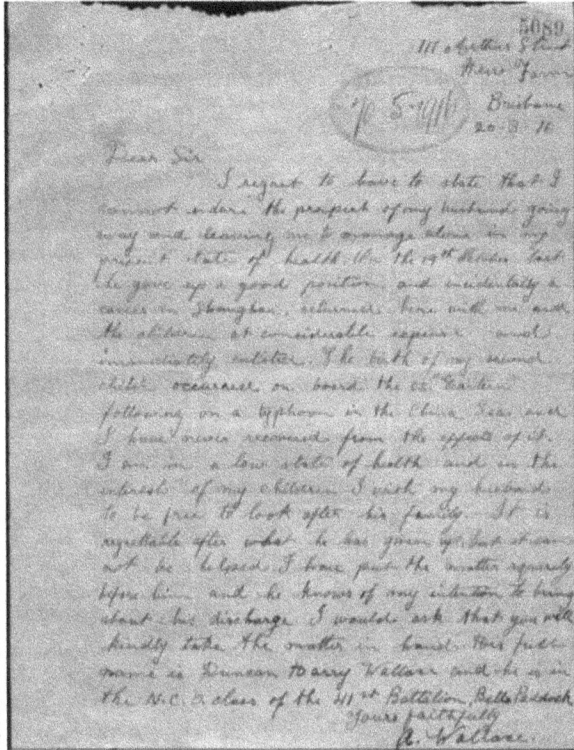

The Letter

How much did this letter change the course of one family's history?

L ife contains many unknowns, many variables, yet when Greg unearthed this document from the War Archive, the first thing that seemed obvious is that, while it was Annette's handwriting, she wasn't like this. It seemed likely that Duncan, after seeing the hell of the WW 1 trenches first hand, dictated to her what he needed to have written.

If such a letter were to have been seen as coming from him, it would be cowardice and thus would be reason for hanging. He survived the war, but came back a different man. Was this the pivotal point that changed the destiny of the entire family? Was the apparent insanity and bravado of Duncan Harry coming from his fear of being seen as a coward?

Sydney Town

Geoff had fond and remarkably clear memories of his early childhood. Merrylands was a real back-water in those days: Semi-rural and close to nothing. It did have a train line running through, a school down the road and a few shops. It was not much, a type of housing commission area, but it was better than Broken Hill. It would seem to be a time of relative calm in young Geoff's life.

From what we understand, Duncan had become excessively abusive, striking Annette and threatening the children for no apparent reason. I suspect he didn't hate his children, but he surely had a strange way of showing he loved them. PTSD is what they call it now, but back then it was Shell Shock. Many people, not just Duncan Harry Wallace, came back from WW1 with concussive injuries and trauma. They simply did not function as reasonable human beings after that.

Yet, for a good stretch of years, none of this affected the family, because they left Duncan for a new life in Sydney. Yes, they were poor, extremely poor and in the middle of a depression. It was also true that their mother, Annette, was anything by gentle and kind, but they were clean and housed. Things were tough, but none of them starved. Of course, none of this meant anything to a four year old. The thing that Geoff remembered most vividly about Merrylands was the "lolly shop", with its display of mouth watering sweets. He longed for these, but the family had almost no money, so such luxuries were out of the question.

When he told me about this, his mouth was watering. "I really wanted those sweets, but it was like a pauper looking at a Rolls Royce. There was no way to reach that lofty goal of a penny's worth of sugar. But still I would go to that shop outside the train station and just stare at them."

There are a good many stories from this time, between Merrylands and the short return to Broken Hill some seven years later, then soon after this the whole family moves to the Black River. Perhaps one of the clearest insights into young Geoff's mind at the time came when his mother had a head ache and asked him to go get an aspirin.

Geoff did so, noting there were only two left in the medical cabinet. And as it happened, Geoff liked the taste of this aspirin. It was almost like one of those sweets he longed for, so without thinking he eats one and takes the other to his mother. She looks at the lonely pill, sees that Geoff is sucking on the other one, and says "What use is ONE aspirin going to do for my headache? You may as well have eaten both!"

So he pops the other one in his mouth and eats it! "There were consequences for that, but I just can't remember what my mother did. It's a complete blank." Geoff told my late in his life.

They were so poor that aspirin was like candy and the entire household could not even afford that. "I didn't realise we were so poor, I just knew everything I wanted I could not have." Geoff paused as he related this story. Gazing back to where the memory was coming from, he commented, "I guess Duncan didn't provide much, seeing as we all left him there in Broken Hill."

What he DIDN'T say at that point was something I had long understood. Geoff didn't HAVE to provide for his family. There was no court order telling him to do so and being separated for some thirteen years before the divorce itself went through, at any point during that time he could have said "Tough" and walked into a new life. But he didn't. He stayed, partly because he did love his kids, partly because a divorce may well have been more expensive, but mostly I believe it was because he really took his personal responsibilities very seriously.

Unlike his father, if Geoff did something wrong, he would admit to it. Here is a secret, a violent man does not believe in personal accountability. The act of accepting responsibility formed a fundamental shift in thinking that separated Geoff from his upbringing.

The lolly story helped me understand why he always, without fail, gave his kids money to buy little things. He took delight in this, watching your eyes light up with some cash being given to you. In his way, he was giving that starving child inside himself the lolly he never got.

Geoff was not going to abandon his family in the way his father had.

As a curious addendum to the story of the aspirin, when Cousin Geoff was going with Geoff Senior to the Belmont Rifle Range in the 1960's he was asked to pop into a local store and buy some cotton wool. It was to put into the ears to protect them from sound of gunshot.

Well, young Geoff got it into mind that the cotton wool on the top of the old aspirin bottles was just the thing, with the added bonus of having all those aspirin when you were done with it. So he bought the headache remedy, thinking he was killing two birds with one stone.

He reports that Uncle Geoff was not amused, "I told you to get cotton wool, and you come back with aspirin?" There was no explaining the deeper elements of thought at work here, so young Geoff duly went back and exchanged the pills for the ear protection. I laughed when he told me this story, because I could not help but wonder if there was not some sort of echo from the past, where Geoff ate the aspirin his mother needed.

Sausages

We don't think of sausages as worth very much and even during the 1930's, with the backdrop of depression and hunger, they were still not much. Most of the cheap meats, like the local sausages, were largely fat, cereal and salt, with little of anything else in them. But Geoff loved them and, in particular, he liked RAW sausages.

Why? Who knows, but one story he told shortly before he passed away is worth a mention. His mother asked him to go to the shops to get sixpence worth of these said sausages, six all up. A penny a banger, as they say. Obviously, it was to feed the family that night. Geoff duly went to the butchers, collected the goods, and came home with them wrapped up in their butcher's paper.

Without really thinking, he broke open one end, and started nibbling on that delightful raw sausage meat. And he as nibbled, he was dreaming along the road home, happy and content. Sadly, by the time he got home, it was like the aspirin, the sausages were all gone. Geoff doesn't remember exactly what happened next, but we can presume he got a hiding.

"For some reason, I was never asked to get sausages again!" He told me, wryly. Then he added, with that familiar glint of laughter in his eye, "I was never very good at understanding consequences."

Butcher's and other Shops at Merrylands (circa 1950, but very much as it would have been in 1934)

Derelict Corner Store in Chetwynd Road

Mrs Johnson

One of the most curious things Geoff brought up in his recollections of his early life, a memory he brought up many times over the years, was his invisible friend, Mrs Johnson. "She was as real as you or I standing here." He said to me one day. "She is one reason why I don't ridicule or Poo-Hoo people who hold notions that are not the norm. Just because I cannot see what they see does not mean it isn't real to them"

Mrs Johnson featured very strongly during the time he was at Merrylands, in Sydney. Geoff described her as a forty-eight year-old woman, the odd thing being that she seemed very interested in listening to him. No one else was. He doesn't remember her speaking any great words of wisdom, he just remembered that she was there, and that she liked him.

He could tell his troubles to her and she never judged him. The curious thing is: Anyone who knew Geoff knew he was a ready listener and he never appeared to judge you. I feel this is what he learned from his invisible friend. Often what is not said carries the greatest meaning.

"I learned not to speak of these things. This either got you laughed at, or beaten up, or both."

There was another 'friend' or sort, a mysterious one that lived under a roadside storm water grill. At age five, Geoff would sit there and talk to her, 'feeding' her leaves. "I don't know why I thought it was a girl, it just seemed to be. I don't even think I thought it was a human there, but more of a thing. Anyway, I fed her leaves." Geoff told me on a few occasions that this strange thing would take leaves when they were handed to her. "I could feel the leaves being tugged from my fingers," Geoff said, "and occasionally she would pop something back up. It might have been a ball that had gone down there, or whatever." They apparently had a return of favours.

"Did you 'actually' receive a ball, or was it a day-dream you were having?" I asked.

"I seem to recall playing with a ball she gave me, but it was a long time ago. It is very hard to distinguish reality from dreams at five, and memory is really just another dream, isn't it?" Geoff answered with a question.

At the time, though, Young Geoffrey thought nothing of it other than he had a friend. He just accepted he fed leaves to a strange person who lived in the storm water drain. "I knew enough not to speak to anyone about this one. Mrs Johnson was bad enough to explain. I still have no idea who it was, or why they were there. However, I remembered Mrs Johnson when I got into some serious trouble at school."

The Spitting Tree

Geoff's school was essentially a long wooden building. There were trees in the playground, one with a fork in it. This was the centre of one of the oddest games: the students would see how high they could spit over and through, the fork in that tree. "One day, as the other kids were doing their usual spitting, a friend of mine walked by on the other side. I did not intend to, but I accidentally landed one on him. It was entirely accidental but the boy didn't take it that way."

He paused, gathered his thoughts, and continued. "The fellow was called Eric, Eric Delainey. The family lived down the road and were fairly well-to-do. I always got on with him fine. Yet from HIS point of view, one day, out the blue, I spat on his face while he was walking in the school playground. He complained to the teacher and we were both hauled me off to the headmaster."

"Did you spit on Erik?" the headmaster asks.

"It was not really a very bright question. It was a given I spat on him, but the question should have been *'Did you MEAN to spit on Eric?'* ... The only answer I could give to the specific question I was asked was 'Yes'. There was no room for any sort of explanation.

Merrylands School

"The headmaster then insisted I apologise to Eric and say sorry. So I did. I said I was sorry and we both left. Outside the room, Eric asked me 'Are you really sorry?' and I replied 'No'." Geoff looked at me and explained. "He must have realised he was walking past the spitting tree, after all. We both seemed to understand that was the end of it, but to this day I still don't know if Eric thinks that I *meant* to spit on him!" We both laughed at the silliness of children.

"I felt it was better to be honest to Eric than to lie. I didn't feel sorry, because after all, he should have realised I was just spitting over the fork in the tree, like everyone did. Yet I regretted doing it because he was my friend. It is hard to explain this and I still can't, but just saying 'sorry' because you are supposed to is meaningless."

Without actually saying it, I somehow connected the dots of what Geoff was trying to say. Someone was guiding him, probably Mrs Johnson, in how to act in these situations.

And one step further: What I find truly extraordinary about this tale is that in a book Geoff had proof-read of mine, called 'Ratology', I had spend a chapter writing about how just saying 'Sorry' is a pointless exercise. Understanding the root cause of your actions was important and often 'sorry' was used as a way to avoid dealing with the things that were really driving you. You would think, after reading the story I just regaled you with, that father may have understood this.

But he did not. This was the ONE chapter in the entire book that he never got. He was convinced I was saying you should never apologise for what you do, while I was saying the exact opposite. You 'must' apologise in a meaningful way when you do another wrong, otherwise you miss the whole lesson to be learned. I was pointing out that the word 'sorry' in itself does not do this, and worse, it actively avoids a meaningful exchange where understanding might grow.

He disagreed with the chapter, yet he believed exactly the same thing!

Michael Notes: *Dad always had a can of CONDENSED MILK. It was one of those things that were a fixture in any fridge in any house where he lived. It would have become a habit from the tropics of New Guinea, where milk went off so easily.*

At his funeral service, Gillian from Sri Lanka was there and said with surprise, "Condensed Milk! I didn't know anyone used it here!"

I had a tin out in his honour and was glad someone noticed.

Autographed Don Bradman Cricket Card 1930's

The Only Games in Town

Kids in the 1930's had not much choice for entertainment. Unless it was cricket or football, there were only cards and marbles to play with. Blood Alley Agates were the best marbles and signed cricket cards were the top of the pile for card collecting. The general goal of all these 'non-sport' games was acquisition. You tried to get the ones that everyone wanted.

Every boy had a bag of marbles and your social standing was, in part, determined by the rarity and quality of your 'bag'. Poor kids had to be really good at the game to get some sort of street cred. Geoff doesn't recall ever having any prized ones, none that he managed to keep at any rate. "If I did get a good one, my older brothers absconded with it anyway, so it wasn't really worth putting a lot of effort into it."

You played all sorts of games with your marbles and every game had changing rules. Of course, the famous "No Nufinks" (No Nothings) meant there were no exclusions or variations to the game being played. I do not recall all the rules, but there were 'upsies' and 'downsies' and 'dropsies'. I am sure you get the general idea. You had to either knock a marble out of a ring, into a hole, or into a zone where you could claim it.

Cards were a different story. The popular ones were the famous test players in Cricket and the important ships of the day. A little like baseball cards in the USA, you always wanted to get the most rare and a SIGNED cricket card by the actual player was by far the best of them all. But the game you played to get these items was essentially really stupid: You flipped cards against a wall and the one whose card was closest to that wall took the lot.

I mean, who would be dumb enough to throw their most prized cards against a wall? No, you threw the junk ones, the ones you were not worried about losing.

Not much of a game, but there was not a lot else to do. There was no such thing as TV and even a family that had a radio was rare enough in those parts. And a family that had a modern car, they were rich.

Very few people really understand poverty and how a truly poor person doesn't even think about money. They only think about the present day and finding a way to survive it. If you eat and have a safe place to sleep, you are good. True poverty strips you of everything, even your dreams. You are in a world of "no nufinks' and all you can do is hope for a little bit of luck to come your way and bring you something nice.

TRAINS and DREAMS

The train station was where all the shops were in Merrylands and it was pretty much the focus of interest for the local kids. You got the shopping, bought toys if you had any pennies, and generally met to talk with the other children there. It was a bit like McDonalds in the present day.

Geoff remembered vividly the time the remarkable new electric trains were being introduced. They started in 1926 and it seems right that it would be early 1930's when they first arrived at Merrylands. Apparently it caused a huge sensation and you could hear them on the tracks from Chetwynd Road, where the family lived.

These also figured prominently in what was to be the start of Geoff's spiritual journey. Keep in mind, his mother was already attending meetings with the Spiritualist Church, something no-one was ever told about. Perhaps she was opening doors on the inner, but whatever the case Geoff started having very powerful experiences at that time.

One pronounced experience, which Geoff mentioned to me on a number of occasions, was a visitation by someone he knew as "Jack". Geoff knew well the wind in the wires, the sound that moaned and howled for hours on windy days, and he supposed that this roaring sound he was hearing in and around his ears as he fell to sleep was somewhat similar to this. But it was inside him and happened on nights where there was no wind. Then one night it changed. He felt a person, who he thought was "Jack" for some reason, come up from behind.

He was not scared, yet it was not particularly enjoyable. 'Jack' would place his hands on his shoulders and the experience would start. At first he just felt numb, then inflated, and then very, very heavy. This sensation began to happen regularly, often every night for days at a time. After a time 'Jack' began to take him places, but Geoff doesn't remember any details. He only knew he left his body, left the house, and travelled far away. But he understood none of it.

When he spoke of this to his mother, she said "It is all just imagination." Yet here I find it curious. In my first story we discovered she was at that time a long-time member of the Spiritualist Church. She had experienced her OWN visitation by spiritual beings, it was the reason she joined that church. Why did she not support her son in this? We will never know, but all his life, Geoff had a deep spiritual curiosity for what lay beyond this world.

Then, at age Eight, when the family was soon to travel back to Broken Hill to be reunited with Duncan Harry again, the nightmares started. Geoff would now dream there was a huge, roaring train coming into Merrylands Station, only the platform he was on was tilting in towards the tracks. It threatened to push him into the path of the oncoming behemoth and there was absolutely nothing he could do about it. He was doomed, night, after night, after night.

At around the same time, he had fallen in love, with his cousin Doreen. She fell in love with him as well and they would often be kissing and hugging, literally kissing cousins. It really tore Geoff up to leave for Broken Hill but the connection remained and many years later, it was to be Doreen's father Charlie Acherly who got him his first job up in New Guinea. So Doreen, in a sense, was the start of "Dollars Wallace" as this connection is what led to him making his fortune.

Years later, after many fruitless quests for answers with Psychics, the Spiritualist Church and religions, Geoff finally came across the spiritual path that he was destined for, and where he rose to become a highly respected initiate. Not surprisingly, it advocated the ability to leave your body and explore other worlds as part of the spiritual quest. Dream travel, and understanding it's messages were of great significance in the teaching. We will look at this more closely later on.

It is a curious thing, but in western culture, dreaming of trains is so often linked to movement upward, a journey to freedom. For Geoff it represented the opposite: a move to hell.

Suffice to say, at a very early age Geoff had already experienced a deeper reality than the day to day. Granted, he understood none of it, but it gave him a taste for doing more than just fitting in. It meant he had an interest in more than just existing, or working in the Nine to Five world of mediocrity. Perhaps it was necessary for him to have something more than this physical world to hold onto, because soon enough, just as he was torn from his childhood sweetheart, most everything he cared for was going to be taken away.

At Age Eight, Geoff and the family returned to the father, Duncan Harry Wallace, in Broken Hill.

Michael Notes: *One of the things we take for granted now is public hygiene, but in the days of DWH it was not the case. The health inspectors at that time were hated more than the police, forcing the people to clean up or be fined. They were about as loved as a parking officer who issues you fines, but because of their work, we have a clean country today.*

Even so, the TYPE of man who volunteered for this profession was, of necessity, one who cared not at all for another's feelings.

Return to Hell

roken Hill in the 1930's is was what most people with any degree of sophistication would consider a hellhole. Abusive miners, corrupt officials, and loads and loads of money pouring through the drinking establishments gave up two classes of people, the brutal and the meek. If the meek were going to inherit the Earth, let them pray it was not going to be this mining town.

Today we know it as the birth place of one of the largest mining corporations in the world, BHP, the Broken Hill Proprietary Company. There is a fantastic book of sketches of the town done in 1935 available from the Broken Hill Biliton website.

It is free to down load: www.goo.gl/iFLVwB

The depression was still not over by 1933 and jobs were thin on the ground. Duncan Harry did not like his posting to the mining town, but he was determined to make the best of it. Even in a secure government position, you dare not raise your head up and complain because you were easily replaced. On top of this, he had been alone there for almost seven years and had the embarrassment of his entire family decide to up and leave him. You might have imagined he would be over-joyed at their return? He was, for a few weeks.

I have made no great mention of Geoff's brothers during this time, mostly because Geoff himself made little comment. I imagine that as the youngest child he lived in his own bubble, but at around this time he started talking about Reg, Colin and Bob. However, any mention of Broken Hill itself is slight. There was the regular story of Duncan Harry losing his temper and threatening to kill one of the kids, but there was a mention when I was at the farm in the 1960's of him beating up his wife, Annette, and doing so quite badly. While my recollection of this is faint, I do recall Geoff getting drunk one night and talking about how he saw the old man beating up his mother. It affected him deeply. I cannot say if that incident was at Broken Hill, or later.

This must have been a deeply repressed memory, because unlike many of his stories, it was never repeated. What is known is that during the brief period of two years that the family was in Broken Hill, Geoff recalled it as a visit to hell. He did speak of seeing his battered mother, and that this was the reason they all took off to Townsville, to move onto a property near to where his mother's family (The Svenson's) lived. This was the Black River, and there are many tales of this period.

What is unclear is how Duncan followed the family to Townsville and got himself posted there. This was 1935. Perhaps it was because the depression was over that he could apply for and get new postings, but from Geoff's recollection, this was the start of many years of unmitigated terror. The older brothers would have known more, but they are all now deceased.

The thing that stuck with me was how often Geoff would repeat the story of his greatest fear, a paralysing fear: *He would die and his father would escape justice.* "He was such a smooth bastard. He knew all the things to do and say to make himself look good in front of any sort of authority. He tugged the forelock, was unflinchingly courteous and bowed humbly before any figure of respect. They would never see the uncontrollable, angry beast that emerged after a few drinks.

"I could see the future like it was a movie. He would shoot me one day when I failed some spelling test. He would blow my head off, and when the police came by asking questions he would sweetly say, with tears in his eyes, that his beloved but careless son had pulled a gun from the cabinet and was playing around with it when it accidentally went off. He would be so remorseful, so utterly in shock, and so self-recriminating about how he should have kept the ammunition higher and more out of reach, that the police would believe him. They would notch it down to another stupid child.

"I would be murdered, and he would get away with it scot-free."

Today we would call the father bi-polar, or perhaps schizophrenic. Clearly, the man suffered severe PTSD, but knowing this doesn't help anyone connected to the person. Duncan Harry Wallace was hell incarnate for his family. A hell that followed them to the Black River.

Geoff Notes: *When the parents separated, I was sent to Townsville to board with private people, and attend the Christian Brothers school. They were a pretty brutal lot, belting kids for any little excuse. I could spell anything in those days (even can today). We were given a spelling test of 10 words, with the promise of the cane for every one we got wrong. I didn't have a pencil, so couldn't write anything, and was adjudged by their strange reasoning to have got 10 wrong, even though I was a top speller. That got me a 'sixer' with their thick, and much-used strap which was about 20 inches long, half an inch thick, an inch or more wide, with a hacksaw blade sewn in the middle.*

TOWNSVILLE: The Black River

The Black River was not the safest place for raising children, even at the best of times. Apart from the crocodiles that regularly took anyone who swam there, the main danger was the black snake, the thing the river was named after. There were thousands of venomous snakes and inattentive youngsters died quite regularly.

If you go to any country cemetery you will see that between the years 1880 and 1940 the ages of those who died was generally over eighty or under fifteen. Why did so many children die at an early age? Hygiene was one reason, but snake bite took a lot of kids who were out playing in the bush. In regards the Black River, black snake anti-venom was developed initially in 1897 but it was a case of injecting venom into horses, prompting an immune response, then purifying antibodies from their blood to inject into snake-bitten patients.

The anti-venom at that time was not particularly effective. In Australia, the Commonwealth Serum Laboratories (CSL) began anti-venom research in the 1920s. It was not until 1930 that the first commercial Tiger Snake anti-venom was produced and not until the 1950's till a general spectrum treatment was produced. In terms of Geoff and his brothers, the reality was simple: if they got bitten, they died.

Soon after their arrival at the outskirts of Townsville the trouble started. By report, Annette had an affair, and Duncan went crazy.

Geoff and the other boys had a fifteen mile trip to school, on dirt roads, riding pushbikes. None of the boys had any shoes and they all attended a Christian Brothers school close to town. (The farm itself was not far from the present day Nickel Refinery, once owned by Clive Palmer.)

The regular story that was told and re-told many times over the years was of how the old man would get angry, really crazy angry, and start shouting at one of the boys, calling him a cur and a dog and loading up the shotgun to shoot him. It took me some time to understand that this was not a 'once-off' but a regular occurrence with DHW. The boy, and it could have been any of them, ran from the car and walked back home at a point that was just out of shotgun range. The father would drive slowly, keeping up with them, shouting abuse, and pointing the shotgun in their direction.

No one doubted he would pull the trigger. All the boys lived a life under constant threat from their insane father. The others would shut up, stay in the car, and say nothing. They all knew if they spoke, they would be next. The Silence of the Lambs! You can only imagine how insane he became when his wife had an affair.

There is no clear version of events from anyone about this period on the Black River, other than it was traumatic and that it was here that the father packed up and left the family home for good, never to return. Geoff had been sent off to board in town, so from this we might surmise that the family home was possibly a very unsafe place to live.

Black River, Townsville, QLD

Geoff Notes: *If you go north from Townsville towards Ingham (it would be the main northern highway), cross the Black River bridge and immediately turn right. We could immediately (or nearly immediately) cross the railway line there. Between here and the coast, there were NO dwellings or habitation, except our little house. Go along the Black River perhaps a mile, and then go north about another mile or two. That would be where we lived in the bush. We used to go to a creek called Alex Creek where there were oysters in the mud, plus crocodiles.*

I looked up the Black River, and it is pretty much as I described it, and about where we lived. There is a certain amount of distress when one sees how much things have changed. The road in the picture is where I used to ride my bike to school towards Townsville. You can see the railway line paralleling the road. Just across the railway line on the right of the road are a couple of buildings. That's where my cousin, Joe Brabon, lived (and may still do). He and I used to share chewing the lead bullets. We were about the same age. Alex Creek can be seen running into the Black. It certainly brings back memories. There are a couple of big, black patches there somewhere, which I guess to be fish farms.

The Canoe

G eoff was laughing as he recalled some rare memories of childhood at Townsville. "Back when we returned with my father to the Black River, my brothers decided it was going to be a good thing to make a boat and sail out into the crocodile infested waters. Did I mention the snakes? The place was also full of black snakes."

But snakes and crocodiles were a poor second in risk when compared to family members. Geoff told me this story only months before he passed on. It happened soon after they got there, when his brothers decided that building a canoe was the thing to do.

"One this particular day, Reg and Bob got a piece of roofing iron and riveted the two ends up, then tarred them, in order to make a sort of canoe. They duly put me in and all of us went paddling out onto the river." Unfortunately, the thing was full of holes and started sinking, so they all bailed out and swam back to the shore. Which was OK for the older boys, they could swim!" Apparently, only when they got to the river bank did they realize Geoff had not made it.

"The problem was, I couldn't swim, and sank like a stone. They probably only dived in to save me because if I died they would be in no end of trouble, so it was that they dragged my unconscious and already blue body out of the water. Obviously I survived, but from that moment on I was pretty sure my brothers wanted to kill me."

As Geoff later told me, "It was probably only the fear of a thrashing that they went back in to get me, because there were crocodiles in the river. I am told I had already started to turn blue. They somehow got the fluid out of my lungs (Bob knew CPR) and they resuscitated me." I must have looked a little astonished when being told this, because Geoff stopped chatting and gave me one of those looks. "You could be forgiven for thinking I had the idea I wasn't loved by my brothers ... But really, it was more that I wasn't really noticed."

Between drowning and the insane father, you start to wonder how any of the family survived. Yet you can be assured they did, because otherwise there would have been no relatives to write this book for!

This was one of the few stories Geoff recalls of that time after Sydney, between leaving Broken Hill and ending up in Inverell. It seemed to me that a curtain had been drawn over this part of his memory.

Taken

I always wondered about this part of Geoff's life. Geoff had been bordered out to a family in Townsville. He was put into this strange families house with no pocket money, no shoes, and the family he was staying with didn't seem to think they were being paid enough to feed the child as well as house him. Out the blue, Duncan turned up at the boarding home, collected Geoff, and took him to Inverell.

He didn't get to say goodbye to his mother or brothers and he didn't hear from them again for many years. "Why did you father just take you?" I was curious. There were other children he could have taken and my guess was that losing Geoff would cause his mother the most pain. Dad simply said, "He needed a slave to do everything and I was it."

He never mentioned the fact his mother traded him for her freedom. (I presume he didn't want to say anything to put his mother in a a bad light.) It turned out that Annette had been having an affair and agreed, under some sort of pressure from DHW, to let him take her youngest as part of the divorce. What we DO know is that Duncan put Geoff behind a sofa, brought in his brother, Colin, and got him to say horrid things about his mother. Part of a mind game to convince the young child, I suppose.

In a letter to his brother, June 2004, Geoff wrote, "*I had never, ever, held anything against her. My firm belief back then, and now, had always been that anyone who had an opportunity to get away from that psychopathic bastard, for whatever reason or at whose expense, should cut and run.*" From what I am given to understand, Duncan was excessively brutal, beating her and the other kids on a regular basis, and Geoff was effectively the price of freedom for the rest of the family.

Why Geoff? I suspect Duncan considered the youngest 'less corrupt' and more trainable than the other boys. I only discovered the letter from Geoff to Reg as I was about to have this book published. In it he clearly states how his mother lived with guilt her whole life for striking this bargain to get rid of Duncan. (It may well have been to save their lives)

It was now that the real terror for the young child started. For five years he was the sole focus of his father's insanity and lived in perpetual fear of a man that was not just dangerous, but who also loved mind games.

I suggested to Geoff that perhaps his father hated to see fear in his children and it triggered him to go crazy, thinking in some warped way this would 'toughen them up'. Geoff replied, "Or maybe he was just sadistic and brutal and enjoyed having power over a helpless child."

Geoff becomes "Stink Foot"

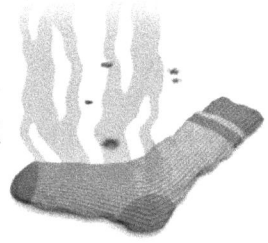

I nverell was a lovely place, set on the northern tablelands of New South Wales. It was very cold in winter, but for most of the year Inverell had a very pleasant climate. Geoff was going to school and his father had bought him shoes. Yet he had no idea what to do, how to keep a house, or how to raise a child. Geoff was expected to clean, wash, prepare meals and be the dogsbody for whatever needed doing, but neither he nor his father had training in any of it.

As a result he got clipped over the ear a lot. The oddest story of this period is that Geoff remembered how he only had one pair of socks and that they almost never got washed. His socks used to smell, which gave him the nickname of 'Stinkfoot', but he also got called 'Tomato Rack' because when he DID take his socks off, his feet were red raw. "The socks were stiff," Geoff recalled as he related the story to me. "And they really did stink. I have no idea why I didn't wash them."

Why were they never washed? It was never explained, but one thing is certain, living on his own later in life, Geoff was meticulously clean and tidy. I recall the liberal doses of Old Spice he would splash his face with and how everything was sent out to be ironed. No shirt was worn twice. In the 1960's it was not common for men to use deodorant and cologne, but no one was ever going to refer to Geoff as 'stinkfoot' ever again.

Existence in Inverell was hell. Geoff told me that he was regularly beaten for the smallest error, but the worst of it was when the father got drunk and decided to give him a spelling test. It was no ordinary test, as Duncan would load up a shotgun, show Geoff the shells going into the chambers, then hold up the gun to show he was clicking the safety off. Duncan then levelled the gun at his son's head and started the spelling test.

As related earlier, Geoff had no doubt he would die. What caused him constant fear was the fact that his father would murder him and get away with it. However, on a positive note, as a direct result of this training Geoff could spot a typo or spelling mistake on a page just by looking at it. Yet not if HE wrote it. It was a mysterious fact of human nature.

"I can spot a grammatical error or spelling mistake at fifty yards." he said to me on many occasions, "Yet when it is my OWN writing, I can't. We never see the faults in ourselves, even though we see them easily in others."

Once more he would quote Robbie Burns, *"Oh wat gift the givvee give us, to see ourselves as others see us."* I guess he was going to keep saying it until I got the message!

One of the funny stories about this time was when Geoff escaped. He ran away at age fourteen by stealing a push bike and riding off. He had no idea where he was going, maybe to the next town to see a relative, but he remembered the incredible freedom he felt while doing this: The open road, no one to tell you what to do. Finally, the world was his oyster and life was wonderful.

"I had absolutely no thought of consequences," said Geoff as he related the story. "All I knew was that I was getting away from that bastard, but after a few miles I pulled up at a railway station and came across a fellow who was sitting there utterly dejected. I don't remember what the conversation was, but I had finally found someone worse off then myself. In an act of incredible generosity I gave him my bike!"

"The one you stole?" I asked.

Geoff looked up with that twinkle in the eye, "I don't think it occurred to me at the time that if the fellow was picked up by the police for any reason, they would automatically assume he was the thief. He would say *'This kid came along and gave me his bike'* and the coppers would just laugh as they hauled him off to prison. Anyway, I didn't get very far, because in an act of remorse I went to report the fact I had stolen the bike to the local police. I can't remember much, but they took me back home, where I got a thrashing."

The details are unclear, but Geoff ran away more than a few times. Usually he was back before the father would notice him gone. There was mention of how the 'old man' would drink and that this would trigger off the worst episodes. The general idea was to not be around at those times.

The thing was, Geoff never knew when his father would lose it and go too far. Every beating he received could be his last. The old man, in a blind rage, might just pull out a gun and shoot him.

Yet it was a calculated rage. As previously mention: *Duncan knew his way around the powers that be. He would say that the child picked up a loaded weapon and accidentally shot themselves. He would do so with such a remorseful, sad face that the authorities would believe him.* Geoff had worked out the game plan and knew if he stayed his fate was sealed. There was only one option: He had to get away.

"As soon as I was able, at age fourteen, I got myself a job delivering letters with the Post Office. It paid very little, but it got me out of home. A year later, I was offered a posting to Tenterfield, a good distance from the old man, so I took it."

From the perspective of a child, the man was evil. What else could a child think? Imagine what anyone would say of YOU if you gave your child spelling tests with a loaded shotgun at their head? Remember: Duncan always made sure to show Geoff that the shotgun WAS loaded, and that the safety WAS off. As mentioned this did have a positive side effect, Geoff's grasp of spelling and punctuation was second to none.

In later years he did a lot of proof reading, so he put that early training to good use. I certainly know how much effort he put into fixing up all the errors in the books he checked for me. We were chatting about Duncan one day, a few years before he passed on, when Geoff asked what I thought of the whole scenario. *"Why would he do this to a child?"* he asked, referring to Duncan

He didn't expect me to answer, but it occurred to me that his father was confused. I was unaware at the time that DHW had been in the trenches of World War One, yet I suspected the real issue was that Duncan had a utter disdain for weakness of any kind. If he saw any trace of fear in the children, he made it his personal mission to beat it out of them. I suggested to Geoff that his father may not have been evil, just driven.

I now suspect that what happened inside Duncan's head was not all that unusual for returning soldiers from WW1. First, there is a guilt you survived when all your friends died. Second, you don't fit in, and will never fit in, with ordinary society. Third, you were schooled in ultra violence, and having survived this, you now saw everyone else as weak.

Regarding my comment that his father was driven to extinguish any fear he saw in his children, Geoff didn't say much, only, "You never knew him, did you?"

However, back to Townsville and the time when the marriage of Geoff's parents irrevocably broke down. This was when the darkest days for Geoffrey John Wallace began, and they were dark indeed. The fear and anxiety that was impressed into his spirit after being plucked from the family haunted him his entire life. It was not that he was locked in with the insane father, but that his mother had willingly handed him over into this situation. No one loved him, no one cared. Dark days indeed.

Yet this stress also created his humour and gave him the ability to see things from the perspective of others. When you are imprisoned with a monster, and Duncan was surely this in the eyes of his children, you learn to find gaps in reality that your consciousness can escape through. Humour, compassion, and understanding can become shelters from the storms raging outside.

On escaping a trapped situation: Geoff had Nelida staying with him in the period just before he passed on. She had made a promise to come back and look after him in his old age and keeping this oath meant that she found herself sleeping on the couch in his tiny, one bedroom flat. She kept this up for eighteen months until he passed. My visiting every week was her one great escape and Dad laughed about this on more than one occasion, commenting, "I suppose you coming gives poor Nell the same feeling I had of escape!"

Geoff always tried to see things as other people saw them, and it gave him an extraordinary sense of humour. Why? I am not sure, but regardless of how it came about, he found a lightness and humour in simple things.

Inverell was hell. This period affected Geoff his whole life, giving him a sense of extreme anxiety that he could never shake. The father seemed hell bent on instilling fear into the child he had taken from the rest of his family, but there is one clear and distinct incident that can, perhaps, give us an insight in the to day to day fear Geoff suffered.

"Well, I'll be. ... I must've been holding
the dang work order like *this!*"

**"Living with my father was hell. At age thirteen,
every day with him was an eternity you suffered,
one that you truly believed would never end."**

The Hair Cut

Like many Australian families, parents tended to cut their own children's hair. It saved money and who cared what you looked like as a kid? One day, Geoff was on a stool, towel wrapped around his neck, when his father received a letter from Annette. The effect was to send him into a rage.

It appeared that she and the boys had the temerity to go visit relatives in New Zealand. *How DARE they up and leave like that, the curs, the dogs!* Duncan was cursing blindly while slashing at Geoff's hair, saying, "If I for one moment thought you would turn out like those DOGS I would kill you right now, right now! The DOGS, how DARE THEY!"

Duncan was ranting, red faced, and incredibly angry, yet at the same time he continued to cut his son's hair. The scissors were being waved at random in threatening motions towards the unfaithful family that not only didn't love him, but dared to go overseas while he stayed home. The occasional snip would slice a few more hairs, but the problem was that in between these were many random swings. slashing at phantoms in the air.

Now, this was just Annette and her kids going to New Zealand to see relatives, but Duncan saw it as a betrayal of some sort. Geoff just sat there in fear, frozen. He knew that at any moment the scissors would slash his throat and he would die, bleeding out in pain on the ground. He didn't die, obviously, but his hair was murdered: a thatch of long and short bits. It would probably be quite a fashionable cut in the present day.

"At fourteen or so, every day is a week, every month is a year, and every year is a decade. All I saw in those days was a destiny of never escaping this hell, of being there, locked in with the old man, forever. But then the war started (WWII) and everything began to change."

Geoff gathered his thoughts, "By fifteen I had managed to get a job in the post office, delivering mail on the pushbikes. Then the local one closed and I was transferred to Tenterfield. I was not at all unhappy to get away from the old man, it was the perfect excuse, but he would not sign the form that would allow me to get the away from home allowance. I guess he was trying to force me to quit and go back home.

"But I was never going back. I had enough for board and very little else. I didn't even have enough money to eat, but I was away from that bastard. Occasionally, I would have a few pence in my pocket and the thing to do was the local cinema.

"I went to see a film in town, *'In the Navy'* it was called, and it was the most exciting thing I had ever experienced. At that moment, I decided the only thing for me to do was to join the Navy. In 1942, when the local recruiting officers came to town, I marched in and signed up. I must have lied about my age, but the war record shows me signing up in April 1943. (This places Geoff at Age Seventeen - acceptable for the Navy at that point) I got in and this is what got me out of Tenterfield and away from the grasp of the old man."

It is such a small thing, cutting hair. Yet it became a life threatening event. A common and ordinary thing that shows perfectly the abject fear Geoff lived in and the madness of Duncan. It tells us clearly how an uncontrolled insanity could completely take over Duncan Harry, yet the 'other' side was possibly worse. The controlled and calculating D.H.W. was an evil S.O.B.

Remember, he made sure Geoff's own brother said terrible things about his mother, and made sure he heard it. He wanted to destroy the bond between mother and son and get complete control over the helpless child.

As a note: Years later, "In The Navy" was on TV and Geoff watched it. His only comment was, "I can't believe that piece of crap got me so excited to join the Navy."

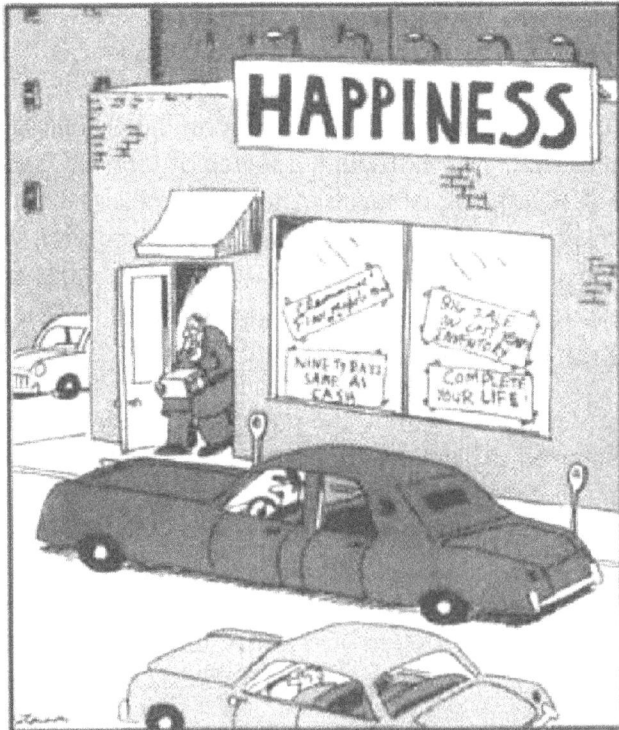

His few friends had told him he could never
buy it, but Mr. Crawley surmised that they just
didn't know where the store was.

DUNDERHEAD

D underhead is such an old fashioned word. It means idiot, or fool. To be called this meant you were incapable of any task above the mundane. Duncan Harry used the term a lot, as he had a very sarcastic and critical personality. One such case was evidenced early in Geoff's life when D.H.W was talking about him passing his intermediate.

This was the exam that allowed you to pass from primary school to secondary school and was considered an essential certificate to ge, in order to proceed with your education. Your report would read "John Smith: 1:A, 2:B, 3:A" and so on. One = English, Two = History, 3 = Geography. These were the core subjects, the rest were mathematics, etc. "1:A" meant an "A" grade in English.

At age Nine during the first year back with the old man, in Broken Hill, Geoff had just passed his intermediate with good grades. For a child, this was a significant event that meant you carried on to higher learning. However, his father looked over the pass, and said, "This is no big thing. Even poor old *Dunderhead* Reg passed his Intermediate!" And that was it. Not one ounce of praise or recognition. Maybe Geoff had turned up with a hopeful look on his face that needed to be dashed? Who can say, but the reality was that the first significant academic achievement he reached was treated with disdain.

In Geoff's memory, the only time he ever recalled Duncan Harry handing out any sort of praise was when the kids proved to be good with firearms. A good shot elicited some sort of compliment. Is it any wonder that all the boys were first class shooters? All the brothers had exceedingly fine weapons and all were capable of packing their own ammunition and pulling down (to repair or clean) any gun, pistol or rifle they had.

After he took Geoff away from his brothers and mother, Duncan bought him a shotgun. Why? Maybe it was to cover the shock of loss, maybe it was to give the boy a distraction. Maybe it was to cover up an accidental killing of the child? It is an unknown as to why DHW suddenly found a generosity of spirit, but the result was immediate. Geoff fired off a couple of rounds that killed six quail. Turns out, Geoffrey was a natural born shooter. This deeply impressed his old man.

Guns were very important to Geoff. When growing up, I recall the first time I was handed a dummy rifle. I was drilled in every aspect of how to hold it, how to load it, and how to clean it. I was drilled in everything before I was so much as given the responsibility of an air rifle. (I was to kill many Coke cans with that rifle) Only when I proved to be adequate with this rifle, which to Geoff was merely a toy, was I allowed to use the Mauser .22 and some years after that, the shotgun and hunting rifles.

I loved that Mauser. It was a beautiful thing, German telescopic sights and amazingly accurate. Geoff kept it, even after the gun laws changed, and only reluctantly handed it in during the very last years of his life.

Geoff was always looking for the funny side to things, but there was not an ounce of lightness about him when he drilled you with how to handle weapons. Even at the time, I knew this was Duncan Harry filtering through. Dad lost any sense of levity, and was dead serious when handling a gun or rifle. Of Note: He had a WALL of weapons at the farm, each for a specific purpose.

The rules of gun safety were simple:
- *A: Never point a gun or rifle at anything you do not intend to shoot.*
- *B: Never walk around with the safety off.*
- *C: Where possible, give warning to other members of your party before you discharge a weapon.*
- *D: Carry your weapon with the barrel pointed down to the ground, or pointing directly into the air. NEVER carry it horizontally.*

I asked about carrying the gun with the barrel pointed upwards, and Geoff just said, "You point the barrel upwards to shoot birds, or let off a warning shot. Point the barrel down towards the ground at all other times, until you are ready to take a shot. Otherwise, you only lift the gun upwards when you are turning to talk to people in your party."

I know it was the same drill they got from their old man and it was the only time I saw Geoff without his trademark glint of humour. Possibly a good thing, considering the seriousness of making a mistake. There were other rules, all common sense. When you were finished for the day, you unloaded your weapon, pulling back the bolt to ensure that any cartridge still in the chamber was removed. You removed the magazine, ensuring that the safety was ON, then you removed the bolt itself to be certain it could not misfire. Then you could clean your weapon, oil it, and rack it.

When not dealing with weapons, Geoff was light and happy. Not so with his father. Duncan Harry was unerringly sarcastic and critical of everything and anything anyone did. It was not just aimed towards his own family, it was everyone. No one was free from his cutting comments. Perhaps this came from HIS father, an officer in the British Army (like Duncan had been before coming to Australia). The attitude smacked of the English belief in personal superiority and the subsequent inferiority of everyone else, something so typical of the Raj in India.

Yet I also wonder if Duncan's aggressive stance came about as a defence from his own inner turmoil. I wonder if he was so harsh on Geoff in Inverell because of his OWN fear. Why do I ask this? Duncan would have seen how terrified his youngest was and instead of being kind, did he decide that to beat the fear out of the child? Perhaps he believed he had to, otherwise, how would the boy survive the harsh world?

This is not to ameliorate or downgrade the child abuse Geoff suffered. It is not an excuse, however, we know the misguided mind of a man trapped by his own internal fears does strange things. Priests who molest young children are an example of this. They are preaching love, but they deal out abuse. Why? Internal demons are driving them. How much of the cutting, vitriolic nature of Duncan came from HIS father? How much fear? It's called a MEME and I remember my uncles could be incredibly caustic to their children and, in earlier years, Geoff could be quite sarcastic.

One of the reasons my ears perked up when told this story about Reg being called a 'dunderhead' by DHW was because I had heard Reg call 'Young Geoff' an idiot, a fool, a DUNDERHEAD. Perhaps because of this my father (who young Geoff was named after) took my cousin under his wing. He encouraged him to learn new words, take up martial arts, and do things that built up your confidence.

Many years later, towards the end of their lives, Cousin Geoff organised for me to bring up my father to meet his father once more. They had not met in person for some twenty years, and quite frankly, I had expected more of the same sarcastic wit I had seen from Reg for most of my life. But I was surprised, there was none of it. More to the point, the brothers were laughing, happy and enjoying themselves. The video of this is up on You Tube: **youtube.com/watch?v=-RyuKJEEC4g**

You will hear me laughing a lot on this video. (You know how it is, you try not to, and it just gets worse.) It was a wonderful day. Yet, joyful as it was, the real miracle occurred as I was leaving. Reg asked if I remembered Uncle Colin, a prisoner of war like Reg had been. Of course I did, Colin was quite mad, but a lovely man.

Reg commented. "Well, I used to think him a fool, an idiot. He just didn't care what anyone else thought ... He did not give a stuff. But now I know he was RIGHT, he was bloody well RIGHT!"

In that moment it dawned on me. All that sarcasm was a defence! In his case, a defence against what people thought. Was it fear of what others thought that drove Duncan as well? We will never know, but one thing IS certain: Duncan hated any sign of fear in another.

For now, Geoff's next stage in life was World War Two. By 1943 he has joined the Navy and found himself working as a telegrapher in New Guinea.

In The Navy

H is time in the Post Office proved to be the starting point of an entirely new career. As he already had some experience with telegrams (decoding Morse and delivering the sad news of someone's death to relatives was a standard thing in the early days of the war) Geoff ended up in the telegraphy room. Morse Code is something we never hear of today, other than the dot dot dot dash dash dash dot dot dot of the SOS signal, yet that complex system of dashs and dots was the mainstay of communication for decades and nowhere was it more prevalent than the Navy. Geoffrey John Wallace became first class operator, one who was considered to be the best in the entire Australian Navy.

He used the notoriously difficult three button Morse key. Only a handful of operators were up to the standards required by this difficult instrument. As a result, he could work with a speed and efficiency that was unsurpassed. Geoff had finally found something he was good at and could be proud about.

Geoff joined in 1943 and was posted to a secret island in the bay off the coast of Madang, New Guinea. The name of the island was "Bil Bil" and it stood just South of Madang. It was used by the navy specifically for communications and had no standing army to defend it, other than basic weapons and a few anti-aircraft installations. It was here that he met lifelong friend, Max Turner and through Max, Frank Wintle. (Later to meet Frank's cousin, Joy Wintle, who became Geoff's wife)

Bil Bil was a place Geoffrey absolutely shone. Training officers used to parade new recruits in to watch Geoff at work, saying that this was an example of almost perfect morse. It was here that he mastered the 'Three Switch Key', the Rolls Royce of Morse Keys. Groups would be brought in to watch him "perform" and other operators would leave with their mouths agape. It was not thought possible to be so fast and so perfect. P/N S8544 Telegraphist Geoffrey John Wallace had mastered the art.

He would talk about related subjects on odd occasions. "Morse operators had a pattern. You learned to pick who an operator was by the WAY you heard the Morse coming through. The various styles were as defined as a fingerprint. I could tell you who it was on the other end in just a few seconds of hearing an incoming message. However, most people receiving my signals thought it was one of the new machine-based keys, because it was just so perfect." Geoff was not bragging, he was simply stating the facts. He was proud of this achievement to the day he died.

Max and Geoff were larrikins of the highest order. There were many stories of how they simply did what they wanted and suffered very little punishment because, as first class telegraphers, they had to be on call 24/7. There was no locking them up! But I was curious about this island in Mill Bay and we tracked it down on Google Earth. It was a tiny thing, barely a few football fields in size, nether-the-less it had a one hundred strong compliment and was central to ALL communication in the South Pacific during WW 2.

Specifically, it was this little island that was feeding the US navy the essential information that allowed the US forces to take Guam and track the Japanese carrier fleet, as some examples. What they did there changed the course of the conflict and yet, with his usual flippant ease, when my sister asked Geoff what he did during the war, he said, "Nothing much, just hung about. In fact, I was given an award by the Japanese - for not contributing to the war effort!"

My four-year-old sister believed him and lived for years under the illusion that her father was in some way a supporter of the Japanese during the war. Amazing what a child will accept as truth and from that acceptance a whole garden of beliefs will grow.

We had Google Earth loaded up and we were checking the general area as we discussed this period of his life. As I looked at this island on Geoff's computer, something you could only describe as 'the obvious' struck me. I asked, "So it was only communications, all on their own, on this tiny island? Do you think you were put off away from everyone for a reason?"

Geoff looked puzzled and said, "I never really though about it. It was where we were sent, it was what we did. You didn't question orders."

I looked at him and suggested, "Seems to me that out of all the operational things going on during the war, that you were the most easily traceable. As you were using wireless and Morse all day long, perhaps you were put there to NOT be a danger to everyone else?"

"I suppose that is correct," Geoff said. "It would make sense."

"So, throughout your entire war experience, you were essentially a target." I pointed out.

"Well, no one ever told us that!" Geoff answered, then added, "But they wouldn't would they?"

I laughed, Geoff laughed, then he added, "No one wants to be told they are a bunny in the gun sights, do they? But even if we were advised of the obvious, there was no questioning orders. And at any rate, the place was incredibly busy. There was simply no time to even think of anything but the work and when you weren't working, you were drinking, or sleeping. The island was absolutely non-stop."

Exactly when Geoff met Frank Wintle's cousin, Joy, is unclear, but it was at some point after the war when they were on R&R from the Navy. He and Frank were in Sydney and they called by to visit the cousins. The thing is, the one Geoff was interested was Veronica, Joy's sister. The quiet religious girl was not his type, but the bold and brassy Vonny (Veronica Wintle) smoking her long-stem cigarettes, drinking brandy, staying out late and partying, this was HIS type of woman.

I asked Geoff why he married Joy and he said, "I honestly don't know. Because she was willing, maybe?"

The war came to a close and somehow all the brothers had survived. Colin was a POW in Europe, a member of a flight crew that had been shot down. He came back with issues, schizophrenic by all accounts. *(Note: Colin was unerringly kind towards myself. I can only go by reports from other family members regarding his problems.)* Reg was a skeleton. He had been taken prisoner by the Japanese, and worked to the point of death, yet he had somehow survived. He was in a work camp outside Hiroshima when the bomb dropped, and saw the mushroom cloud.

To his great credit, he did not think "Good, they are killing Japs!" instead his thoughts at the time were simply that this would end the war, and that because of this, many of his friends would survive.

Geoff was at a loose end, and moved to Sydney because both Frank and Max were there. He took up many odd jobs before finding his feet, which was back in New Guinea.

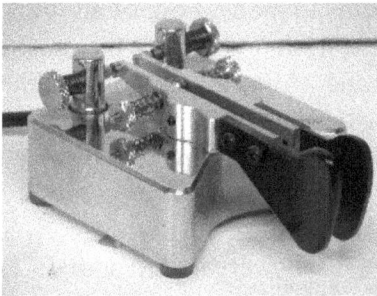

Geoffrey John Wallace entered the Australian Naval Reserve as P/N S8544 and worked as a Telegraphist. He received the following medals:
1939-45 Star
Pacific Star
War Medal
Australian Service Medal

Four Brothers - One Father - Two Wars

It is worth noting a truly remarkable thing. The Father, Duncan, survived the World War One trenches, and somehow his four sons all came through World War Two. Not unscathed, Reg survived the Burma Railway, and Colin survived Nazi Germany, a feat which in itself is remarkable, but for all four brothers to have lived when so many families lost at least one of their loved ones is almost unprecedented.

War casts a long shadow. And this shadow is never more potent than when it is hidden in the dark recesses of the mind. We know Duncan came back a different man after the trenches, what we cannot know is what he might have been were it not for that experience.

But we must be grateful he survived! Geoff always said that gratitude is the cheapest thing you can pay, and if you pay this one small thing on a regular basis it gives the greatest reward, contentment. *Bless the small things between the cracks of trouble, and trouble falls to pieces.*

Note by Michael: *There was a friend of my father and myself, an Eckankar connection, who summarised Geoff's sense of gratitude. Erwin Baudzus was a sailor, like Geoff, but he served in the German navy. He survived three sinkings of the ships he was on, and one day when talking about shadows in the mind, he said, "Hardly anyone lives after their ship has gone down. Yet it happened to me three times! I had no idea why I was so lucky, but guessed that a silent hand was helping in the background.*

"Everyone had a difficult childhood, everyone has problems, everyone suffers in some way or another. Dresden at the end of the war was worse than the war itself, if this were possible. Eva (his wife) and myself could not get enough food to eat, which is why I took to option to emigrate to Australia. I made a decision, to put my focus on where I was going, and bless every moment I am alive. It could have so easily been otherwise."

"The greatest turning point came when I came to Australia. I was fairly certain I would be thrown into jail, or shot, but at least Eva would be able to have a decent life. Yet when I landed in Sydney and came off the boat, the clearance officer looked at my file and said 'Oh you are a mechanic! Can you fix Mercedes cars?' I said 'of course' and they said this was great and that I already had a job waiting for me.

"I said, 'But the war?' and the fellow replied, 'That's done with mate. We won, you lost, it's over.' I survived three ships going down, the humiliation of defeat, starvation, but this cheerful acceptance and happy Aussie attitude destroyed my ego. I was overcome with gratitude, and right then, I decided Australia was my home. I bless every day I live here."

After the War

Geoff worked initially at the Post Office, as a travelling operator. This meant he was on call to go to wherever the PO needed him that day or week. They did not pay for fares to get anywhere, and certainly did not cover the time spent travelling to some oftentimes distant postings. Geoff was not happy about this, as the pay was poor, and he was a little bit over telegraphy, at any rate. It was dull compared to the Navy.

He was living in Bondi, but being sent all over the place. Finally, it was to the Western Suburbs, Canterbury to be specific. This was a train and bus journey of some hours, which meant very early starts and late returns. And this was unpaid time, not even the fares were reimbursed. Geoff was getting excessively tired. One Friday afternoon he was the last to leave the Post Office and he completely forgot to lock it up.

People were reasonably honest in those days, but to leave a post office, with all the valuable stamps and equipment in there, totally unlocked for the entire weekend was a serious offence. He was dragged over the coals, called irresponsible and other insults. It was a reprimand too far. He was jack of it and with no plan for the future, he quit. Did the Post Office realise they just lost one of the best Morse operators in the world? No. Did they care? Not a whit.

Max Turner was at Bondi now, and together they went out looking for odd jobs. Working as a builders labourer was the first serious gig, one that Geoff was entirely ill equipped to do. They had to gather the hot bricks, delivered to site soon after they came out of the furnace, and carry them to the brickies. Then they had to make the 'mud', the sand and cement mix that was the mortar that held the bricks in place. After this you carried it all up to the waiting brickies. You had to be quick, it was your job to make sure there was no downtime for the highly paid bricklayers.

In the 1940's a bricklayer was paid four times the wage of an accountant. They were not to be kept waiting or idle for even a minute, but Geoff was a bit of a klutz, and the work was incredibly hard. By weeks end, he was jack of it, and made up a fictitious excuse that he had a sick relative he had to see, so he could not make it back by next Monday. Geoff laughed when telling me this story. "The only comment the foreman on the site made was, 'Good!'."

"I gathered they were not particularly impressed by the new guy, and were quite happy for me to leave." Geoff joked. "I then got a far more suitable job, as a bar useful at the Coogee pub. You did anything they needed done. Clean the loos, sweep the floors, serve drinks, shuck oysters, wash aprons, whatever was required.

"This went quite OK for a while, but one day some of my mates from the Navy happened to walk into the bar. Obviously, I did what was natural and went around the other side to sit and drink with them. When the boss came out and saw his barman downing a beer with the customers, I was fired." We both laughed, because it was so typical of Geoff. He added, "There was not a lot of understanding given to an employee who not only shirked his duty, but who also stayed to drink the profits!"

Geoff was in fits at this point, gasping for air in between the peculiar and quiet laughter he had, "I was never very good with consequences. This was when I decided I needed a real change, and I had an offer from the husband of Mum's (his mother, Annette) sister to go work in New Guinea. I was already engaged to Joy by this time, and as there was certainly no sex before marriage with that one, so hanging around penniless was no great option. Picking up the extra cash would go a long way to helping us get a start.

Thus, from the humiliation of being a lousy employee with no future, the journey to becoming "Dollars Wallace" began!

Coogee Bay Hotel Circa: 1946

Michael Notes: *Geoff loved his comedy shows. All the old American performers like Red Skelton, Bob Hope, and shows like F Troop, Bilko and Get Smart. He had 'Get Smart' on his VHS tapes, and had all the episodes, but he ignored them and always watched it on TV. All his life, even though he had seen them a hundred times, he would laugh at the same routines. "Missed by THAT much!"*

New Guinea Bound

G eoff's aunt was Ida Acherly, a lovely lady. She was married to Charlie Acherly, the same family mentioned in the "Merrylands" chapter, where Geoff had fallen in love with their daughter, Doreen, at age eight. It was Charlie who had written Geoff (probably on Annette's prompting) and suggested he make his way to Moresby, to work on the docks organising the shipment of goods onto and off the wharf. Geoff already had a basic understanding of Pigeon English, the simplified language used to communicate with the natives, so he could work with the labourers and tell them what to do.

The job meant very long hours, from seven in the morning up to eleven at night, but it paid incredibly well. Geoff loved it and for the first time in his life he felt free. It was not just the independent nature of the job, but the nature of the country. New Guinea was a place not constrained with social do's and don'ts. It was a world where he flourished. He decided that this was the place for him. He liked the people, he could cope with the humidity, and he was paid really well.

The task was simple. Everything came in mesh baskets, which were craned on and off the waiting cargo ships. You started early, finished late, and all day long, sixteen hundred pound baskets were being craned off ships, then shifted up, down, and across the docks. This is how it was before containers, baskets lifted by cranes with mesh nets. Everything involved a lot of physical labour.

At first Geoff stayed with the Acherly's for three months, after which he moved to a boarding house, with pigs in the back yard. "They were nice pigs, though I barely got to know them, as I was working such long hours." I really don't know why Geoff seemed to think this mention of the pigs was important, but I suspect it was where he learned one of the great secrets of diplomacy in New Guinea.

It was possibly at this place where he was told how to get on with the locals. If you had to work in a tribal area, the first thing you did was to go see the head man, in person, and take him a pig as a gift. This ensured he gave you approval for being there, which meant you were under his guardianship. Such a simple thing, but the gift of a pig in their culture was something worth more than jewels and gold. They were even more highly prized than wives!

There is a 1950's Chips Rafferty movie made in Port Moresby up on You Tube that you may find interesting:
https://www.youtube.com/watch?time_continue=10&v=LYOux58UT2g

After Nine months on the docks he returned to Sydney. After all, there had been a wedding organised and, as the groom, he was expected to turn up. He had already made some two thousand pounds, a small fortune in those days. To relate it to current values, this was enough to buy five houses in the Western Suburbs of Sydney.

However, soon after he arrived, his future wife, Joy, had a falling out with her uncle, the man who was going to be paying for the wedding. Rather than scale things back, Joy convinced Geoff they should spent the lot on their wedding. "Looking back, not the smartest move." He said to me, sardonically.

"Spending all that money?" I asked.

"Getting married," he replied.

"Why didn't you marry Aunty Von? I know you fancied her."

The Kanimbla

"I have no idea why. I much preferred her to Joy, but I don't think she was the marrying type."

She wasn't. Aunty Von, beloved by the family, a virtual mother to Geoff's kids, never married, never had children, and never seemed to regret this. At any rate, the wedding happened and Geoff convinced Joy that New Guinea was the place they had to be. She went with her new husband, sailing up there on the Kanimbla. This was a passenger ship recently converted from a Naval Troop carrier. On board, Geoff counted the cash, they had the grand total of thirty pounds left.

It was at this time that he broached the subject of children with Joy. He explained to me, "We were going into rough territory. I have been accepted into the government administration, looking after native labour. What this meant was that we will be getting some remote postings. It was not the place to raise children. So I said to Joy that, when we stopped over-night in Port Moresby, that she needed to see a local doctor and arrange for some contraception."

Joy proceeded off ship to do as she was asked by her new husband, but the problem was she was a devout Catholic. Contraception was a sin. She didn't go to the doctor, she went to the local priest with her serious concern. He would have told her what to say. (I am obviously paraphrasing but the following is known to be a general conversation priests had with Catholic women in the day). "Just tell your husband the doctor found you could not have children. It is not a lie or a sin when you are acting to obey the word of God."

"But what happens when we have children?"

"It is God's will if you have children. After he has them, he will learn to love them." The priest would have answered.

Geoff was reminiscing about that time. "She came back and told me that she could not have children, therefore contraception was not necessary. Foolishly, I believed her." The newly weds were posted up to a grass hut at Manus Island. This is no exaggeration, it was literally a grass hut, with a wooden floor. And can you believe it! God's will be done! This was where the first son, Peter, was born.

Then they were moved on to Kokopo, where the second son, Greg, is born. This place is a beautiful part of the world, truly a dream to behold. It is on the outskirts of Rabaul, but it is a deceptive paradise. Volcanic eruptions from Tavurvur are a regular and life threatening event in that area. After the last eruptions of 1994, Kokopo became the defacto main city, though Rabaul is slowly being rebuilt.

After two years they moved to Lae, where my oldest sister, Julie, was born, then onto Port Moresby where my sister Trish was born. I think it is fair to say that Geoff had realised by now that Joy had lied to him about not being able to have children. At this juncture, he was also getting jack of the native labour business. There was no future in it, and it offered no permanent position where you could settle down.

The next posting was to be Higaturu, a place with only thirty white people. It may not seem to be a place you wanted to go, but as the only other option on the table was Goroka, a godforsaken backwater up in the hills, it was a no-brainer. "No one in their right mind wanted to go to Goroka. It was the dead-end posting and I really fought hard to get Higaturu. It was a much better option." The family was due to fly out the following day, but Geoff came down with a terrible flu and was unable to leave. This was Saturday the Twentieth of January, 1951.

That next day, just after their plane would have dropped them off, Mount Lamington exploded. It wiped out the entire settlement of Higaturu, killing every one of the thirty white residents and thousands of natives. Not one white person within 16 miles of the crater survived. Geoff paused in telling me this tale. We had looked up the eruption on Google, and saw the photos of devastation. He simply said, "*Not my will, oh Lord.*

"One day people will learn to trust that life maybe has a better idea than we do about the right place for us to be. If it were not for that flu, the whole family would have been wiped off the face of the earth. And so, despite all my efforts to the contrary, as a result we were posted to Goroka."

Mt. Lamington Eruption 1951

Goroka

G oroka worked out to be much better than expected. It was where "Dollars Wallace" got his nickname. The place was, despite the rumours, a beautiful and friendly place. One of the reasons things worked out so well for him was an old hand had told him the way to have a trouble-free existence in New Guinea. (As mentioned: When dealing with native labour you to go to the headman of whatever village the workers were coming from, and give him a pig. Once you did this, the workers gave you no trouble.)

If you showed respect in the correct tribal way, you were given the keys to the jungle, so to speak. It is no different in our society. You grease the palm of the person in a position of influence and things work better..

In New Guinea, the white people were, for the most part, honest to the bone. You simply did not tell your neighbour a lie, or say you were going to do something you had no intention of doing. People like that were fairly quickly ostracised from normal society. However, there were other ways to be ejected from the local scene and the most significant of these was to have children to native women. This was considered as "going Tarzan" and was seen as entirely unacceptable.

There was one such man up in the hills behind Goroka. We will call him Bob Jones. He had a few "wives" and lived a little like a tribal chieftain up in the hills. He was one of the few that got in early and actually owned his land, whereas most settlers lived on land leased from the government. (The Australian Government, right at the outset, had the view they were caretakers until the New Guinea people could look after themselves)

Geoff had no bias towards Bob and, unlike the previous fellow in charge of native labour, Geoff sent up workers to help the man out. As long as a plantation owner paid the going rate to the men, he would do his part and find them suitable staff. This was not organised slavery, but local men who were willing to work for wages. Granted that the wages were not particularly high, but for a the man doing the work it meant he were well ahead of his fellows and could buy things other men in their village could only dream about. (See 'WanTok': www.goo.gl/XdeXtg)

Shortly after arriving at Goroka, Geoff won a motorcycle and side-car in a poker game, so he had transport. Plus soon after, in another game, he had won some five hundred pound, which was enough to consider branching out into farming, where the real money was. This is where the "Dollars Wallace" saga gets underway. Geoff was up in the hills talking with Bob, seeing if he needed anything, when the man, out the blue, offered him the use of some land he owned that was closer into town. He wasn't using it, Geoff was welcome to it.

Dad planted beans, a very humble crop, but it was a vegetable not grown in the highlands. In fact, most people did not believe commercial fruit and vegetables COULD be grown in New Guinea and just about everything was flown in from Cairns. It made this type of food valuable and beans were a fast growing, easy to sell crop. The problem was, there was no market system set up. Geoff went a different course. He had to, there were bushels of beans he needed to move! So he sent them direct to the local stores in each of the main towns with a note, saying they could pay him a fair price after they had sold them. No one in their right mind flew out fresh vegetables on consignment, but Geoff did.

It was either that or plough it back in. Well, as a result of this unique way of selling goods, he made a lot of money from the beans plus having access to native labour meant he could plant and harvest it while still doing his job. In fact, he made so much money he was able to buy the lease on a property that came up for sale, Kamaliki.

"I never thanked Bob for giving me the use of that land. I knew nothing about gratitude back then, and feel regret that I never properly told him how much I appreciated it," Geoff said in his last months.

I put a different light on it. "Perhaps you DID thank him by not judging him. He was isolated, alone, yet you accepted him and helped him when no one else would. Perhaps him offering you the use of that land was HIS way of being grateful to YOU?"

Geoff was not convinced. "There is that, but gratitude is never one way. I feel grateful now, yet that is easy. Looking back and then counting our blessings, or cursing our regrets, this is the easiest thing in the world to do. Being grateful and appreciative in the moment, that is something else and it is much harder to achieve."

There is not a lot you can say, but I put myself in the place of Bob Jones, and I know what he felt. Someone who did not judge him was the gift of a gold worth more than any prize. It meant acceptance plus, as a result, he had the workers he needed to bring in the coffee.

Geoff Notes: *The thing about New Guinea, there was no government that got in the way. There was no tax, no complication. You could just go and make money, and create a life for yourself. It was freedom at a most basic level.*

And it worked! Everyone was happy, everyone made money, and no one suffered for it.

HIGHLAND VEGETABLE GROWERS
(G. J. WALLACE, PROPRIETOR)
GOROKA, T.N.G.

STATEMENT OF ACCOUNT FOR

MONTH OF ....

ACCOUNT ....

DATE	INVOICE	PARTICULARS		DEBIT	CREDIT
1956		January K. Kan			
		Bee O'Brien Bag		7.16.8	
Charged.		Gibbes	4	8.13.4	
		Bush	10	10.3.4	
		Woodward	4	5.13.4	
		Madelon	8	11.6.8	
		Pendland	21	31.0.0	
NOT Charged		D.C.A. 1st 4 bag			
		19th 4			
		25th 4			

Invoicing Record: Goroka 1956. The cost of this one receipt is over Fifty Nine Pounds, more than five times the average weekly wage of the time. These vegetables were all sent by air to the various plantations around Goroka, and this would have been only one of many that month.

Coffee Judging

Goroka was all about the coffee. It produces perhaps the finest beans in the world, having the perfect climate and growing conditions for Arabica, the premium strain. However, the locals were paid half what growers in Brazil were getting. Geoff, having bought Kamaliki, was now a coffee grower, and he knew they were all getting paid less than the true value, but what to do? The ONLY company buying coffee was Nescafe' and they set the price. So Geoff, along with the local growers cooked up a simple idea.

The next time the man from Nescafe' came to town, they would say they had been having an argument as to who grew the best beans. In reality, the beans the man would be judging had been gathered from the best plantations from all over the world. He was 'really' judging the value of New Guinea coffee.

And so the trap was set and the short, bald man that no one liked was surprised to find he was cordially received. He was a taciturn little soul, not prone to any sense of joy, but they plied him with drinks at the local bar that night and regaled him with their woes. In particular, their big argument: *No one here could decide who grew the best bean.*

He was asked if he might possible set aside some of his time on the morrow to do a taste test, as HIS was the only opinion that could properly settle the matter. The little fellow agreed and so, on the following day with banners above them regaling the inaugural Goroka coffee-tasting contest, the Nescafe' man stepped up and, one by one, sipped each bean after it had been brewed.

It was almost like a Paris wine tasting and all were watching out for the result. To their delight, the man pronounced the local Goroka coffee as the best of the bunch, and everyone cheered. Then it was explained to him what had actually just occurred and how he had just chosen 'their' coffee over the best beans from around the world. As a result, the price the farmers were paid doubled overnight.

The trap had been set, the mouse had taken the bait, and the jaws had snapped shut on him.

But then, against all current wisdom, Geoff did the most remarkable 180 degree turnaround. He decided to pull up half the coffee beans and turn his hand to what had already proven to be easier and more profitable. He did something completely radical for that part of the world, something that had never been done before! He planted vegetables.

Vegetables

Tribal Gathering at Goroka 1970

It was 1953, Geoff had been in Goroka close to two years and had decided that the life of a pubic servant was not for him. He had a block of land in town, where the family lived. It was little more than a grass hut with windows, but it had a tin roof and a wooden floor. He had already been growing beans on the 'borrowed' land and was shipping the crop all over New Guinea. He had a significant income stream from this endeavour. On page fifty seven you will see a typical record of invoices, amounting to many pounds of income every week. He was earning significantly more than his government wage, which allowed him to buy Kamaliki, a property to the South of the town.

This was an established coffee plantation with mature trees and a steady income, but the goals of this new farmer stretched past being a servant to Nestle'. He didn't want to have any sort of boss hanging over him. By report, it was Joy who suggested to him the obvious, that everyone grew vegetables in their back yards, why should Geoff not expand the farm into growing vegetables?

Geoff agreed that growing vegetables was a better and more profitable idea then growing coffee. While many in Goroka considered him half mad for doing it, with dire warnings that you could not possibly grow commercial levels of produce in the highlands, this is exactly what he proceeded to do. He pulled up half the beans and planted all kinds of European vegetables, the things that were expensive and flown in from Cairns.

"Joy made sense on this. Every single one of the locals had a garden in their back yard, growing exactly the vegetables I intended to grow commercially. Why they imagined they would only grow in small numbers was beyond me, but that belief suited my needs. So I planted everything, and it worked!"

The vegetables grew like weeds, as Geoff and Joy knew they would. In retrospect, it was obvious. On the original plot of land, his beans went like rockets, so why not other crops? Plus, the growing conditions meant two and three crops a year. Added to this he had all the native labour to help out. Soon enough he had harvests a-plenty and was filling up all the existing shops to overflowing, yet still more produce was coming in.

So, he started selling direct to plantations, flying them direct to their farms at rates around half what they would otherwise pay. I have seen his meticulous log books that kept a record of every shipment that flew out, how much it was, cost of transport, etc. There are BOOKS of these single line entries, all for seven pound, fourteen pound, twenty pound and up. Many, many books with Geoff's meticulous record keeping showed individual shipments, each one invoicing the client a fee that was many times higher than a weeks wage in the real world.

"Did you have many non-payers, shipping things out like you did?" I asked.

"Precious few. Most problems were simply argument over things arriving damaged. I just sent the same again free of charge. In the end, I don't recall there was a single debt unpaid."

The year was 1954 and life was good. Business was booming, so Geoff decided to build a 'proper' house on his property. And he did! Geoff started building a modern European home in those back-blocks of Goroka, one that was second only to the Governors house in Port Moresby. By today's standards, a fairly modest residence, but in Goroka at that time, a virtual palace. And it was expensive!

Geoff had never used the local tribes for labour, they were extremely lazy. Instead, he chose natives he knew and had worked with in Native Labour from a neighbouring valley. This decision had an unexpected benefit. When the locals saw the 'big house', as they referred to it, going up, they were amazed. In their culture, because their 'chief' had the best house in the entire highlands, this increased their personal standing and esteem over the other tribes. They wanted to repay him in some way.

Building the house had the most extraordinary side-effect, these natives wanted to GIVE Geoff two hundred acres of prime real estate, situated right beside the farm he currently owned. By law, this was not permissible. However, Geoff could make an offer to purchase a leasehold, which then had to go through a variety of government channels.

"It caused a major issue with the local administration. Had I bribed the tribal chief? Had I threatened people? Why did they want to give me such valuable land? People were suspicious. Many forms had to be filled in, and many questions had to be answered. It took something approaching two years for it all to go through."

But all this activity created a different sort of concern. The problem was that the supervisor of the government department that oversaw native labour complained to Geoff that he was abusing his position. As a government employee, you are not supposed to use the natives in your own business. It was not illegal, just frowned upon.

"I was ordered to stop, which was extremely inconvenient because I was in the middle of harvest and I was still half-way through building the house. Another five months and I would be good, but right then if I lost the government organised labour force, I was dead in the water. So I told the fellow that I understood completely where he was coming from and to make sure I caused him no further concern, I would give five months notice. This would give him time to arrange for another person.

"This was the perfect 'out' for the fellow. He could accept the offer and turn a blind eye. The supervisor was grateful that I was so reasonable, and in the meantime, as I was soon to be a private contractor, I was therefore permitted to continue using the native labour. That is the stupid part, because I quit the job it was all now OK, as I would shortly not be a government employee. Technically I was thus using the labour in the proper way. Even though I was still an employee for five more months, it was all ticked off and approved."

Geoff looked at me as he remembered this time and added, "Government officials are in their position because they have no imagination and if I had stayed, I would have ended up like them. It was time to go and I never looked back."

What is more, because Geoff was so 'reasonable' the supervisor signed off on the application to lease the adjoining two hundred acres and over the course of around eighteen months (with a lot of paperwork going into various government departments) the transfer of title took place. There was now 400 acres to grow vegetables on!

This was 1955 and over the next two years, 'Dollars Wallace' earned his nickname. By 1957, the year my sister Sue was born, the Wallace family were well established as fully-fledged plantation owners of the most profitable farm in New Guinea. All thanks to humble vegetables and a couple who ignored convention to do their own thing.

New Guinea Trivia: By 1959 American missionary Father Leo Arkfeld, the man who was to buy Kamaliki, had been flying in New Guinea for eleven years. When travelling home to USA on leave, he went via Europe, and arranged to visit Dornier's works near Munich to inspect the Do 27, intending to add capacity to the mission fleet of Cessna 170s ands 180s.

After a demonstration flght, Father Arkfeld was highly impressed. When he returned to New Guinea, he was negotiating the purchase of two Do 27s, and in agreement with Dennis Buchanan of Territory Airlines, placed an order with Dornier for three aircraft:

(Goroko Plane) **Do 27H-2 VH-CHR for Goroka Catholic Mission**

Technology

One thing Geoff always had a hankering for was the latest and best toys. He loved technology and, in the case of Kamaliki, he imported the worlds best sound system. It was not stereo as we know it today, but a system with tweeters and woofers and large speaker cabinets matched to a multi-valve amplifier.

He also had the very latest two-track reel-to-reel tape machine. Obviously, I go by what my oldest brother tells me on this, as I was not there. But I remember the reel-to reel-because, years later, we kids used it as a toy to create little family plays.

If there was a gadget that was new, Geoff wanted it. Many years later this same desire translated into him buying the first PC that was user friendly. (With the brand new and exciting Windows 95 operating system)

The thing was, when people came to visit, what they saw was the latest and the best the world had to offer up there in a remote part of the world called Goroka. Geoff even imported a French car, the Peugeot 403, because he had studied what was the best thing for the family in their situation. That car survived many years and came back to Australia with the family when they went to Brisbane.

The family was finally out of the grass huts and into a proper house. It was at this point that Dad really missed good old fashioned carbonated drinks. They were simply not available in the highlands so, once more, his interest in technology changed the family's way of life.

Rather than import an expensive product, he decided to make his own. He bought the equipment to make 'fizzy drink'. For bottles he used old beer bottles, or whatever was to hand and for which he could find a suitable cap to seal it.

To say it was popular was an understatement. Everyone wanted some. Soon Geoff had the oldest boys, Peter and Greg, helping out in the production. He even set up a small shop in town to manufacture and sell it from. He called it 'The Trading Post' and, with Joy at the helm, this store rapidly expanded and became a very profitable business.

Portable Reel to Reel system, similar to what Geoff had in New Guinea

The Trading Post

The store was Joy's domain. She ran it, organised the staff and oversaw every detail. The place is still running today in Goroka, so it is a testament to their foresight. I recall Joy speaking at length about the things she had to do to stop the natives stealing everything. In New Guinea, taking things from a shop was not seen as 'theft'. The locals knew the white people frowned on it, but it was almost a game to see what they could get away with.

The Trading Post was extraordinarily successful. To keep it that way Geoff made regular visits to Hong Kong, in order to find the latest and most interesting things for people to buy, from fashion to kitchen utensils.

Geoff and Joy were making money hand over fist and he got the nickname 'Dollars Wallace'. Everything he touched turned to gold, though it must be said, he would have the vision, but it was Joy's persistence that would see it through to reality. As business people they made an excellent team, though the same cannot be said for their personal relationship.

Dad never quite got over the betrayal of that initial lie that lumbered them with so many children and yes, he loved them, but it added a great deal of pressure. Joy had the burden of personal issues and concerns over early childhood abuse at the hands of a step-father. So, in business all was good, but personally the pair were fractured individuals. .

One day I asked Geoff what the real reason was for him selling up and coming to Australia and he said, "The truth? I came to Brisbane because Joy had no interest in sex. Here there were women who did and that is all there is to it. Stupid decision, really, but what can you do?"

The Trading Post still exists in Goroka. Kamaliki still exists. Dollars Wallace, however, is just a memory to everyone up there now.

Geoff sighed as we looked through Google, finding the old property. "Navigation in New Guinea was largely by landmarks. To get to Goroka, for instance, you flew in from Lae, up the river then across towards Mount Michael. Then you picked up the Asaru River and followed that all the way up to the blue porch, which was the house at Kamaliki. From there you turned due north and you went straight to the Goroka landing strip." Was he interested in going back? Not really, who would know him now?

"The real problem, no acquisition gene. I didn't have a commercial bone in my body. It was a great adventure, making money, and in New Guinea there was no tax, so anything you made was yours. I felt liberated there, free, and then it all got turned upside down, because the old man decided he wanted to visit."

Duncan Harry Returns

D uncan had written Geoff, begging to come up to see his wonderful property. Geoff, the eternal soft touch, paid his airfare. Airfare? Of course, because the ship was going to be too hard for his old bones. It was an incredibly expensive thing in those days, flying out from Brisbane to Cairns, then hopping to Moresby before jumping to Lae, then all the way to Goroka. The Kanimbla sailed direct to Moresby, then Lae, and took 10 days. It was a fraction of the cost, but what the hell, he was Dollars Wallace! And so the day comes, soon after the house is built, that Duncan Harry Wallace sees his son for the first time in over a decade.

It is all smiles and warmth and friendliness and he is so well-behaved that even Joy sets aside her reservations. The next day he asks if it is OK to wander about and take in the sights. Geoff agrees, but asks that he has nothing to do with the locals. For the present Geoff is 'the boy who made good' and D.H.W is all smiles as he trots off to see for himself the lay of the land.

It took just three days, just three days and the place is in an uproar. Native workers are threatening to quit and are at each others throats. DHW is accusing the locals of theft and threatening them with guns. The police are called in! Geoff finally gets to see with adult eyes the type of mischief-maker his father really is. He had come up here with one purpose, to create trouble. There was nothing for it, the old man is packed off into the town to sit at the bar for the rest of his stay. He is banned from the property and from having anything to do with it - which was the entire reason for him coming up.

This episode is what finally removed the old man out of Geoff's life. He may write him the odd letter, call to see if he was in the area, but never again would Geoff allow the conniving bastard to stuff up his life. "We may not choose our family," he said, "but we can sure as hell choose whether we want to know them."

That was it. Duncan was packed off 'back to civilisation' and everyone was happier. The locals stayed, no one killed anyone, and harmony returned. The ones that suffered most under Duncan were the household staff and they, in particular, were glad to see the end of him.

And yet, his accusation of them being thieves was to prove itself to be accurate

Spanner: It was the oddest name to give the house boy, but there it was. He was no mechanic, no one seemed to know WHY he was called

Spanner, but he was. He looked after most of the household chores, the washing, cleaning the floors, doing the yard, etc.

As the boy in charge of laundry, he had a peculiar way of making the job pay. If there ever was any money left in pockets, he would pull it out and place it under something. If asked, he would say, "Yes massa, I did find that. I put it HERE for safekeeping." He would then pluck the one pound note, or whatever it might be out from under its hiding place. If you never asked, he figured you would never know and eventually it got pocketed.

Duncan, the canny Scot born in India, could spot a chiseller and called him out. Anyway, Geoff sort of knew what was happening, but as they all worked for pence, he didn't really mind. Spanner stayed on while the father departed Geoff's life, but not his mind..

The interesting side-bar about this event came after a conversation with my oldest brother, Greg. He pointed out that around this time he and Peter had been given a right thrashing for going down to the Asartu River, a dangerous place. It seems to be that before Duncan arrived, Geoff was following the traditional model of the stern father, spare the whip, spoil the child, etc. But after his father leaves, there are no more reports of him ever seriously hitting one of his children again.

There is something that happens in Goroka that changes Geoff's internal compass, but exactly what we may never know. Perhaps he saw the need for a different path? One thing is certain, when he returns to Australia a few years later, he is a spiritual seeker. A person interested and dedicated to things other than physical world pursuits. Was it this last visit from the father that changed things? He never said.

Geoff Notes: *My final time in the Administration was at Goroka, which had not long been opened up to the first white men. This involved running the Highlands Labour Scheme whereby native highlanders could go to work on the coast under certain conditions. Had charge of up to about 1,500 of them at various times awaiting processing as well as the local native labourers in a compound. So my whole 12 years in post-war (from 1948) New Guinea involved close association with natives, and I deeply realise now what a really decent lot they were, albeit often frustrating. Kembu, the house boy at Kamaliki, I admire more than anyone I have ever met as a superior human being. Also the boss boy Nomi (pron. Normie).*

Dollars Wallace

G eoff now legendary ability to make money had him generally referred to as 'Dollars Wallace'. Everything he touched turned to gold and everything around him seemed to turn a buck. One notable story appeared when the Commonwealth bank loans manager, Bob someone, was in town. This was a time when all the farmers would queue up, cap in one hand, with the other one outstretched looking for a loan. A notable exception to the appointment list was one Geoff Wallace from Kamaliki.

The initial loan Geoff had taken out was already fully repaid, and the current list of assets were considerable. As a result, the man from the bank approached Geoff at a little soiree' put on that evening as a 'meet and greet'. "I notice you didn't put your name down for an appointment, Geoff. Was there anything we can help with, regarding a loan, for any purpose?"

Surrounded by friends and locals, Geoff looked up over his beer and said, "Gee Bob, I have so much money I really don't need any more. But, I want you to know, if there is any way I can help, with a loan, feel free to come and see me!"

Everyone laughed, including the butt of the joke. New Guinea humour was a staple diet of dry wit. A small example of this is the true story of the concert pianist in Port Moresby after the war. He had turned up fresh from Carnegie Hall on a paid-for tour of the provinces, a way to educate the yokels in a bit of culture. The man played his classical set, as was required, and at the end of it he turns to the audience. He says with a sneer, knowing they will ask for 'Roll out the Barrel' or similar, "And what would YOU people like to hear?"

A voice comes from the back of the room and shouts "The soft, dull thud of the lid closing!" The same sort of laughter erupted around this bank manager as had happened when that man stormed off stage, insulted as you might expect.

Well, the bank man didn't storm off and took it with good grace. For the first time in his life he had met a man not interested in grovelling and finding favour with the bank. Geoff didn't need them, at that point he could buy pretty much whatever he wanted with cash. He had defied convention, made his own path, and life had rewarded him for the risk.

Later in life, he would be better known for his ability to spend money, but for now, he was rich, had a settled family life, and the future looked golden. If only he had gotten his father out of his mind, not just his life.

Raising Kids

To his surprise, Geoff found he liked having kids. After the father left Goroka, he changed from a disciplinarian to someone who just liked to enjoy their company ... when he had the time. The truth was, he preferred the bar and having a drink to sitting at home being a father. Occasionally Joy would insist he pull the boys or girls into line for some reason. One such occasion happened in Goroka when the oldest boys, Peter and Greg, were caught smoking.

They were all of seven and eight at the time, just kids, and Geoff recognised it for what it was. Rather than spank them, he went the other way and lit up more cigarettes for them to smoke. He insisted that they smoke every last one he gave them. Well, Greg went down in coughs, and gasping for air, Peter was tougher and kept on smoking, for a bit. Soon both were green and agreed it wasn't something they wanted to do.

Greg did end up being a smoker, so it half-worked. Peter wasn't but this is possibly because he didn't live past eighteen years.

Was it that early intervention? Who can say, but while many will disagree with the practice, no one can argue that showing kids the end result of what they are doing is a whole lot more effective than telling them not to do it.

Geoff was never a pick-up-the-baby type. Kids were all well and good, but he never felt comfortable holding them for too long. Apparently this changed when I came along. He used to come in and pick me up, and just hold me for hours. He told Joy it was because all his worries left him and his anxiety disappeared.

I suspect for the first time in his life he had been secure in some emotional sense. He had money, a wife, a family, and a feeling he just might have been, for the first time in his life, loved. Perhaps he could afford to love another?

It was probably this early bond between us that meant I never missed dropping in to see him whenever I was in the area, not once. This still

The Wallace Family 1959

held, right up to the day he passed on. The same could also be said for his anxiety as that, too, proved to be a faithful friend that never left his side.

End of the World

There were people in and around Goroka who needed help with workers. The position in Native Labour had required Geoff to call out to some fairly remote places. One day he mentioned to me the most curious story about a visit to a woman, one who was quite removed from the small social scene up that way.

Her place was well out of town, in a very remote spot. She was the wife of a plantation owner that lived there virtually on her own. Her name was Joan. The husband worked in Moresby, making the money needed to keep everything running, and she had to run the highlands farm with only native helpers for company. She was on her own for many months at a time.

Shortly after the war, Geoff was up seeing what she needed. He knew Norm, the husband, was away and that she had only the radio for communication. She had not responded to a call, so he drove out through the bush tracks to say hello and see if she was OK. It turned out to be a fault with the equipment, the woman was fine. As he was standing on the front porch, chatting and organising a few things, one of the brand new army jets made its way across the sky. There was a roar that echoed around the valleys and a contrail. This is something we are all familiar with, but back then jets were extremely rare and contrails non-existent. In fact, Joan had never seen one before, or even heard of them.

"Oh no," she said, at first shocked, and then saddened. *"It's the end of the world and Norm's not here to share it with me."*

In her mind, for some reason, the jet with it's contrail represented the apocalypse. Maybe she associated with that new terror, the atomic bomb? Who can say. "Why would someone think a jet in the sky was the end of the world?" I asked Dad as he related this story.

"She was lonely, and afraid," he replied. "Fear does strange things inside your head, loneliness tells you stories of even worse things. Finally, it is the jealousy that drives you mad."

I was left with the sense he was telling me something which had nothing at all to do with the story. It was one of those really odd little tales that he mentioned only once, whereas he often told and retold other stories many times. To this day, I still have the image of that woman, all alone in a foreign land with no real connection to anyone or anything. I believe Geoff was explaining himself and some of his odd actions, but he was also warning me. *It can happen to anyone.*

For some reason, I had the impression that the woman had later committed suicide. Dad never said it, but I was left with this impression.

Selling Kamaliki

The native staff at the Kamaliki house were very good with the children, and I believe genuinely so. Not that I can recall much, because I only lived in Goroka up to my second birthday. Yet, by the time I was to be arrive Mum had had enough of natives and decided that her next child was to be born in Brisbane. And so, heavily pregnant, she got herself on board a plane and flew South. Apparently, she went into labour ON the plane, but her will was so strong she held me back till she got to the hospital.

However, the 'good hygienic western private hospital' was full to the brim with infection. So it was that just two weeks after I came into this world, I was extricated from that Ashgrove clinic by Doctor Anderson. I was then filled up with penicillin, saving me from what would have otherwise been a terminal Staphylococci infection. It's a longish story, but essentially, the head nurse was covering up the contagion. As a result, the hospital went into quarantine and was shut down. I lived, needless to say, to write this book.

So if you don't like it, blame Doctor Anderson.

This was when Geoff bought the Brisbane house at Seventeen Stewarts Road. (As a side note, Geoff's mother lived there before she purchased her Red Hill house.) It was to become the family home for many years. For now, he had decided to put Kamaliki up for sale and move back down, but it was to take some time. It had gotten a lot more complicated because the manager he had installed suddenly won the lottery. Now thirty thousand pounds richer, he no longer needed the job. Geoff had to return to sort things out and, in the process, organise the sale of the property to the only interested party, the Catholic Church.

Arch-Bishop Leo Arkfeldt was the man making the decision. He was a tall, gaunt man with the notable reputation for never smiling. Geoff confirmed he certainly never saw even the glimmer of humour in the man and any attempt to bring it out was met with a frown. In order to determine the price the Bishop sent in his best man, a fellow who had absolutely no concept of how a farm ran. His name was Brother Romule. The man was a boot-maker and he was to spend endless months learning every aspect to being a farmer. In the process, he insisted on a formal lunch every day.

To this end he would arrive on his BSA bike with side car mid-morning, learn nothing, sit down for lunch, and proceed to discourse about the wonders of Christianity to all who had zero interest in listening. However, you had to be polite, as the sale of the property and getting the poor man to some level of competence was reliant on it. "In retrospect, he put Romule in there to bring the price down. By stretching it out and making me frustrated, I was put into the position of accepting a lower offer in order to just get out of there, which is exactly what happened.

"I sold all the town building that we had for whatever we were offered. I didn't even think to dicker for a better price," said Geoff. "I don't have the acquisition gene. What they offered I took. I think back and could have easily gotten more, but at the time I just wanted out." In the end, Geoff sold Kamaliki for half it's true worth and it was set up as a Catholic Mission in the area.

This meant the family moved back to Brisbane, but it also brought Geoff's charmed run with money almost to an end. From that point on, apart from a small stint installing the new Hills Hoist, the tide of cash seemed to flow eternally out.

Geoff Notes: *Kamaliki is the correct spelling (no R- the other spelling is correct) was on the Asaro River about 5 miles in a straight line from the bottom end of the air strip which had a distinct downward slope. In bad weather with little visibility, pilots used to fly up the Asaro River until they found our house, and then turn immediately right to land at Goroka (countless lives saved here?) It was the Divine Word Mission through Bishop Arkfeldt at Wewak, a tall, austere, humorless figure, with endless, endless negotiating. They installed to run it all a Brother who was an ex bootmaker (not bookmaker) and not exactly executive material.*

I had 4 years in the Civil Administration, initially as a native labour supervisor at Port Moresby, then got married, then to Manus Island at Lorengau as acting District Labour Officer running the government native labour compound (hundreds of natives) as well as administering the Native Labour Ordinance which stated all the conditions under which natives were to be employed by private enterprise. I had to provide native labour to the RAAF at Momote and go over there to pay them.

I have a newspaper photo of me paying the natives there (it is in poor condition if I can find it). Incidentally, the War Crimes Trials were being held there at Lombrum (I think it was called). High ranking Japs were tried and some of them were hung as a result. I used to go in and watch the trials at times. Manus was mainly coral islands, and was a HUGE American Base on Seeadler Harbour during the war. You could just go and get yourself a jeep or other vehicle. Out of the bush, I got a big Studebaker truck with 2 lots of double wheels at the back, and 4-wheel drive. Hardly any miles on the clock and drove like a car. I had an American 30.06 service rifle and found a cache of ammo the size of a bedroom in sealed tin cans. I used this to stand on a low bridge and shoot into schools of fish, which stunned them. Natives would dive in and harvest them and they soon recovered (the fish, not the natives).

Hills Hoist

Geoff used to say, "University is fine, but if you want to make money, start a business." Which he did on a number of occasions, most notably up at Goroka. However, one of the most promising of all businesses he started was in Brisbane, with a small job he got as a contractor installing the new Hills Hoist. In 1961 , the Hills Hoist was a very new business. It was just starting up and they needed installers. The management, unaware they were destined to become an Australian icon, had worked out it took almost one and a half days to put up a clothesline and they paid contractors accordingly. Geoff was duly contracted.

It went great guns, and the REASON Geoff did so well was simple. His love for technology meant he thought outside the square, and he figured a better way to install a hoist. He was able to put them up much faster than the factory thought possible, to the tune of four and five every day. The technique was really simple, he set the base post in concrete one day and had the top section ready to pop on the next. The trick was to 'pre-string' the top section and have a batch of these "ready to go" hoists loaded in the Single Spinner Ute. It meant that Geoff was making 1500 pound a week. The average wage in 1961 was under fifteen pound a week, so he was making a fortune. Every week he received two years wage!

Geoff had attended the factory training, which involved a laborious section by section piecing of the entire thing, along with the incredibly slow tensioning that took half a day. This was the real time killer. But logic dictated that, given that all the arms were the same length, then all the wire stringing it together also had to be the same length. So taking measurements from the first one, he would 'pre-cut' the wire, and thread them through the four arms.

He treated the thing like an umbrella, threading all the wires while standing the 'arms' upright. It was so horribly simple. Geoff was doing four and five times the number lesser mortals were struggling to get up. The company was amazed at how many he was getting through, and asked how he did it. Geoff then made the grave mistake of showing the company rep how easy it was.

Hills Hoist fired all the contractors and offered everyone the job back at fifty pound a week. Joy always said this broke Geoff at a very basic level. He really thought he was onto the next good thing and he was! It seemed like his own honesty had worked against him. The next experience of life in the "Big Smoke" was going to be far more painful and even more expensive.

The Nightclub

L ate in 1962 Geoff had left the family home and moved to 502 Milton Road, in Toowong. He lived in one of the front apartment of a block of thirteen mostly single-room bedsitters. No one would have ever claimed he and Joy had a happy marriage, in fact, they were polar opposites and Geoff decided enough was enough. He was off and having many adventures and misadventures, but possibly the craziest and certainly the most expensive of these was the Nightclub.

To be fair, it was more of a Croatian meeting hall, a place where the local immigrant population would have dances at night, but 'Nightclub' sounded much smarter than 'meeting hall'. Geoff used to bring the family some of the commercial boxes of Smiths Chips that got delivered there. These were large rectangular tins full to the brim with potato chips. The Nightclub was to be his next great profit machine, and it was doing OK until one day when Geoff mysteriously just abandoned it.

No reason was ever given, nor did it seem to make sense, and many years later I asked him about it. "What happened with the nightclub?"

"Problems with the staff." Geoff answered.

"But you spent thirty thousand POUND on it? What happened?"

To put this in perspective, that was approximately six houses in a decent suburb at the time. A lot of money. "The manageress/singer there became a huge issue, and I had to leave."

"What sort of issue makes you walk away from thirty thousand pounds?"

"Her husband found out. I figured my life was worth more than the money."

Obviously, to my mind, it had been a set up. The couple had found an easy mark. She had been the one to convince Geoff to buy into the place, and no doubt played her part well. "I never did have an ounce of commercial sense, really." Geoff added.

My brother Greg recollects that it was this madness, losing 30,000 pounds, that really ended the marriage with Joy. I was too young to know, but it does seem a very likely scenario. I can but imagine what I would think if my partner came home and said, "Sorry dear, I just threw away five houses!"

And as if to highlight the lack of commercial sense, the next episode in the Parables of Geoff happened soon after the nightclub fiasco. He bought a farm.

Rochedale

Deep red soil, underground water, with flat, easily cleared land: The advertisement promised a new goldmine! The fifty acres at Rochedale looked just the thing and it meant getting back to what he did best, farming. Geoff threw himself into making a go of the venture and even brought in some hired help, a man called Harry. Harry was about as useful as a three pound note, but Geoff kept him on despite the fact he cost twice that every week.

He put down a couple of bores, cleared the bush, and made the whole property ready to grow potatoes and watermelon, plus he put in some papaya trees for good measure. The three sons, Peter, Greg and myself would go out on the odd weekend and help move irrigation pipes. This entailed walking knee deep in red mud, and generally getting incredibly dirty. After the morning doing this, you would spend the rest of the time with an air rifle or riding the Suzuki step-through posty bike.

There was a large shed at the front of the property which had a 'house' or sorts built into it. This was quite a comfortable little place, with a few rooms, a lounge, bathroom and kitchen. When Geoff bought it the shed was full of antiques. He pretty much gave them away. He believed them to be useless junk no one would want. So he got rid of those and brought in 'modern' 1960's decor: Laminated tables, African women lamps, and the cheap wall art that used 'flock', a sort of velvet painting that was imported from the Philippines. (A big addition came some years later when Geoff acquired one of the new fibre optic lamps from the Brisbane 'Ecca'. Completely kitsch, but expensive and he had to have it. It was something like $400 in 1968. That was six weeks wages at the time!)

After a year, my brothers got tired of helping out for no pay at Rochedale, and soon enough I was the only one to make the journey out from Ashgrove of a weekend. For myself it was a welcome change. I always liked Geoff, he always liked me. But at night it got awkward. I didn't like it when he got drunk and would call me over, saying, "You are a great kid, don't you ever forget that. A great kid!" Then he would reach for his Spanish guitar and play Pearly Shells. It went as follows:

"*Pearly shells, by the ocean* - Burl Ives is a GREAT singer, he is a great singer - *when my heart sees them I think of all those little Pearly Shells* - Great song, terrific song..." And eventually he would collapse into sleep, and I would drop off. I didn't like it at the time, but now I look back and I realise he was trying to give to me what his father never gave to him, kindness.

As I write this, I understand one simple truth. Not one person in Geoff's childhood ever gave him the sense that he was loved. And the other truth was I would never have had anyone tell me I was loved if it were not for Geoff. I cannot help but feel that those stupid drunken sessions were really about his sense of loss: In some way he was trying to make good the deficit of his own upbringing, by telling his son that he was a 'good kid'.

It was certainly a mile away from what HIS father would have said. His father would have gotten drunk and tried to thump Geoff for still being up, calling him a 'useless dog'. "You useless dog, come here!" was a common phrase from Duncan Harry's lips. In some ways I regret being annoyed at Geoff's drunken ramblings. I could have said "You're the best Dad!" or something simple like that, but the truth was, I hated drunks. I hated people not in control of themselves, to be more correct.

Who could imagine an eight year old boy could have SO many opinions about life. I was to learn to be humbler and more considerate, but that was a journey of many years. The real truth is that if I have any humility at all, it is because I learned it from my father. It did not come naturally.

The mornings at the farm were very different than the drunken evenings. Geoff was bright and clear, with none of the emotional baggage weighing him down. The food was the best part: Steak, eggs, corn, lettuce and tomato served up on the large oval melamine plates. We had both scoured Chinatown to find these, and Geoff seemed particularly pleased to serve me up food from them. No one else got that special little smile as he gave me breakfast. It was a 'thing' we had done together, finding those plates. This was the Geoff that knew how to raise a son, and curiously, many years later, shortly before he passed away, I realised ALL my health issues came from the diet most kids ate, bread and cereal. What Geoff offered up was the perfect food as it did not create the auto-immune reaction I got from grains.

This was no miracle on his part. He had a similar metabolism and what he felt good eating, he fed to me. But, despite all the above, the truth was that he had absolutely no interest is raising a child. It was great to have someone around for a bit, but full-time parenting? He far preferred drinking and blondes.

Despite a huge effort the farm was not really producing cash. It produced loads of food, Geoff just didn't get enough of a return from what he sent to market. Many times he sold things in what amounted to a loss, it didn't even cover the costs of growing. My father was discovering the utterly corrupt world of market traders. These people are a world unto themselves and they way they work, which they continue do so to this very day, is just unbelievable.

You deliver your fruit and veg to them at the Rocklea market. They tell you what you will most likely get for the days trading, and at the end of the day, they then tell you what you got. Invariably, they didn't provide paperwork, and looked shocked if they were asked to provide same. Often farmers would be carting in goods and get paid less than the cost of production, and furthermore, it was all done on trust. You never got any proof at all that the trader sold your goods at the price he claimed.

Geoff did not do well, so he decided that, rather than not use the market system, or to not run a farm, that the problem was he needed something new and unique. He came to the notion that the solution to all his worries was Cantaloupes, or rockmelons to you and me. Brilliant idea, and he spent a lot of money developing the market, but the problem was people only knew watermelon. As yet they had no idea about these 'cantaoupey things' and he could not get them sold. It was another fail

Yet just three years later 'rockmelons' became all the rage. Once again, Geoff was right, but he was a few steps too far ahead of the curve to profit from his insight.

Geoff Quips: *Light travels much faster than sound: Which explains why some people appear bright until they open their mouths.*

The 'New Fangled" thing called a Hills Hoist

Harry the One Toothed Farm Worker

arry must have been in his sixties, but he looked more like eighty. He had a weather beaten crinkled face, hard and brown from sun, but you barely saw it because of his enormous smile. And when you saw the smile, all you saw was the extreme lack of teeth he had. "How would you be, Geoff!" he would say whenever Geoff turned up. Often there was a message left from someone, "Ah, there was a fellow here to see you, he said somfink, I know he said somfink, I just can't put me finger on it exactly."

This is when the standard quiz began. "An older or younger man?"

"Bout in the middle."

"Tall or short?"

"He was tallish."

"Dark hair, or fair?"

"Oh he was dark, and slick, you know, all combed and pretty with the hair, and he had a hat!" (said as if that really nailed it!)

And so it would go, but rarely if ever was the individual clearly identified, and almost never was the message actually remembered. Eventually Geoff got Harry to get the person to write down what they wanted, and it had to be the visitor to do the writing because Harry

This is not Harry, but he looked like this

could not read or write. Even so, he didn't see much importance in that writing stuff, and he usually forgot. He was likely brain damaged from too much alcohol, but even so, he was a real character with a very kind heart.

Children can always tell if an adult is cruel or kind. No words need be said, you just feel it from people. Harry carried not one ounce of malice in him, nor an ounce of common sense, nor an ounce of responsibility. He just lived moment to moment, loving the sun, liking the rain, enjoying whatever life threw in his direction. He was the type of Aussie you just don't see anymore.

He may have had no memory for messages, but he never forgot the day he was supposed to call into the unemployment office. Once every fortnight he had to go 'collect me pay' as he used to say. Now Harry didn't have a car, so Geoff usually took him in, because on the buses it was an all-day job, and there was work to do! So, on top of the wage Geoff was paying him, Harry also collected a subsidy from the government. I reckon, in the end, he was making more than the boss.

The farm was now Geoff's permanent residence. He still had the flat, which he would use on occasions, but he lived at the farm. Harry, along with a friend of his, whose name I can't recall, were now his permanent staff. Harry was paid seven pound a week and I reckon Geoff thought that two pound of that was worth seeing that smile everyday: A huge, almost toothless grin and a welcome face.

There is a part of me that suspects Geoff hired him not to do work, but just to see that smile. It lifted your spirits. I loved old Harry, he was a real character and in his day I am sure he was a hard worker, but at that particular point in time he was mostly a hard drinker. But he was also a good talker, one who had the most peculiar way of getting on with people.

No matter what Geoff spoke of, Harry would add, *'I was just thinking the same thing meself'*. Geoff might say, "I was going to set up irrigation for the back paddock on Monday."

Harry would reply, "Geoff, I was just thinking the exact same thing to meself, just as you said it."

"I might go into town and get some more overalls."

"Funny that, I was just thinking about new overalls, I was!"

It didn't matter WHAT you said, if you were the one paying the wages, everything you said or thought about was confirmed as the right thing to do. I understand now, it was a survival tactic. Harry had lived all his years at the behest of some boss and by agreeing enthusiastically with everything the boss says, you were guaranteed not to be fired.

Some thought Harry was an idiot. He seemed stupid, but really he was a wise old owl who knew how to negotiate a world where education and money were becoming everything and of which he had neither. What he DID have, however, was charm. Rough, down home charm to be sure, but because of it you never felt Harry would do you wrong.

Of course, he was also pilfering anything that wasn't nailed down, and did get caught on occasions, but his standard response was: 'only borrowing Geoff!' In other words, if you got caught, you handed it back. Dear old Geoff really was a soft touch, but at the same time, Harry was company of sorts and helped him through in a really lonely stretch.

Rochedale was a period of extreme isolation for Geoff. He used to get so lonely that, late at night, he would call telephone numbers at random, just talk to people.

It should be noted, Joy did not want the girls staying at the farm. No one is entirely sure why, but most likely based on the fact that Geoff did get extremely drunk at nights during that time. There was never any question of sexual impropriety and it may simply have been that she didn't want them doing farm work for him.

The Two Thousand Pound Phone Bill

The special long-distance beeps were very familiar to Geoff. There was a particular sound the old land-line phones would give when you called interstate or international. STD was long distance in Australia, ISD was international. Geoff wanted something more interesting than another Australian, so he called ISD, most often to the States. Late at night, alone, and usually very plastered, there was a game he liked to play. Pick up the phone, dial numbers at random and see who you get!

He would choose a country and dial those numbers first. After that, it was random. A curious game, but for a few months this seemed like the best possible way you could pass the evening hours at Rochedale.

"You are ringing from WHERE? Australia? Why?"

"I just wanted to hear an American accent," Geoff might say. "I fought alongside you people in the war, you know, in New Guinea. Yes, near Guam ..."

And so the conversations would run. Sometimes he found a very friendly ear and he would talk for hours on end. It was just the most marvellous thing to do, but then, after three months, he received the phone bill. It was huge.

Two Thousand Pounds in the late 1960's equalled two brand new cars, one third a house, or beer for over a year. It was an incredible sum of money to spend on nothing but talking to people because you were lonely. It would have been far cheaper to go to the local whore-house! I remember as a kid that he mentioned the bill, with a slightly ashen face, saying he had to stop making those calls.

But he still did, on occasions. Who knows why, but I suspect that just meeting someone who had absolutely no idea who or what you were meant that, for a brief period of time, you had a clean slate. You had no luggage to cart, opinions to rise above, or people that needed pleasing.

Many years later, when he was connected to the net, he joined a number of chat lists. The thing is, he never once replied to any of them, but he liked reading what people from other cultures thought and wrote about.

Mind the Muffler Dad

T he '66 Chevy was green with a white roof. The back seat was huge and often when I was picked up latish on a Friday, I would fall asleep on the way out to the farm. One night after some grading had been done, one of the water levies put into the entrance to drive rain water off the road was a little too high and the exhaust got knocked off.

I woke with a start, hearing the loud sound. Geoff was fully plastered and failed to notice it. This is, until the next morning when he started up the car and it made such a noise he almost had a heart attack. "What the hell was that?" he asked.

I am only young, but I knew when you knocked off the exhaust the car became loud. "You hit a bump in the driveway last night. I reckon you knocked off the muffler."

"Can't be. I would have noticed that, the driveway you reckon?"

"Yeah, where they just graded it." I answered.

A brief inspection, and the offending muffler and tailpipe were located, rather damaged. Harry was about, so he wired it into place, enough to get the car to the shop to have it fixed. You think nothing of these things at the time, they are just passing events, but every night when I was being brought to the farm, half asleep, I used to call out when we turned off onto the dirt, "Mind the muffler Dad!"

This became a thing of joy for Geoff. A silly, small detail of life, but he found absolute delight in it and he never tired of the little boy who wanted to be helpful in some way. You have to give him this, he may have been a drunk, he may have been confused, he may have been depressed lonely and gullible, but he was always good to his kids.

Not one of Geoff's children ever lived in the fear of him. Peter and Greg certainly got some smacks, but Greg does not recall it as being anything other than fair punishment for stepping out of line. I recall no stories of any of us being punched or beaten. I can't speak for all families in the clan, but Geoff, for the most part, appeared to consciously choose not to follow the path of the authoritarian father.

Possibly because he was more interested in his own life than wanting to try and rule another's, who can say.

Carol the Neighbour

C arol was a strange name for a man and he was a fairly odd fellow. To give you an image that fits I would point you towards the farmer with the pitchfork in "American Gothic" by Grant Wood. He was a very gaunt, odd fellow who was as miserly with a smile as he was with money. He would do things like find a sunburnt pumpkin in a field of pumpkins and offer Geoff a penny for it, saying, "It's sunburnt, you'll get nothing at the markets for it."

At one time Geoff found he was low on nails for crates, so he asked if he could buy a few off his neighbour. Carol would want Geoff to nominate a specific number and then count them out, one by one, charging Geoff for what they cost. These small details were the sort of things Geoff never thought twice about. He was more of a 'have the damn pumpkin' sort of guy. Yes, it was true that he couldn't sell it at market. Yes, it was commercially worthless, but offering a penny was not really worth anything either. It was done purely so Carol did not feel any sort of obligation, nor any need for friendship, towards his neighbour.

There used to be a lot of this type in Australia. They counted every penny, gave nothing away, and were content to scratch an existence from the dirt. But they were not all as sombre as Carol. Nothing appeared to give him joy, except perhaps when he went to church on Sundays.

We just don't see this type of man anymore and I have to say, it's no great loss.

Michael Notes: *One of the odd things I noted when looking through some of Dad's books, the word "FEAR" was constantly underlined. This was in book after book, so Geoff must have truly believed he lived a life of fear.*

Antoine de Saint Exupery (Author of 'The Little Prince') once said, "True courage is not flying a plane into a hurricane. You do that to survive. You have no choice, you fight on, or you die. No, true courage is found in walking up to two pretty girls at a fountain, knowing they might ridicule you, and saying hello."

One thing is certain, Geoff had no problem going up to chat to girls. I remember clearly one day at the ice skating arena he was standing beside a blonde, and said, "What is that perfume, Fidgie?" The poor girl fell for his charm instantly. So he had courage in areas most men do not.

Goodbye Rochedale

Geoff eventually sold the farm, trading it for a house on the water at West End, and some cash. It was never really a go, despite all the effort and time put into it. The place is still there, undeveloped largely because the council put orders onto the surrounding fields that made subdivision impossible. The reason was to retain farm land. Unlike so many other areas, the farm would not be broken up into 'little boxes full of ticky tacky', as the song goes.

I dropped in when working in the area a decade ago, the shed was still there. I wondered if *'the house inside the shed'* was still there, but probably not. A large, two story brick house had been built and not a lot of agriculture seemed to be happening, but it was essentially the same. It had been upgraded to a bitumen driveway, with some gardens and small improvements.

There seemed to be no one home. There was not anyone who wanted to come out, at any rate. I sat for a few moments, looking at the past through the lens of my now adult eyes. I am quite sure no one really appreciates what they have got until it is gone. (Pave paradise, put up a parking lot)

I thought of the gun rack, with all the various shotguns and rifles sitting there. There were twenty-seven at the high point, but no pistols, and sadly, not the Luger. Apparently there was too much bureaucracy to get it through customs when returning from New Guinea. Proper German post-war sports model, with the long barrel. Accurate as a rifle, Geoff used to say. They are worth a small fortune now.

The stencils to mark all the fruit boxes, they were quite possibly still hanging up on the tin walls of the shed. These are what the farmer uses, with shoe polish as paint, to mark the boxes and bags as coming from that particular farm. The red soil was some one hundred and twenty feet deep at that point, good for farming the land for hundreds of years. You plant anything, give it water, and it grows.

I imagine the old aluminium irrigation pipes are gone. Too much labour in moving them and new systems were most likely being used. The past was looking back at me, peering in from the 1960's to the present day. I don't miss it, but how different life would have been if Geoff had kept this place. Water under the bridge is hard to measure, however, so I turned and left, just as my father had done so many years ago.

Fortunately, I didn't have to mind the muffler, as under-road pipes and bitumen now made a nice flat road in and out of the place.

Stewarts Road

There is one incident I recall clearly. I was still maybe three years old, but I heard raised voices coming from my parent's room at the Ashgrove house, Seventeen Stewarts Road. Geoff spent most of his time away from the home now and when he came back there was a good deal of tension in the air. I heard shouting and without a reason as to why, I opened the door to their room and walked in. I saw Geoff angry, raising a fist towards Joy. "That's not right!" I said. Geoff looked back, I could see it hit him hard. I didn't know emotions at the time, but now I recall that face and it would seem like guilt mixed with regret. He dropped the fist, stopped the shouting, and left without saying anything. Mum was in tears.

I had never seen my father angry before, and I don't think I ever saw it again. I am sure he had the emotion, but that was the first and last time I had personally witnessed it. I am guessing that what I saw was a man remembering a vow he had made to himself, to not be like his father. I am guessing that my presence at that time, as a young child, reminded him of what HE had seen as a boy. And here he was, repeating the cycle.

I know Geoff had deep and dark frustrations with Joy. Many years later he told me that she had no interest in sex and though she loved Geoff, she hated the fact he found release in other women. It was all a recipe for disaster. It was around this time that Geoff moved out to the flats at Milton Road. He only visited after that, to drop in money to Joy and talk with the kids. But really, you could tell when he called in that he didn't really know what to say.

As an example: He would put one daughter on his knee, and say "You are my favourite!" Then, on another day, a different daughter, and THEY were now his favourite. (He never said this to myself or my brothers) For the most part, Geoff spent most of the next decade stoned on some drug that his latest psychiatrist provided. Plus he often drank a few beers to wash them down, just to complicate proceedings.

Testing out new drugs seemed to be his specialty. Finding that one pill didn't affect his anxiety, he would go to a different doctor, and then another, and then another one. Each good doctor put forth their 'cure', invariably in the form of a drug. While you cannot cure depression and insecurity with a pill, you CAN make it a whole lot worse, however. There was no answer to the brutality of his father that Geoff could find in a bottle or a prescription, but you have to give it to him, he looked hard and long into that world, convinced there would be a solution there.

How he survived no one knows. One of the drugs he was on, when mixed with a little booze, had a curious side-effect. I was watching one day as he walked into the wall, thinking it was a door way. I remember it clearly: Geoff walked into a wall and said, "I thought that was the doorway?" After this he got into his 61 Chevy and drove home! The 1960's were a period when "anxiety" was treated with a plethora of various medication, many of which had side-effects far worse than the issue they were treating.

I recall when I was around ten years old. My oldest brother, Peter, had died a year earlier, and all the kids were taken in to see Geoff in Lowson House, the mental ward of the Royal Brisbane Hospital. He had admitted himself after he apparently tried to kill himself. What had happened was that while watching TV he decided to drink White Spirits, and then turn the old fashioned bar radiator face down onto the carpet. He realised he was a danger to himself and others, so booked himself into care.

"I have no idea why I did this. It all just seemed to be a very good idea at the time, even though the back of my brain was saying it wasn't. But when I came to later, I thought the only logical conclusion was that I have cracked, and gone mad."

Thank goodness Geoff had the good taste to only use wool flooring. If it has been acrylic carpet, the fumes would have asphyxiated him and most probably burned down the flats, with the likelihood that many innocents would have died. He had no idea why he was doing it, but his luck saved him. He fell asleep and dropped off the chair. Purely by chance he hit the heater, which caused it to unplug itself.

Years later he discovered the prescribed anti-depressant drug he was on was known to have these sort of side-effects, but at the time he thought he must have cracked. Maybe he had finally snapped and fallen off the edge? So he booked himself in as a voluntary patient to the mental asylum, only to realise within the first day that the good doctors in there were far crazier than either himself or his fellow inmates.

Soon after the families brief visit to see him he apparently walked out, got in his car, and left. As he said later, "I forgot to get my certificate of sanity before I left, though. So I cannot be certain I am OK. Isn't that a crazy notion? When you are booked in to a mental asylum by a doctor, you can't get out until you receive a 'certificate of sanity'. Someone has to officially find that you are not looney tunes. Do YOU have a certificate saying you are sane?"

I laughed, and Geoff continued. "You get a certificate to say you are capable of driving, you get a certificate to say you can practice law, be a doctor, etc. but who gets a certificate to say they are sane? So the question is: *'what does this say about the rest of us?'* "

Geoff always found the funny side of things. But as I look back I can only imagine how alone he must have felt at that time, possibly at all times. He had no idea what was going on, only that he felt incredible anxiety and stress and that this could be triggered by the smallest thing. Even a possum could do it!

Certificate of Sanity

by our signatures below we do hereby certify that to the best of our ability and subject to the vagaries of data collection and analysis that the following person

Name of the Sane Person

is deemed to be sane within the meaning of the word as defined in the Psychiatrists Bedside Companion 25th Edition Revised. Further, we herby declare that the above mentioned person is considered fit and qualified and should, given clear and concise directions, be capable of catching a bus on their own and be quite adept at using a knife and fork while eating.

Name of the First Signatory

Name of the Second Signatory

Geoff Quips: *Many people think we are descended from monkeys, whereas in reality our ancestors were Four Bears.*

Michael Notes: *Food was a thing for Geoff. So often he would get take-out Chinese for the family, or we would go to the Gold Coast, and he would stop and buy a couple of kilos of prawns and a crab. He discovered YumCha (Chinese Dumplings) in Hong Kong and in the 1990's I had a great deal of delight in taking HIM out for YunCha on the Gold Coast.*

He loved it, out with the family, eating Chinese. "Oh, the deep fried wontongs, Let's get those!" He would say, almost drooling at the sight of them. It was like a kid in a candy store. He had such tremendous enthusiasm for every interesting thing that went past.

Possum Magic

There is no particular reason why I laughed so much about this story, but even now, I find it just extraordinary. It says so much about Geoff's quest for true love, only it is a story about the possums he regularly fed at the Milton Road flats. The possums that came down most nights were delightful creatures. They would sit on the window sill, looking in to see if Geoff would make them a honey sandwich. He loved showing any who visited the trick: He would put honey on bread and hand it to a possum waiting there. "Watch this!" he would say expectantly and sure enough, the possum would take the bread and fold it over double to make a sandwich. Then it would eat it while holding it in both paws. But Mr. Possum never ate the crust!

A whole family of possums would come to his window, look in expectantly, and when handed their treat they all folded over their piece of bread, making it into a sandwich, and then ate it like a human. I had never seen anything like it.

It was one of those small things that absolutely delighted Geoff and he never tired of the scene. Then one day I visited, and noticed there were no possums coming down in the early evening.

"Where are the possums?" I asked.

"They left," was all Geoff said.

Many years later he confided to me the real story. One night, when very, very drunk, he decided that, after years of feeding the possums, they were now his friends. So he picked one up to cuddle it. Of course, it bit him. Accusing it of being ungrateful, Geoff wrapped the little bugger up in a towel, put it into a box, and drove the car miles away and released it into the bush near Mount Cootha. Then he went back home. However, he couldn't sleep and found himself feeling very guilty.

It really wasn't the possums fault. After all, it was a wild creature, and must have thought it was defending itself. Full of remorse, the next night, and the night after, and for many more nights after that, he drove to the same spot with a honey sandwich. He stood there calling his possum, offering it the bait, telling the little fellow that he was very sorry and could he please come home.

"So let me see if I have this right: You beat it up, threw it in a box, and cast it out into the bush away from friends and family. Then you go back there hoping it will fall for the same trick? It might be a tad cautious about trusting you again, wouldn't you think?" I was weeping from laughter.

Geoff added, "It must have seen me as the evil ogre, luring it to come in and get beaten up again!"

It was not that he felt that the possum would trust him. Even after feeding the little fellow for years he realised it was not tame. But he thought it would love him! However, the issue wasn't that it bit him, or that he got incensed and tossed it out into the wild. The real concern was that Geoff knew the past could not be undone. However, by going out and making a peace offering he had hoped Mr Possum would forgive him. If the fellow would just accept his apology by way of the pro-offered honey on bread, he might sleep better at night. I still laugh about the craziness of this little episode.

Mind you, who knows how things pan out in the invisible worlds! That was in 1976 or so. It wasn't long after this the book "Possum Magic" was written. It is all about a possum who is made invisible to protect it from the dangers of the bush. The book is about his journey to re-find that visibility. Geoff's possum surely suffered the same fate, that of vanishing from plain sight.

Michael Notes: *One time Geoff took me fishing at West End. I know he must have thought it was just a way to keep me occupied, because we had no bait. I said I would put some cheese on the line, because I liked cheese, and why wouldn't a fish want some? He laughed, thinking it a great joke.*

Well, I caught myself a two pound catfish. The look on his face was delight, he could not believe it! "Cheese!" He exclaimed, "Who would have imagined a fish would go for cheese!" We tossed Mr. Fish back, as Geoff said they were not good eating.

The Iconic Wood Burning Crown Stove, manufactured in Brisbane

Crown Stove Property

Geoff went into real estate as a way to earn an income after the farm. He worked for H&M homes, got his license, then got his principals license. This meant he could run his own office if he wished. Selling 'spec' houses for H&M proved to be a bit of a winner and he was their top salesperson for most of the time he was there.

But he wanted more, he wanted to be his own man, so when the opportunity to sell the Crown Stove industrial property came up, Geoff took it with both hands. He left H&M and the solid income, and ventured into the high risk world of industrial marketing. Geoff paid for the advertising, he paid for everything to do with the marketing, even the printing of leaflets. He wanted to make sure he was going to collect his quite enormous 10% commission.

The sale of that property, which had been the manufacturing site of the failed Crown Stove business in Brisbane, would set him up for life. It offered a fifty thousand pound boost to his finances, which had been draining away since Goroka. Poor Geoff! For seven years he got offer after offer, but the only thing that happened was that the seller wanted more. Finally he realised the simple truth: the owner never really intended to sell it. He was using the offers Geoff brought him to negotiate better loans through his bank.

Geoff was his patsy, the guy who was making him money by increasing his properties valuation. This is why he gave him such an incredibly good deal: *Sure Geoff, you can have ten percent commission, just as long as you pay for all the marketing.* The guy was, quite literally, laughing all the way to the bank, carrying every offer he received to his bank manager, which increased his capacity to borrow against the property.

Geoff earned no money at all for those seven years. He was mortgaging the flats, living off a real estate asset like the crown stove man, and getting into a slightly higher mortgage every year. He was using that borrowed money to support the family. He didn't HAVE to, no one ordered him to do it, but he had agreed to give Joy money every month to raise the kids and he did till the youngest, myself, turned sixteen.

This episode proved to be the end of "Dollars Wallace". The blood-sucking nature of the man who ran the remnants of the Crown Stove empire, a once great name in Australian manufacturing, broke Geoff's once inexhaustible bank. Now he was living in debt, and getting desperate.

Houses in the Flood Zone

The simple truth, as Geoff often told me, was that he just didn't have the acquisition gene like most people. Money was for spending, not investing. It meant he had to go back to working and he started with a new business that started just down the road for m him, with Author and Spero Conias, of Conias Apollo in Toowong. He was doing very well, working in the Western suburbs of Brisbane right at the time before they became the fashionable place to live. He had let go of his dreams of selling commercial real estate and settled down to make some money doing the more conventional home market.

He spent many happy years there, earning quite a good income, and earning the respect of his principle, Spero. Years later, Spero was to say to me that Geoff was the most methodical and trustworthy agents he ever had. "He did everything by the book. He wrote up the listings, dealt with the clients, and prepared contracts in a way that never had to be checked. If Geoff did it, it was done right."

And around this time the big 1974 Brisbane flood hit. Taking time off, Geoff took all the kids up to the lookout at Mount Cootha, where we could see the enormous lake that had engulfed our city. It was a remarkable sight, gazing down over a huge flood zone. The water had snaked right through the heart of Brisbane, with houses dotting out on the edges of it. Such things stay in your memory for a lifetime and it highlighted the fact that Brisbane very much exists in a flood zone.

In the days after the water had receded, Geoff took me around in his '66 Chevy, and pointed out the homes that had gone under in Toowong and Auchenflower. "See these!" He said, waving his hand in their general direction, "They are all worth ONE THIRD of what they were only weeks ago. But give it a couple of years and everyone will forget, then the price will go back up to what it used to be."

I am all of fourteen at the time, but the obvious here is the obvious. "Well, why don't you buy them?" I asked.

Geoff's answer clearly proved the complete and total lack of commercial sense that ran his thinking. "But they are FLOOD AFFECTED!" he exclaimed, which put an end to that nonsense talk.

Two years later, the price was higher than they were pre-flood. Everyone had forgotten, as Geoff correctly predicted. What's more he was the one now selling a lot of those flood-affected houses … at three times the price he could have picked them up for.

Remember that at this time he was working as an estate agent! The part that amazed me, and still does, is the way he knew what would happen, yet could not see the wood for the trees. Yes, he fully understood human nature and how things worked, yet at the same time he could not see the obvious course he needed to take in order to profit from it.

When presented with the opportunity of a lifetime, Geoff decided to completely ignore it.

It is not entirely his fault. In many ways, the notion of making money out of housing did not really exist in the psyche of the 1970's person. Houses were what you lived in, or rented out, and eventually they were worth more, but what did that mean? Every house in the street was worth more! You bought a property because it was better than renting and it gave you stability, not to make money.

When Joy was selling up in Ashgrove to buy a house on the North Coast, I suggested to her that, as the Ashgrove house was already set up as two flats, why didn't she rent those out? She could then use the income from these flats to buy a second property. Her response? "That would be THEFT!" Joy cried.

Can you imagine a time when people thought they were stealing from people if they made a profit out of renting a house? That world, that type of thinking, has long departed.

Scenes from the Brisbane 1974 Flood

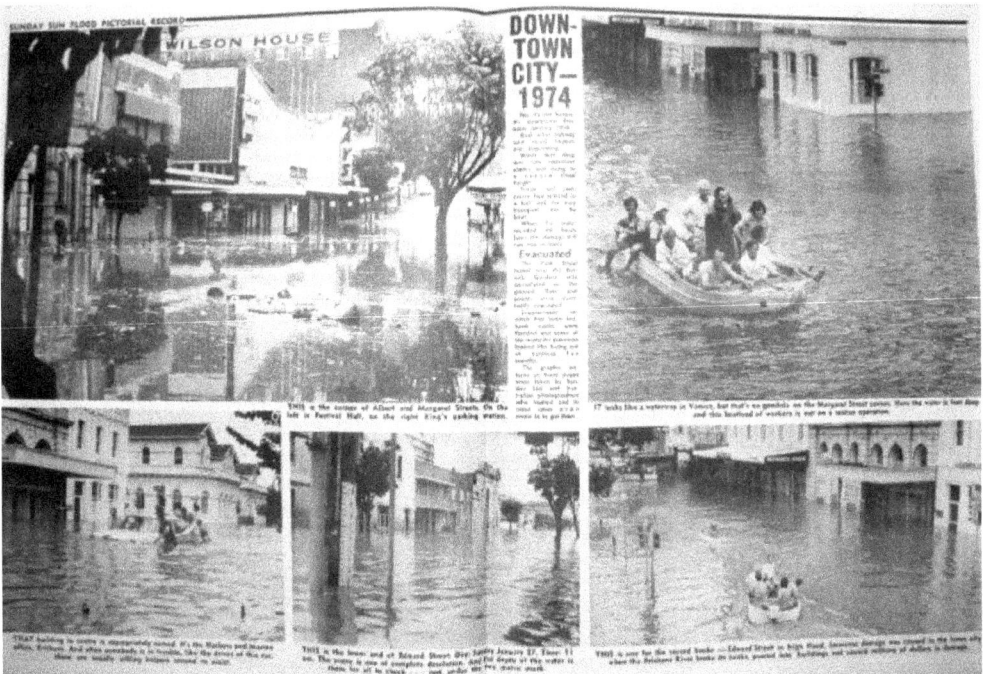

The Bush Wedding

My Brother, Greg, married a country girl, Marg, and they had the wedding reception in a hall out in the middle of nowhere. The place was full and, apart from the plentiful food, the brother of the bride had made up his own home made wine. I was not drinking, but everyone else was into it. Mulberry wine, apricot wine, you name it, if it was once a fruit it was now a wine.

Geoff really hammered down quite a few glasses, as did Joy and Vonnie. It was only when it came time to return home that Geoff realised he had not a clue where he was or where he had to go. He was also so sloshed that he had to cover one eye with his hand to even see the road in front of him. Fortunately, I had a good sense of direction and could read the odd road signs.

"Turn left in 100 yards. Slow down, turn left NOW." And so it went all the way back to Brisbane with Joy and Vonnie in the back, giggling away. They were oblivious to the fact that Geoff was driving along with one hand over one eye, following directions from a thirteen year old. We all made it back, somehow.

Everyone said what a great wedding it was.

Imagine today if you did the same thing and told everyone on Facebook. What would happen? You would be reprimanded by people around you, and get told you were being socially irresponsible.

I had remembered that episode with Geoff one day, years later, when he commented. "Since when have footballers and rock stars become role models? It was considered the thing to do back then, if you were famous, to trash a hotel room, get drunk and abuse drugs.

"Slowly the axe has fallen. It is hovering over our necks as we speak. Don't do anything, or be anyone different from anyone else. It's like our cars, they used to once be individual. Now, they are all the same as each other.

"You used to look at a Buick, a Chevy, a Roller, and KNOW what was coming. Now they are homogenous, like our milk. Safety is our prison and the wardens that keep us in gaol are not big business and government, it is our own minds. The only real safety in life is gratitude. This is what insulates us from the harsh reality. It is very easy to become bitter about what we have lost. The hard part is being grateful for what we have."

I suspect he was thinking of all the wasted money that would have provided security in his old age. "I can't complain, I have a pension and a place to live. It's more than most of the world."

Does Yez Take Super?

Geoff and Reg & Ford Ute

G eoff's favourite pastime was hunting. He was an excellent shot, but the real reason he went out West was not to fill the fridge with game to eat, it was to escape phone calls and responsibilities. The trip was all about walking the bush during the day and sitting around the campfire at night, drinking. Both meant you were free as a bird and living the good life. One of the funniest episodes came about with an early expedition out West. He was out in Central Queensland with his brother, Reg. It was a Sunday and they were making their way back home in the single spinner Ford ute when a serious reality started to emerge.

In every town they passed through, nothing was open. There was no petrol to be bought but surely the next town would have something open? No, it didn't. Sunday in those days meant everything was shut and you went to church, ate a big lunch, and did nothing. Out there in the middle of the bush, their situation had become difficult. They had painted themselves into a corner: There was not enough fuel in the car to get to the next town, nor was there enough to get back to the last one if they turned around.

Around this time, they realised their only option was with buying some petrol from a local farmer. Reg then spotted some fuel tanks at a station. Thankfully there were two of them, which meant one would be diesel, the other petrol. "Pull off here and see if we can buy some fuel off the man," suggested Reg.

They do so, approaching the homestead cap in hand, asking if it were possible to purchase some of the man's petrol. "Nah," the farmer answers, "I don't think so."

But why? They would pay over his cost price (Back then the farm fuel was half the price of the bowser) and more. They begged and cajoled and pulled every trick to get the man on side. They explained that they were desperate and had no fuel to get to the next town, but this had little effect. "Nah," said the farmer, "Cause if I sells it to youse lot, then theys all will comes a knockin, they will."

Geoff and Reg promised faithfully to tell no one, and make sure that the sale of this fuel was not advertised. They will guarantee the farmer, on their mother's grave, to stay silent about it. The talk went on for hours, some four hours in total. It was already beginning to get dark when the man finally relented, "Wells, alrighty then, if'n you really needs it," he says.

Geoff and Reg were relieved and expressed their profound gratitude. Finally, they back the car up to his refilling tank. But then, at the moment of triumph, just as he puts the nozzle to the fuel filler on the car, the farmer stops and takes it out. What on earth could be the problem now? *"It's super, does yez take Super?"* the farmers asks.

Geoff and Reg had to make sure not to laugh. Four hours of dickering, four hours of begging, and the old farmer thought they might have rejected the fuel? "Super! Damn, no way, we are out of here!" Geoff just said, solemnly, "No, she is good with Super."

They got enough in there to make it back to Toowoomba where there was petrol at a twenty-four hour coin-operated station. They finally get home in the early hours.

"Does yez take Super?" was the catch-cry of the brothers for many years after that.

Geoff Quips: *If you must paint yourself into a corner, try to pick a decent corner.*

Note from Sue: *When Dad visited me would give me a hug and physically check me out – "You've put on a little weight". I remember one day being very sick of this and saying something like "Do you want to check my teeth too, like a horse."*

The Rubber Snake

Geoff had the odd notion to scare the wits out of Cousin Geoff, or 'Young Geoff' as he was generally known. In some junk shop he found a near perfect rubber replica of a death adder, only it was green. The thing looked amazingly life-like, but it was green. The plan was to put it into the boot, on top of everything, and then ask young Geoff to grab something from there as they were setting up camp.

Well, it worked a treat. There was a shout of alarm as the boot opened and a loud, "Quick, get me my gun! There is a snake in the boot!"

Everyone had a good old laugh. The snake was held up, inspected, admired for it's life-like qualities and it's general rubbery-ness. Then, when the attention was elsewhere, young Geoff tossed the thing onto 'old' Geoff's bedding without him noticing. Drunk and happy, father was climbing into the camp-bed when he shouted and jumped up in fright. "You bugger!" He called out, knowing who had done it.

Geoff swore it scared him sober. It meant he had had enough of the snake. He put it in a bag and stuck it back in the boot of his car, whereupon he completely forgot about it until, yes, you guessed it: We were unpacking and it leapt at him. He had completely forgotten that the rubber snake was in the bag and he looked in there, wondering what it was. Another trip to the chiropractor but this time Geoff had more than enough of that damn snake, so he threw it high into some overhead cupboard.

There it sat, patiently waiting, for well over a year. Then one day Geoff is getting down some bedding and the snake leaps at him one more time! Another huge fright, a leap backwards, and another trip to the chiropractor. As if this were not enough, he threw it under the house, where it lived to get him AGAIN some months later.

In all that rubber snake ended up costing three trips to the Chiropractor. Logically, therefore, it would seem reasonable that any Chiropractors needing extra income should invest in rubber snakes. Maybe they could even start a second business, selling rubber snakes?

Geoff notes: *DHW used to say, 'I gave you all good bodies'. He was also prone to belting the shit out of my particular body. I suppose, as he had given it to me, he had the right to give it the odd disciplinary belting.*

Never Come Between a Wallace and a Dollar

After Annette had died and probate was settled, all monies had been distributed amongst the sons, apart from a small living allowance. There was a matter of some two thousand dollars left in Annette's holding account. Geoff wrote the brothers, suggesting that instead of him sending out four hundred to everyone that he keep this balance, to offset the costs of his travelling to see her every week for many years.

In simple terms, they all acted in unison, and did so with an extraordinary sense of bile towards this suggestion. Geoff was called a money-grubbing cur and many other quite vicious insults over what was a paltry sum. Really, Geoff just wanted recognition for all the effort he had put in. The small amount of money was simply a way they could have all said 'thank you' for his years of assistance on their mother's behalf.

At first he was upset, then he gathered himself and saw the funny side to it. This was when Geoff took a quiet revenge and devised a coat of arms for the family, a new family crest if you will. He researched his Latin, found snippets of the Wallace heraldic symbols, and put it all together a new coat of arms, with a Latin inscription that translated to, "Never come between a Wallace and a Dollar"

The whole thing was so stupid and the reaction so out of proportion to what anything was worth. I asked him, "Why do you bother with them?"

He said, "Because, they are my brothers. Despite how they act on occasions, they are still my brothers. We all have issues and it is better not to judge."

It took me a long time to get what Geoff was really saying here. Your true measure comes in keeping to your principles when you are insulted, abused and treated unfairly. It is easy to love those who are lovable.

The really funny twist to this tale, Bob's daughter upon hearing this dreadful tale was all sympathy and concern for poor Geoff. Yes, her father was a tightwad, she knew it as well. When he passed on she got millions in her inheritance and, as she was the sole heir to both the father's and mother's fortunes, the girl was rather rich. In response to the terrible miserly nature of her father, she duly sent Geoff a cheque for two hundred dollars ... Exactly half of what she had said her father should have given him way back when.

Geoff laughed and sent the cheque back. He no longer took her calls, which were all largely complaints about this or that anyway. The sad addendum to this tale came when Bob's daughter passed on. Despite her cousin, Gabrielle, looking after her, caring for her, and staying in constant contact, the woman left all her money to a cattery.

In truth, I gather that the poor woman had some sort of mental issue at work in the background. It is not for us to judge another, but surely she could have at least given SOME of that money to a family member who had gone out of her way to care for her?

Never come between a Wallace and a Dollar, unless you are a cat.

Numquam veni, et inter Wallace a pupa

Geoff Quips: *I ponder sometimes at our language, how there is a stipulated way to convey certain nouns. For example, you must scream abuse, hurl insults, battle cancer, wreak havoc, cry foul, and if you are emerging from a fog, you must loom out of it. You can't just walk out of a fog, you have to loom out of it. It's marvellous what sometimes occupies your mind after a few snorts. After a lot of snorts, I sometimes get amazing revelations of wisdom and write them down. On reading them the next day, they are absolute bullshit.*

Note from Sue: *One very hot Christmas when Dad was in his seventies, I was explaining that my yoga teacher had shown a method of cooling yourself by curling your tongue upwards on the outsides and breathing through the curl. I can't curl my tongue. Dad discovered for the first time in his life that he could do it and mentioned some days later that he kept looking in the mirror and curling his tongue.*

The Texas Camp

G eoff and myself, along with Cousin Geoff, would, once a year, make a pilgrimage to the bush. The goal was ostensibly to hunt pigs and ducks, but really, it was a matter of not being chained to the convention of the day to day

The usual camping site was a place on the Dumaresq River, near to Texas, QLD. It was a place of extraordinary beauty, a real gem that had the added advantage of having ducks fly past. However, staying there required a lengthy and extended "book in" and "book out" period with the property owner, Old Col. This was an extended affair of some hours and always the conversation was about the same thing, nothing. The weather: 'yep, she's been dry'. The politics: 'Nah, not one of them bastards can be trusted'. And so on, and so forth, for many hours.

It was not until one of my last trips out West with Geoff and Cousin Geoff, when 'Old Col' had passed away and his brother 'Young Tom' had taken over the reigns, that I realised the deeper secret behind it all. It was the very same reason it took Reg and Geoff four hours to get petrol into the old single spinner ute. These are men who are intensely lonely. Just having someone there meant a whole lot to them. Just having someone to talk to about nothing was everything.

Old Col passed away from some disease and his brother, Tom, took over the property. He already lived there in a different house, but as these holdings are many square miles in size 'Young Tom' could as easily have been in a different State. The point was, nothing changed but the name you used. It was the same sign in, sign out, procedure.

It was also the same process, year in, year out, to organise the pre-flight check to travel out there. Geoff had a list, typed and organised, of every single thing that was needed. Before it went into the boot of the Chevy it was ticked off and confirmed by two sets of eyes. "Tent?" check, "Tarpaulin?" check, "Griddle?" check, "Beer?" check, and so on. Every little detail was covered, so that nothing would be forgotten.

And when you arrived, two people went to get the firewood, one would set up the campfire. Once that was done, everyone set up the tents. Ice was already in the Esky, with the beer and coke put in there to cool back at Inverell. When all was prepared everyone sat down, cracked their can, and relaxed. It was an all-day effort to get there and the first words out of Geoff's mouth was invariably, "Finally, no more phone calls!"

Yet, just three of four days later, when we were all packing it back down into the boot, Geoff was wondering what had been happening. He now needed to get back to call people up. It was as regular as clockwork. The need to escape was in some way married to the need to have some purpose. It is everyone's story in one sense, but with Geoff it was accentuated.

Texas was freedom. You took the rifles and guns, and you went hunting pigs or ducks. The ducks you waited for, the pigs you walked through the bush looking to find. Occasionally you might smell a fox and Geoff had his fox whistle ready to call one up. I can't say we ever shot one, I can't say we ever shot very much at all, but that was not the point. It was the experience of freedom you were having. Let's face it, if you really needed to hunt to eat, well … hunt in the butchers shop. It is cheaper and easier.

The ducks were for eating, however, but the pigs were shot simply because they were feral animals, like foxes. You did the farmer a favour by putting them down.

**Dumaresq River, Texas, QLD.
An extremely picturesque and
beautiful river.**

Note from Michael: *For years I thought this was something that really happened. I was on the Dumaresq River, camping with Dad, when I decided to go fishing instead of hunting. I went to a nearby bridge, and threw off a line. A yellow Belly Perch took it right away, but surfaced, looked at me, then ran the line around the bridge pylon. Then it came back up, snapped the line, and swam off. The fish clearly told me, right into my mind, "Do not kill for sport!"*

Because of this experience I never wanted to kill anything, and never fished again, or shot any animals. The thing is, there was no bridge near our camp. It must have been a dream, but it was so real it changed my entire life.

DUCKS and the Orange Dot

L ater in life, Geoff felt bad about the ducks. He discovered that the Wood Duck mated for life and shooting one meant a very lonely solo duck had to go on living. Sitting in his flat, alone, he felt for the departed and regretted killing them. "Still, they were good eating!" He said, by way of explaining things.

I remember the first time I was out at Texas and given a duck to clean up. This meant gutting and de-feathering. I had never done it before, but I understood the principle. What I wasn't prepared for was the stench. Wild duck, when you start to gut them, stink in a way that is just extraordinary.

Geoff and cousin Geoff were laughing their heads off at the look on my face. No doubt this is exactly what happened to them, then they showed me how to do it ... You gut them underwater. "Food for the fish, and you cover up the stench." said Geoff.

To be fair, I personally offered absolutely no advantage to the hunters. I was a reasonable shot, but I really had no desire to shoot ducks or pigs. My job there was mostly to drink coke, then shoot the empty cans, a task I found enormously satisfying. But the men took their task seriously and calculated the correct ammunition and rifles needed for every expedition.

After the duck cleaning exercise, Geoff decided he wanted to try out the new 'polycore' shell, a single one ounce pellet of lead in a shotgun casing. This was the old elephant gun concept and the ammunition was developed as a way to bring down large pigs. But first there was testing! So we put up a target and over a sixty meter range, Geoff fired two shots. He looked through his binoculars and seemed surprised. "Looks like I missed one," he said to Cousin Geoff and myself.

We walked up to the target, and discovered quite the opposite. The polycore was so accurate that, even over sixty meters, Geoff had grouped one shot over the other. He tore that section of cardboard off and kept that little trophy for years and years. It was a thing of great pride that he could achieve what was, for most, an almost impossible task.

However, the next test for this new bullet was to see how much it dropped over a range. To this end we were walking up the river and saw what looked like some orange plastic on a tree. Geoff lined up the shotgun, aiming straight at it, to see how much the pellet dropped over the three hundred meters between us and the target.

He steadied himself, flicked off the safety, and was about to fire when he flicked it back on. Looking up, and squinting, Geoff says, "I thought I saw it move."

"Probably just the wind," I suggested.

Geoff went to line up the target again, but dropped the gun back down, saying simply, "If in doubt, leave it out."

As we walked further up river, we realised that the orange dot was really a vest over a fisherman sitting by the river. He waves at us, calling out, "Bet you shooters are glad I wore my orange vest, hey? Too easy to accidentally shoot someone!"

Geoff manages to not laugh, and replies, "Yeah, you can't be too careful with shooters about, can you. You really stand out at a distance with that orange." We continue on, laughing at the absurdity and how the very thing the man thought was going to protect him was what marked him as a target.

But the story did not end there. I have the whole thing recorded on tape, because one of the things Geoff loved to do out West was record conversations for later. Of course, with a little booze to lubricate the humour, what happened were little 'play acting' scenes where everyone partook in a performance. That little portable cassette deck caught some funny moments. One example: Cousin Geoff and my father would play act out the Westerns, "I am calling you, Kincaide!!" "What are you calling me?" I am CALLING you!" You get the idea, a general overall silliness like this.

But the orange dot fisherman had more in store for us! When we got back to camp we found his car had been parked near to ours and late into the afternoon, as evening fell, we heard a splash, with a voice from the river calling out, "It's OK, I just fell in the water!"

"The fish aren't supposed to catch YOU," called out Cousin Geoff, "You are supposed to catch the fish!" And for the next ten minutes, a general conversation was made into the portable tape deck regarding the close call the fellow had on the riverbank.

Then another car pulls up just as it falls dark and, in the middle of nowhere, they manage to drive into the fisherman's car. "Hey, who's running into me car!" He calls out, mysteriously knowing that it was 'his' car that got bumped.

"If in doubt, leave it out."

"It's only us, dear. Brought you some tea and supper." And the man's wife and her friend amble past, nodding to us as they go by, thermos and esky in hand.

What is the likelihood of an accident here? There were just three cars inside fifty miles of each other and one of them manages to run into another when it is parked! Soon after, the dripping wet fisherman and his wife straggle past and Geoff comments, dryly, "Better be careful, you could catch your death out here on the river bank."

"Lucky I am not prone to the flu, hey?" the fisherman calls back, laughing.

We are all laughing, and Cousin Geoff says when he is out of earshot, "He needs to be more worried about catching a case of severe lead poisoning or getting run over by his wife."

Geoff adds, "You know, he doesn't even realise how lucky he is. In his mind, today has been a bad day. His wife ran into his car, he fell in the river, all bad things. He has no idea how much worse things could have been. The lesson is clear: It pays to be grateful, even for the things we think don't deserve gratitude."

Note by Michael: *Geoff loved the old song made famous by Pete Seeger: "Little Boxes, on the hillside. Little Boxes made of Ticky Tacky. Little Boxes, on the hillside. Little Boxes, all the same"*

He would comment on how awful the new subdivisions were, how soulless the new world was becoming, and yet within a few years he had sold the farm and was making a living selling those "Ticky Tacky" houses that "all looked just the same".

Cousin Geoff

My father got on extremely well with his namesake, my cousin. As mentioned, the two were distinguished in conversation by Geoff calling my cousin "Young Geoff. (When my cousin was sixty years old he was still "Young Geoff") "Uncle Geoff" and "Young Geoff" referred to each other by these terms and all their lives.

Geoff really liked his nephew and treated him as one of his own. Before you cheer too much, what this meant was when Young Geoff visited he got, "I am glad you are here, there is some furniture that needs moving out of one of the flats." No one in the 'inner circle' ever got to visit without some task being required of them. The oddest thing was that if you were 'just a visitor' you were not expected to muck in and help out with whatever it was that needed doing.

"I could not recall a time when there was not a *'Good that you are here, this needs doing!'* coming from Uncle Geoff," said Cousin Geoff when I asked him. This was a guarantee that you were liked and accepted, but not many realised it at the time. Visiting Geoff was like asking to do work that never got paid, but you were paid in other ways, like trips out West.

"We had some great times," Cousin Geoff regaled me with a few of the occasions. "Remember when the 900 pound Sow was charging me after I shot it's babies? You can't blame it, but that was scary. Thank goodness your Dad was there while I was reloading. He was my guardian angel."

It was a serious reminder of how dangerous the whole business of hunting pigs could be. One time, when Reg was with us, we were walking through the bush when a Taipan reared up to strike Reg. Without thinking, Geoff shot his 22/250 from the hip and hit the damn thing in the head just as it was about to strike. My cousin was truly amazed at how anyone could have pulled off that shot and many years later he researched it.

Apparently, what happened was not as unusual as you might imagine. Taipans are so fast they can see the bullet coming and they STRIKE at it. So, just fire close enough, the snake attacks the projectile, and kills itself. A good thing too, as Reg was dead if Geoff's bullet had missed. We were over an hour away from the nearest hospital and miles into the bush. A Taipan bite paralyses you and inside 30 minutes you are gone.

Cousin Geoff had the most wonderful way of passing the moments: he would sing old Country and Western songs, with a passably fine voice. It was not just about not having uncomfortable gaps in conversation, there was something really wonderful about sitting around a campfire and hearing "Yellow Rose of Texas", or Johnny Cash, or Burl Ives. Young

Geoff knew all the words and Old Geoff loved hearing the songs of his earlier years.

"You are two great kids," he would say, happily drunk, soaking up the stars and moon, listening to the splash of the odd fish in the river.

"I felt like I was his son," Cousin Geoff said to me years later. "Geoff always treated me like family and I always felt welcome at your Mum's house as well." The modern world seems to have snipped people off from their extended families. The smart phone has connected everyone, yet made so many of us feel more alone.

Geoff loved this photo, saying: "This is a 100% certified way to drive a man to drink!"

Note from Young Geoff: *Uncle Geoff sold me my first gun, and Over and Under Winchester, for Eighty Pounds. A fair sum in those days, but a really first class shotgun. One day when we were both going out to the Belmont range, he stopped at a shot and asked me to get some cotton wool, for the ears. Well, I saw the aspirin bottle had cotton wool at the top, and as a plus, all those aspirin. Two birds with one stone, I thought! Uncle Geoff was not amused, and told me to go back and get what he asked for!*

Visitors

Geoff had a cadre of regulars who would call on him. Some of these were people he once taught how to use a computer and who were now personal friends that liked to call by. Others were professional persons, like the Podiatrist who did his nails every six weeks. She was a very kind woman, and such visits were one of the benefits of being a D.V.A. (Department of Veterans Affairs) gold card holder.

As a note: Because he served in WW2, Geoff was given the tremendous benefit of a DVA Gold Card. This meant ANYTHING that needed doing, dental or medical, was taken care of. This is what covered his visits to the chiropractor, his knee operation in a private hospital, etc. Geoff often spoke of his deep gratitude for this country and the kindness it showed its veterans.

John Grattidge was a student who became a friend. Geoff offered very cheap computer tuition and setup for people new to computers. He would advertise his services on shopping centre notice boards. John called him, and after a few sessions they became fast friends. Even after he had stopped lessons, he would still call by, every Tuesday, to see Geoff.

"He is one of the most honest people you will ever meet," Geoff said of him one day. "The thought of taking something he didn't pay for would never even occur to John."

There were also the locals in the block of flats where Geoff lived. For the most part they were a very friendly crew. There was one abrasive fellow, but Geoff always kept a polite conversation with him, because, as he said, "Someone else's opinion and experience of a person is not mine, nor should I make it mine. It is better to stay on good terms with others." Then he paused and added, "Especially those who can be troublesome."

Peter was a fellow from upstairs who used to drop in regularly. He had a ready grin, and, like Harry the Farm Worker, more than a few teeth were missing from it. Peter loved Geoff and looked up to him as a wise soul. I suspect it was because Geoff never judged him, but also because he was good for a small loan on occasions, which Peter always paid back. He came from the wrong side of the tracks and had survived drug addiction and alcoholism. Under Geoff's quiet guiding hand, he slowly turned it all around and was studying to be a counsellor. He started accepting personal responsibility, stopped talking about himself as a victim, and started talking about where he was going more than where he had been.

Gary lived on the floor above. He was looking after his Mum, and was regularly out the front, bottle of beer in hand. He would always ask me as

I walked past how Geoff was going. There were also the ladies who (unpaid, purely voluntary) looked after the gardens, they were always asking if he needed anything.

George from upstairs would call to see Geoff for advice regarding computers. He was another good soul living out their days in Government sponsored housing. Keep in mind, the block of flats in Palm Beach was a stones throw from the beach and though the places were small, they were well appointed. If Geoff ever felt any embarrassment for ending up there after being so wealthy, he never showed it.

The specific thing about visiting Geoff was that you had to be on time. Punctuality was extremely important to him. If you said one o'clock in the afternoon, he expected you there at that time. Calling up and saying "I should be there around two-ish," was barely acceptable, but to say this and be there at 2.30 was a definite no-no.

I did ask him one day, "So what are you doing that makes arriving at a specific time so important?"

"That is not the point," he responded. "The thing is doing what you have agreed to do."

"Absolutely father, and this is why I am doing what I agreed to do, which is to call in. What I am not doing is promising you I will be there at a specific time. But honestly, what is the real concern? You are just sitting at home anyway, and it matters not a whit if I am there at one, or two."

Geoff was clearly not happy with this sort of arrangement, so I compromised, "OK then, I faithfully promise that I will be there at two, but if I arrive early, is that OK?"

He grudgingly admitted that it probably was, knowing he had fallen into a trap. "But if you are here early I may be out. I could go to the shops, so you would have to wait." His counter argument was the potential threat of him not being there, therefore proving the rightness of setting a time that everyone agrees upon!

I was prepared for this rebuttal. "No problem, I have lots to do and have a key so I can let myself in." There, he was trapped. Instead of saying 'between one and two' I can just say 'two' and as long as I am not AFTER this time, I am good. The main thing, of course, was visiting, and visiting with a regular and trustworthy regularity on a specific day.

But you had to be the right person to get visitation rights. Most people, if they said they were dropping in to say hello, would get a cagey response from Geoff. He would say "I am out that day," or "This is not really a good time to call by," or any number of other reasons to avoid meeting you. I suspect it was simply that he felt stress being with people he did not fully trust.

Occasionally there were obligations to be met. A grandson would 'book in' to call by with his wife and kids, and Geoff would be OK with this, as they were family, but he also wanted a definite time period. "So, you will be staying an hour? That's good, because I am old and tire easily." In other words, don't stay longer.

He did appreciate that people made the time, but he also knew that it was most probably obligation on their part. However, this is not necessarily a bad thing. But if you were not a family member, it was like booking a seat at the world's most popular restaurant. Unless you were Clarry! Clarry was a bushey, a country lad, who met Geoff and liked him. Clarry could call in any time he wished. He was not family, nor even a particularly close friend, but there you have it. He liked Clarry, possibly because he reminded him of people he knew in the past.

What I really think is that Geoff only wanted honest people around him. Most people, and they are largely unaware of this, put on airs and graces. They pretend to be something they are not, or they carry a sense of self-importance that rubbed against his natural humility. I really can't say for certain, because he never said anything specifically, but I noted the pattern over time.

If you were down-home, friendly and were able to 'give space' you were welcome. It is hard to describe this concept, but there are people who are just very accepting and allow others to be whatever they wished to be, these are the people Geoff liked to have around.

But if you DID visit, the one thing that was an absolute certainty was that you were needed for something. "I am so glad you called by. I have been meaning to get some help doing (whatever it might be)." Geoff has a list of things that needed doing, or at the very least, subjects he wanted to canvass when any particular person dropped by.

It is only now that I start to 'get it'. Geoff was prepared. He wanted a specific time and place, because he had very specific things he wanted done or talked about and he had them all written down. He would have gone over these in his thoughts, and really given your visit a great deal of deep consideration.

People who turned up willy-nilly threw his clock out of whack and more to the point, this did not give him time to consider things. Geoff was not an improviser in social situations, but had the entire show organised, down to an internal script of the things he wanted to say and do. My job in life it would seem, by being random and not always on time, was clearly designed to throw a spanner in his works.

Punctuation

From Punctuality to Punctuation: Geoffrey had a deep love-hate relationship with grammar and punctuation. He loved the language, but hated how people abused it. It was a war he continually waged, a constant battle to get the written word correct. To this end he had an arsenal of style books, dictionaries and thesauruses ... And he hated the use of Ellipses. This was particularly difficult for him as I used this a lot in writing.

There are two rules for the use of Ellipses. The first is that when you REMOVE a section of a quote you are using, it is appropriate to insert three dots to let the reader understand you have taken a section out. The second use is a literary pause, which was it's original purpose.

It did not matter that I explained to him the history of the Ellipses, and how it came to be in use. Most will know the name of the famous Roman, the foil to Julius Caesar in the Senate, Marcus Cicero. He was a self-made man who rose up from the commoners to strut the world stage as one of the most famous lawyers of all time. He invented the Class Action, for one. Many of the legal principles we abide by today are as a direct result of his arguments.

His secretary, Tiro, was also a very extraordinary man. And all the above is to highlight this one resounding fact, he invented the elipses. He also invented shorthand, but that is another story. The man would go with the great orator and attorney whenever he went to meetings. Without anyone realising it, his secretary would have wax tablets in his pocket, and scratch the conversation down in his own form of shorthand. The 'three dots' were an indicator of a pause in conversation.

They symbolise one of the greatest advances in legal history, note taking. When a solicitor could quote EXACTLY what you said in a meeting, it was a powerful instrument. The pen was mightier than the sword for the first time in human history. Marcus Tullius Tiro is rarely acknowledged, but this man changed the world, and he also invented the Ellipses.

(From the wiki on Marcus Tullius Tiro) Aulus Gellius says, " [he] wrote several books on the usage and theory of the Latin language and on miscellaneous questions of various kinds," and quotes him on the difference between Greek and Latin names for certain stars. Asconius Pedianus, in his commentaries on Cicero's speeches, refers to a biography of Cicero by Tiro in at least four books, and Plutarch refers to him as a source for two incidents in Cicero's life."

See: https://en.wikipedia.org/wiki/Marcus_Tullius_Tiro - cite_note-9

Did this matter to Geoff? No, I was over using this particular punctuation mark. It was not correct. However, he accepted I liked it, even though he disapproved. Even so, he made a note in all proof reading he did for me regarding 'overuse', though he accepted that the final inclusion was my decision. A wrong one, of course, but my decision. FINALLY, I got the message. It had nothing to do with the grammar being correct, and everything to do with how it would be seen. And 'der' ... (you like my use of Ellipses, don't you?) The whole point of writing is that it is SEEN! HOW people see the written word is extremely important, and the entire purpose of writing is wrapped around this.

I did overuse the Ellipses, and I underused commas. So many small, little details in my writing were not correct and Geoff was right: It was not the error itself that was the issue, it was the effect this had on others. It was a form of arrogance to presume the reader would overlook the peccadillo of my penchant for the Ellipses. (Isn't that a nice string of words to throw together!)

Once again, Geoff was right. Yes he was picky and fussy and all of those things. Yes, this could be annoying. Yes, it was a matter of seeing the trees but not seeing the forest. But the fact remained, he was right. I changed my writing style and guess what? I started to write more clearly. What is more, it did not stymie my creativity, or cramp my style in any way. It just made it easier to write.

So often Geoff would look at me and comment, "Of course, you know everything, so it is pointless trying to convince you otherwise." It was possibly the greatest single task Geoff ever undertook in this life, getting his son to write better. Perhaps he knew I would end up writing his story and it was all done purely through self-interest? I am sure he is laughing about my stubbornness now, with the paradox being that I believed HE was the stubborn one.

Geoff was determined to get punctuation right and yet, as he stated on many occasions, he could not see the errors in his own writing. In a letter he wrote to Telstra, he meticulously went over it for days, to ensure everything was correct and his point was clear. Then he posted it. He showed it to me and I point out a spelling mistake! He was shocked, but added with resignation, "We can never see our own faults. The blind spot rules us."

Later, I found myself wondering: *"Did he do this on purpose, to get a message across?"*

PROZAC

Worthy of note, there are prescribed medications that can have extraordinary and adverse side-effects. Earlier we noted how an anti-depressant Geoff took when he was living at 502 Milton Road had caused him to drink White Spirit and turn a radiator onto the carpet. He put himself into the asylum after that, thinking he was mad.

Many years later, after Geoff had moved himself to a rented flat in Kirra, he was utterly exhausted and went to see his doctor. The man believed his symptoms exhibited extreme depression and he put him onto a drug called Prozac. This is a Nitrogen-salt based anti-depressant. Geoff took ONE pill, and promptly forgot where he was, what he was doing, and how he ended up in what was a fairly seedy flat with awful furniture.

I had called round to see him because he had not answered his mobile. He had forgotten to turn it on and when I got to the door, he seemed confused. "Where am I?" he asked. He did not even remember my then wife, though he did remember myself and my youngest son. Otherwise, he had absolutely no recollection as to how he got to where he was, where his furniture had gone, or anything.

I was seriously concerned. He had exhausted himself moving to this flat, insisting of doing a lot of the shifting himself, and maybe something had given way with the stress? On impulse I asked about what pills he had been taking and he pointed to the new one, Prozac. A quick check told me there was a high incidence of side-effects with this drug. A further check with a nurse well acquainted with a variety of drugs confirmed my suspicion. "They say 30% of people have side-effects," she said to me, "but in my experience, it is more like 90%."

The effect lasted three or four days and finally Geoff began to remember what had happened. However, the strikingly powerful effect of that one pill he took, a pill that had been prescribed, left a lasting impression. I did some research on the drug. Turns out, even in the final clinical trials where it had been approved for use, the side-effects such as memory loss, suicidal tendencies, and the desire to kill other people had occurred in the control group, but these were not reported.

Why? Under the rules of that time, the company was not required to report negative outcomes for the control group that did not exhibit depressive tendencies. Only the people that were depressed were reported, and they exhibited an extraordinary decrease in symptoms.

I began to wonder about all those mass killings in the United States. How many of those people who committed those heinous acts were under the effect of a drug like Prozac? The desire to kill others is, after all, a known side-effect of this specific type of anti-depressant. There is no research and this area is an unknown, but I can personally vouch for the dangerous nature of that specific drug.

When Geoff had come back to his senses after a week or so, he looked around, and asked. "How did I get here? I used to be rich, but now I am living in a dive, dependant on a pension."

I didn't know what to say. A series of bad financial decisions was the obvious answer, but while I sat there Geoff answered himself. "The good news is that I am not suffering from people who only want to know me for my money!"

As always, the trademark sense of humour pulls him out of the nosedive. However, things were not looking good for Geoff. He had sold what remaining property he had and largely spent that money paying rent and costs living in a mobile home site in Burleigh. Nell had divorced him in early 1989 and the famed cash cow had finally run dry. Geoff later rented a better apartment, but costs were going up and his income was fixed. He was starting to fret about how he was going to survive.

Then fate intervened by way of a Housing Commission flat coming up at Palm Beach. This was a godsend, and a further gift came when he qualified for a Veterans pensions, which topped up his government one and meant he could now afford to live. This meant that the last decade of his life could be spent in security and comfort. And yes, the little place got cluttered, because Geoff still wanted two of everything.

I remember he had an old and useless printer that he had been holding onto and I said, "I can fix that printer. Would you like me to show you how?" He was really interested, so I picked it up and asked him to follow me. Whereupon, I took it to the disposal bin and threw it in. "There, your printer problem is now fixed!" I declared.

He bought two new ones to replace it! To give you an idea, we carted out seven wheely bins full of junk from that little flat when he passed away and still had barely made a dent. Geoff did say, "You are just going to throw everything out when I go, aren't you?" We did.

This is my impression of what my sister thought when we were there to clear out Geoff's flat

Questions as Advice

W hen Geoff wanted to say something to someone, or to make a point, he rarely would say things directly. Instead, he would ask a question that circulated the point he wanted to make. "People hate to be told anything," he said to me. "Everyone gets their back up when you suggest they are wrong, but if you ask about why they do something, or what purpose it was for, then they start thinking, and stop blaming."

Inside the question was the message he wanted to say to you. As an example, rarely, if ever, did Geoff say anything directly to suggest you were wrong. An example was my use of the Ellipses, the question would be, "Do you feel your reader will find this annoying after so many repeated examples of the same thing?" Or it might be, "Is there a purpose for using this ellipses so often?"

Another odd question came when I was having a bad patch playing poker, "Do you think the others might be working together as a team?" He was really saying "You need to be a team player!" and poker was only the excuse he found for this to be brought out. And again, he was correct. When you work together with others, finding agreement and direction, things work for us far more easily.

Yet poker would seem to be the least 'team game' you could imagine. It is you against everyone and everyone against you. Again, under that question was a deeper meaning. Am I understanding the motivations of those sitting with me? Am I considering what THEY want, where THEY are going? Am I paying attention to the world and how it sees me?

I started playing each table like it was a team of people, each with their individual goals and aspirations, and I started winning games again. One step further, I also learned to make bets in the way that I was asking people a question. I started to ASK when I made a bet, "One thousand?" I would ask. It made a tremendous difference to how people responded. They no longer saw me as an aggressor, but as a friend.

This meant the table was no longer so willing to gang up on me. All because I started paying attention to everything there that was not myself, and asking questions instead of making statements. It all changed because I started to walk a mile in their moccasins.

The thing is, I only fully understood this question after he died. You see, Geoff asked, *'Do you think they are team players?'* three months after he had passed away, in a dream.

Mick Knows Everything

G eoff often laughed about the fact that I apparently knew everything. He would ask my opinion about something, or ask a question regarding some notion he had been wondering about, and add, "You know everything, so you are the best person to ask."

He always referred to me as 'Mick' which I found extremely funny because when I was born my name was going to be Michael John. Geoff decided at the Births Deaths and Marriages counter, where the birth certificate was issued, that Michael would become Mick, and that is an Irish fighters name, which he didn't want. So he reversed it to John Michael. No-one ever called me John and from age two, I was called 'Mickey Mouse'.

The only person who called me Mick was my father, ironically the same person who changed the name so I would not be called Mick. Be that as it may, when other kids were reading comic books, I was reading science magazines. I loved reading books, and would read one a day. I was consumed by a need for information, facts, science and though a terrible student at school, I was an excellent reader and researcher.

Geoff fuelled this by providing books on a wide variety of subjects, and because of him I was studying Buddhism and comparative religions at age sixteen. At the time I possessed an eidetic memory, something innumerable motor cycle accidents and several near death experiences beat out of me. But my powers of recall in the early part of my life were remarkable.

However, Geoff's somewhat cynical "Mick knows everything" was a bit of a standard comment on the fact that he did not believe I was humble enough. He was right, in his way, but it was his fault for throwing so many interesting books my way.

Geoff Quips: *I'm always curious. Why do they put a use-by date on sour cream?*

Note from Sue: *Dad would always ask 'How do I look?'*
He enjoyed telling the story that went to the doctor one day saying he had holes in the inner corners of his eyes. The doctor replied that they were his tear ducts.

Eckankar

Few people knew it, but Geoff was a highly placed and respected member of a spiritual teaching, called Eckankar. The story of how he found it, or how it found him, is worthy of mention. The first stage of this journey coincided with his spiritual searching, soon after he departed the marital home.

He had bought the Rochedale farm and I would travel with him in the Chevy on weekends to stay there. As we drove through Stones Corner there was a large blue and white sign that read, simply, "Eckankar". It got Dad curious, so he asked a friend who worked in the newly opened Circle Bookshop, located in the CBD of Brisbane, what it was about.

She knew the name because there were books relating to it. "It's a spiritual teaching," she said. Geoff bought some books. I remember these because they ended up in his bookshelf at Milton Road and I used to pluck one down on occasions to look at the smiling face of the guy on the back cover. He seemed to be looking at me and was very friendly. I don't know why, but I often pulled down the book, called "In my Soul I am Free" by Brad Steiger.

Many years later, I encountered the teaching again but all I remembered was the name. I saw this name. Eckankar, on a book at a fellows house and I asked what it was. He gave me a copy. I read it, liked it, and joined. Later that year, I dropped into Geoff's and mentioned I joined a teaching called Eckankar. He said that this sounded familiar for some reason. So he read one of my books and then told me he was sure he had read it before.

Well, I look on his book shelf and there are his books from the late 1960's. Suddenly he remembers the sign! After he re-reads his books, he goes to a few meetings and also joins. At the time he said to me, "I have no idea why I didn't sign up back then. This is the only thing that ever made sense."

There was a peculiar thing about the meetings he went to. He had gone, listened to what people had to say, but the thing that struck him most was the old woman that sat there, knitting the whole time. He would chat with her afterwards. After a few visits he eventually asked her what she thought about the whole thing and she gave a curious reply.

"I am not particularly smart and don't have any answers for you. Plus, I really think you just have to decide these things based on their merits."

Can you believe THIS is why he joined? He loved her humility. He loved that she wasn't airing her opinions or giving him advice. She was simple and honest. The thing is, after he told me this I checked around. I asked friends who were there about a woman who sat in those early intros just knitting, because it seemed odd. The people presenting the talks at that time told me that there was never anyone like that during any presentation that they were aware of.

"You don't suppose this was a little like Mrs Johnson?" I asked. Geoff looked at me, it was not something he had ever really considered. He was not long from passing away at that point and I had the distinct impression that, perhaps, this WAS Mrs Johnson, his invisible childhood friend from Merrylands.

I know I first met the current leader of the teaching when I was age four. He called me by name and we chatted for a bit. Eckankar did not even exist at that point, it was registered by Paul Twitchell some two years later. So who can say, the cross over between spiritual and physical reality is something that no one can prove, or disprove.

Of course, things can happen 'on the inner' that are so real we feel that happened out here in the 'real' world. As a child I often didn't know if I was in the physical world or one of the inner planes. For example: I thought I could fly and got frustrated when my body decided it couldn't. On the 'inner' I would spin on the Hills Hoist and take off. I would be flying! But on the 'outer' no matter how much speed I gave it by spinning around on the Hills Hoist, there was no flying. It was excellent for getting giddy, however. The message: We can experience things inwardly that appear for all the world to be a physical world event.

Did you ever have a dream where you were 'really there'? It is not uncommon, and called Lucid Dreaming. But where were you? Clearly, your physical body and your being disconnected for a bit and your consciousness went 'somewhere'.

I also worked back over the history of this 'sign at Stones Corner' business. Who put it up? There was no organisation in Australia in those days. Not one person I spoke to recalled such a thing, nor was there anyone in the teaching at that time who could fund such a large cost. The thing was, the place where we both saw the big ECKANKAR sign was above a residential block of flats, which just happened to be the same building I was in, many years later, when I met the fellow who gave me my first Eckankar books.

Make of this what you will, but a silent, guiding hand seemed to be at work. It is certainly a basic tenant of the teaching he belonged to that there was help for every member should they but ask for it. In fact, even people who were not members could ask for help and receive it! Despite Geoff's poor sense of saving and finance, he was looked after his entire life.

Which brings up his poor fiscal sense. People with money used to ridicule Geoff, quietly, for his incompetence with money. It is true, he was never good with saving and, as he himself admitted, he just didn't have the acquisition gene. Yet he was never a burden to anyone. What Geoff DID have was a connection to invisible worlds. Why is this important?

For one: This allowed him to step into another's shoes, and see how they felt about something. As a result, this allowed him to see himself a little as others saw him. Because of this, he was essentially honest, humble and kind. Or perhaps it is the complete reverse of this, the honesty, kindness and humility is what allowed him to feel how others might feel. I am not very good at those things, so I can't be too certain, but I have a sense this is how it was.

Why Don't We Tell Them?

Being of mature age, I have been to many funeral services. At these services, the following thoughts always occur to me, and I would like to share them with you. There has never been one of these occasions when at least one speaker has not stood up in front of the attendees and extolled the good qualities of the deceased. And not once have I heard anyone recount his faults!

But, unfortunately for the deceased, he or she is able to hear *not one word* of this praise and appreciation. It's too late! He or she is totally oblivious to the esteem in which he or she was held by many of those present, who are now dabbing their tear-filled eyes. What a difference it may have made to his or her life (which is hard enough for most of us) if they could have heard those same expressions of esteem and love whilst they were living! Probably most of them would not have known that many of those present even saw good in them, let alone loved them.

Wouldn't it be better to have told them while they were alive and could hear the words that they now never can hear, rather than live with the regret for what we neglected to say? Or to have done something for them while they were alive?

But the opportunity has gone, and now that we would like to say the words that are in our hearts, there are no ears to hear them.

Perhaps we don't tell them because we *assume* that they know, when indeed they may not. Perhaps we may feel embarrassed. Does it matter? Why don't we tell them while they still can hear? And who knows when that day will come when those ears will be able to hear no more? Why don't we tell them?

Geoff Wallace

Reg has a Spiritual Experience

When Geoff's brother, Reg, was in hospital he came too out of the induced sleep and found his brother standing there, glowing white, like some angel, at the end of his bed. "It was a vision, an angel!" he said to Geoff later, when he called him up to explain what he saw. "You were standing there, holding out your hands, like you were healing me."

Geoff demurred. "I was home at the time, Reg. What you saw was what you saw, but I was here."

Reg insisted it must have been an angel that at least looked like his brother, or something, maybe just a hallucination from the drugs and anaesthesia. "I am sure it was you, though."

Geoff let it rest. He knew how the Holy Spirit will use any channel to communicate with a person. If, for some reason, it saw fit to reach his brother in the form of himself, then so be it. He had no recollection of such a thing, that much he did know.

Reg was transitioning. His wife had passed away and, not knowing his mother had been a member of the Spiritualist church, he had joined this institution seeking to reconnect with Marie. His heart was opening and the spiritual forces reached out to him, using the form of his brother.

However, this was not the only time some person attributed a visitation from Geoff as having a profound influence on their lives. Another one was Vi, a rather eccentric, bi-polar woman who he met doing Tai Chi. She was wealthy and, possibly as a result of this, she was paranoid and suspicious of everyone. She was also schizophrenic, having a nasty personality that lived beside her normally pleasant one.

She, too, swore that Geoff had visited her in hospital, reaching out his hands in healing. The thing is, Geoff always denied any and all suggestions that it were actually himself these people were experiencing. It was spirit at work and that was that.

It certainly did not stop Vi a few weeks later from writing an abusive and quite nasty letter to Geoff, accusing him of all sorts of things. I started to 'get it'. It WAS spirit at work and whether it worked via Geoff's consciousness or not wasn't the issue. You don't put yourself up on a pedestal, because, as we know, after Palm Sunday comes the Crucifixion.

Stay humble, be invisible, do not seek to be important. Let Spirit, or whatever you wish to call it, do ITS job because it really isn't us doing any of this. At best we can be is a clear channel for ITS will and cluttering this up with notions of self-importance is possibly the worst thing we can do.

The Axe

Few things say more about Geoff than the axe he had in the bathroom. He always had one there, why? Obviously, because he could get locked in. It happened once and this caused a major panic attack. He REALLY hated feeling trapped in any way, and any form of social of physical situation where he felt cornered or not in control terrified him. However, this is all solved by having a small axe that can chop through doors when needed. It provided a security blanket.

Once at a Christmas gathering at my brother's house, Geoff got locked in the bathroom. "He looked ashen when he came out," my brother said. "It seemed that being confined really traumatised him."

He had many other fetishes, like the "Spare Thing" habit. Geoff had an enormous capacity to have two (or more) of everything. As one example: Under the flats at Milton Road I noted one day that he had twenty-one gas heaters sitting there. I suggested this was a tad excessive, even by his standards. Geoff explained: "These particular gas-jet water heaters aren't available anymore, so I have them as a backup replacement."

"You have twenty-one of them, father, and you only have thirteen flats! Do you think they are all going to fail, twice?"

He just looked at me, looking for a reasonable way out of what seemed to be a trap. "I agree, on the surface, it might seem excessive, but I pick them up for very little and they are useful, so really, can you have enough of useful things? Plus, I have the space to store them."

There was no purpose to be had in belabouring the point. He knew it was excessive, but he was a bower-bird. To him, a gas-jet wall-mounted hot water system was a thing of beauty to be gathered up and safely stored away. When he saw things that could be useful, he loved to pick them up and take them home. Like the 'security' axe he carried around with him from house to house, for maybe thirty years that I can recall. It was no beauty queen. In truth it was a genuinely ugly thing, with a rusty, metal handle, and a hand grip that was unwinding. But here we have the secret: This was THE axe which made him feel safe in the bathroom.

Yes, he had several other axes, but 'that' was the one that went in the bathroom. Everything had to have a place and after he passed on, there it was, the trusty, rusty axe. It was still sitting there beside the loo, just in case someone got locked in the bathroom.

This is as good a synonym for Geoff's deep and abiding claustrophobia, not just being locked into a room, but into a situation, or with a social gathering. Geoff never stayed overnight, he would visit, but no offer to stay and sleep over before travelling back was ever taken up. If needs be, he would book a room in a motel before staying at another person's house. There was no way he was going to be trapped in an awkward spot he could not manoeuvre out of! That genuinely ugly little axe symbolised freedom from confinement and thus was a thing of beauty to Geoff.

Even more curiously, that axe was the one thing my sister wanted to keep of his. There I was, hoping the thing could finally be put to rest and tossed onto the junk pile where it belonged.

Though often fraught with anxiety, Geoff was always the optimist, and looked to see the brighter side of things.

Note from Sue: *One very hot Christmas when Dad was in his seventies, I was explaining that my yoga teacher had shown a method of cooling yourself by curling your tongue upwards on the outsides and breathing through the curl. I can't curl my tongue. Dad discovered for the first time in his life that he could do it and mentioned some days later that he kept looking in the mirror and curling his tongue.*

Cheepa Card Company

At around age fourteen, I was visiting Geoff and he asked, "It's your birthday soon, isn't it?" He was never very good with dates. As it happened, my birthday was that very day. Geoff looked about, found a bit of butchers paper, tore off a corner and wrote out a birthday 'card' with a well wishing. To finish it off, he added at the bottom "From the Cheepa Card Company".

"It's the same thing, really, when you think about it," he said, as he handed it over. "People spend a lot of money on cards and they include a casket ticket, which is often half the price of the card. If you are going to do that, why not just give someone three casket tickets!"

Geoff had the view that no one was ever insulted by money, so rather than socks or underwear, he would give people cash. "It must make a great present. I know this to be true because no one has ever sent any back to me, saying it was unsatisfactory!"

I kept the butchers paper and on HIS birthday I duly handed it back to him. I had crossed out the 'Mick' in "Happy Birthday Mick" and inserted 'Dad'. He laughed so hard and said "Fair cop." At Christmas next, I had the same piece of butchers paper returned, with the happy birthday crossed out and Merry Christmas inserted.

This went on for a decade until the scrap of paper had nothing left to write on. By this time, Geoff had computers and Version Two came out. This was a printed sheet of paper with a front that had a variety of greetings and well wishings, with a box beside each that you could tick off as appropriate: Happy Birthday, Merry Christmas, Happy Father's Day, etc.

On the inside of the 'card' was another array of options: Have a great day, Congratulations, Happy Honaker, etc. and beside each there was a little square box you could tick. And on the back, *'From the Cheepa Card Company'*. These stupid little things meant more to Geoff than anything you could purchase. It was in these little things where his simple humour shone through.

When we were clearing out his flat, can you believe I found the ORIGINAL 'Cheepa Card Company' scrap of butchers paper. Little things that meant a lot, and it was put into a box of his special items, things that warmed his heart. The things that he cherished never had any connection to their worldly value.

The Big Ear

In this case of the "Cheepa Card Company" it was never the silly card, but the shared connection it created that mattered. Holding that little piece of paper meant he was not alone in this world. I suspect this was something that lingered in the back of his thoughts.

For years, Geoff used to talk about an invention he should make: the 'Big Ear'. This was a large sculpture of an ear that anyone could go up to and tell their woes. You put in a dollar and tell it your troubles. The 'Ear' was to have a recording loop that had sympathetic-sounding phrases that repeated at random, "Oh, that's terrible." "You don't say?" "I can hardly believe it!" etc.

He talked about this for years, jokingly of course. As he explained it, all people really want when they chat is an ear to talk that hears what they say. There's never any solution for their problem, nor do they expect to find one, they just want an ear to tell their troubles to.

"And it would save all those punters at the race track from having to put up with the guy who is moaning about his bad luck. It is a win-win situation for everyone. What is more, it also means that the person who had once been forced to sit and listen has an option! He can now direct that person to a professional ear, thus solving so many of societies problems in one fell swoop."

Many years later I was working on some projects on the coast, and out the back of a swamp I saw this extraordinary sight. There, above a forty-four gallon drum, was this four foot tall ORANGE NOSE. It had a council sticker, so I followed it up. After so many years of hearing about the Big Ear, this Large Orange Nose tweaked my funny bone.

Turns out a fellow who invented it had studied midges and mosquitoes, and discovered they were attracted to the colour orange, while also to the shape of the human nose. Not just this, these bugs were also attracted to carbon dioxide. Accordingly, the 'nose' was piped to a CO_2 canister that slowly leaked CO_2 through it. The bugs followed this desirable gas in through the nostril of the nose, whereupon they were caught in a water trap.

The 'Big Nose' could clear whole areas of mossies and midges and it was incredibly successful in this regard. Unfortunately it looked so weird,

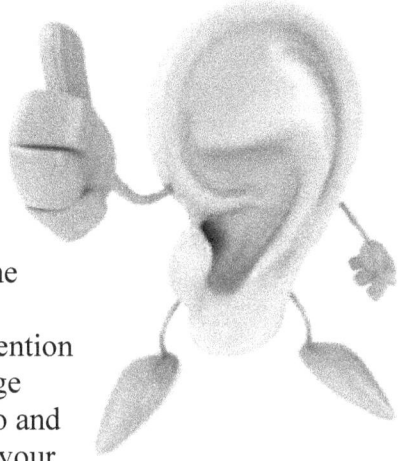

and maintenance of the operation meant more staff were needed than simple spraying, so the whole thing was let go. But I have to say, it brought back to my thoughts the notion of the Big Ear.

I told Geoff about the 'Big Nose' and he really got a huge laugh out of it. It was a thing that just tickled him and he kept breaking out in odd spurts of laughter for the next hour. Finally he said, "People think I am silly with some of my ideas, but that nose just goes to prove I was right! The Big Ear would work wonders at attracting human pests, if they would only give it a go!"

Of course, today it would have to be digital and have a voice responder built in. But I can see it, the "Big Ear App".

It is worth noting, Geoff never laughed out aloud so much as had an internal chuckle. He could be red-faced and gasping for air and in fits of hysteria, but it was a "heh heh he heh heh!" that was more a rasp than a laugh. He never laughed out loudly like most would do. I am not sure if it means anything, but I have a sense it was connected back to the father and not showing too much happiness, in case he knocked it out of you.

Geoff turned up one day in this crazy orange-hair wig, saying "Peace Man!"

The Orange Haired Hippie

One day at Stewarts Road, a hippie came to the door. He was standing on the back verandah holding up two fingers, saying "Peace man ... Peace!" The fellow seemed very odd, just standing there, looking confused. But Rani, the boxer dog, was wagging her stump of a tail in recognition. This was, to a five year old, suspicious. Mum was panicking, however, turning about breathlessly and deeply worried. She was saying over and over, "There's a hippie at the door! There's a hippie at the door!"

He had a cheesecloth shirt and this crazy head of long, orange hair. He just stood there, saying "Peace man". Oh, I got it! I recognised my father where apparently no one else did. Mum was just running around confused. She had HEARD of these hippies, but to see one in the flesh? Up close? It was a scary thing.

I said, loudly, "It's just Dad!"

Finally the other kids started to realise and then the laughter came. Geoff pulled off the wig, saying he found it somewhere, and came inside. Mum was still getting over the panic attack and was now in an 'even more less than pleased' to see him mood than usual. Rani, the boxer dog, had recognised him right away, of course. Dogs have noses and as a result are smarter than people in many ways. She would have known him by his smell, while we mere humans had to rely on face recognition.

Why could family members not see their husband or father standing there? Why did they only see the actor and believe the performance to be real? This is, perhaps, a deeper question than the slightly madcap antic that Geoff employed deserves and I am sure he had no concept of trying to convey some sort of deep meaning, but I was left asking this question.

To him, it was a funny sort of thing to do, and it certainly caused a stir. For me, it started a life-long question. Why do people accept things at, literally, face value? How come so many people accept a person's performance as reality? Why are people so totally unable to see beneath the various sorts of disguises others will wear?

None of this had anything to do with why Geoff put on a wig and cheese cloth shirt. To him, he was just playing a joke. But it does show how small things grow. From the seed of thought planted by a father, purely by chance, it grows in the mind of his youngest son and ends up as a series of books and stories.

As a note: the wig probably came from one of his girlfriends, of which there were many.

Hypnotism and Cucumbers

One day around this period Geoff decided he wanted to be a hypnotist. More to the point, he wanted guinea pigs to experiment with and we kids were the logical choice. He had us all lying down on the floor of the Stewarts Road house, saying to us, "You are feeling sleepy, sleeeepy. At the sound of my voice, you are feeling sleeeepy..."

He went on for a bit, then as no one was moving, he decided to test things. "You are listening to my voice. When I say to, you will raise your right hand slowly. Now, raise your right hand." all the kids must have been attuned, because we all raised our right hands, slowly. "Good, now put the right hand down and slowly raise the left hand."

You could feel him get excited, because all the kids started to raise their left hands. And it would have been good, except Julie started laughing, then I did, then we were all in fits of laughter on the floor. "You little buggers!" Geoff exclaimed, wanting to get angry, but instead he ended up laughing at his own stupidity.

Another time when at Nobby's Beach on the yearly holiday (Geoff usually paid for the family to go away once a year) we were playing 'snap'. Geoff decided that 'snap' was dull and that, instead, we should say 'cucumber'. We all joined in and as we slipped over the next card, waiting for a pair, we started chanting, "Cucumber, Cucumber, Cucumber!"

Right at that moment, some woman came to the door, possibly pedaling religion, and she stands with her mouth agape, looking at what was clearly some communal devil ritual. "Cucumber, Cucumber, Cucumber!" Then a PAIR falls onto the deck! "CUCUMBER!" we all shout.

The woman ran away. We never knew what it was she wanted.

Geoff's Law: *For every opinion, there is an equal and opposite one.*

Note from Sue: *Once dad visited and proudly told us that he had bought us a bag of Clinkers, a chocolate covered sherbet confection, but he got hungry on the way and ate the lot!*

This wouldn't have helped his indigestion. Dad always had a bottle of antacid in the car and would swig on it often.

Rejected by Jesus

A t one point, Geoff was seeking something, anything, to cure the constant depression he felt. A friend went to a 'Born Again' type of church and that person seemed happy enough. Geoff decided to check it out and see if it would solve his concerns.

"Hand it to Jesus my friend! He will take care of all your worries and set you free!" Such a hopeful message and hope was something Geoff desperately needed. So off he went to the new-fangled Pentecostal church.

They were all singing, swaying and praising the Lord, and generally being very emotional about everything. "The happiness is infectious, and you really feel you want to be a part of it." Geoff explained. It all did seem a little odd to him, but hey, they were happy and Geoff needed some happiness. After many visits where he suffered a complete lack of courage, Geoff decided to come forward and be blessed by Jesus. He went to the communal rail to be saved! The Pastor was holding his hands on people's shoulders and forehead, saying, "Let the spirit of JESUS come into you. Accept the POWER of the LORD!"

One by one the people beside him were accepting Jesus and falling over, until just Geoff and the Pastor (along with the aides that caught all the falling-down, spirit-drenched conversions to the Lord) were left standing. The man does the usual routine, holding Geoff by the shoulders and putting his right hand over his forehead. He speaks the words, but Geoff doesn't fall.

The Pastor is undeterred. He goes again, because it means saving this poor lost soul who has come begging for the release that only JESUS can give. But Geoff stays standing upright. The Pastor is dismissive. Obviously he could not fail, nor could Jesus, so it must be that this person in front of him was not genuine. Geoff is told to go back to his seat. He walks up the aisle, with all the eyes staring at him, and the only thing he can think of is that even JESUS won't have a bar of him.

"I even failed to be accepted by the one person who guaranteed he would accept everyone. I was pretty certain all the people there thought the devil must have a hold on me, so I never went back." Geoff told me many years later. "I really thought I was utterly worthless. Even Jesus didn't want me."

I was in tears with laughter and even Geoff was smiling. "Don't we do some stupid things?" He said. "But I was lonely, and there was some pretty women who liked me that went to that church, so it wasn't completely irrational."

Then he paused and thought, "And really, I just could not have done the 'talking in tongues' crap. I was pretty ignorant, but I knew in the Bible that the real story was the person who 'spoke in tongues' was speaking their OWN language. The miracle was that others in the audience, who did not speak that language, could hear the message in their 'own' mother tongue.

"If Jesus came back I very much doubt he would be interested of ANY of the religions named after him. Technically, all that money and wealth has been raised in his name, so therefore he owns it. But can you imagine if he did come back? The lawyers would be over there, saying he could sue the Catholics, saying all their money was his! Could you imagine the kafuffle? And go one step further: Imagine how they would all argue in court against him!!"

Geoff Notes: *"Humour is the lubricant of a difficult life"*

THE FAR SIDE® By GARY LARSON

Professor Gallagher and his controversial
technique of simultaneously confronting
the fear of heights, snakes, and the dark.

Michael Notes: *Geoff was incredibly honest. One day, when given $20 too much change at a hardware, he went straight back in and gave the money back. "No need for an honest mistake to cost him his job," he said.*

The Panel Beater

I was with Geoff the day he went to check out how the rust repairs were going on his Ford. There was an old guy who did the work at Burleigh and as we came up to his shop we found him in a cloud of dust, created by the angle grinding he was doing on some panels on a car that he had bogged up.

Geoff noticed he wasn't wearing a face mask of any kind, and joked, "Breathing all that dust in must be good for you!"

The old fellow smiled a toothy grin, the creases on his face showing up as cracks in the fine powder that absolutely covered him. "If yer gonna die, Geoff, yer may as well die making a dollar."

The car was all ready to go and the panel beater handed Geoff the bill. Dad pulls out cash, as agreed, but adds an extra fifty dollars to the asked-for amount. "You did a great job and I want you to know that I appreciate it." He says.

The man obviously is happy and we leave amidst handshakes and smiles. I go back to my car, but before Geoff goes to his freshly repaired one, he turns and says, "Do you understand why I gave him more than he asked? (I obviously didn't) Well, he does good work and when I come next time he will remember me. Because of that fifty dollars, he will do a better job on my car. That fifty bucks is a little like insurance. It costs very little, hurts no one, but has important benefits in case things go wrong."

I saw Geoff do this again and again. If someone did a good job, or went out of their way, he made sure he recognised it with a tip. He also made sure he complimented them and said the extra he gave them was his way of saying 'thank you'.

I have to say, he collected a bevy of competent and willing trades people all happy to go that extra yard for him. Just a small recognition by way of a thank you, and by way of some cash, was all it took to get into the 'good books'.

He added a simple adage to the story: "A compliment costs nothing, but it can save a lot."

Note from Sue: *We would sometimes play "Get lost" in the car. We would go driving with Dad and he would pretend to let us tell him to go right or left at random in order to get lost. This never happened because our commands were often overridden. He apparently didn't hear us.*

I remember Dad as loving driving but he was always highly concentrated on the task. He didn't like distractions.

The Colt Revolver Company

In New Guinea, Geoff picked up a second hand Colt 45 revolver. It was a really nice pistol that he got for an excellent price. When he got home, he realised the reason for the bargain, the gun didn't work. He stripped it down and the problem was self-evident: A bent firing pin.

Well, it was American made, so there would be parts. He wrote to Colt Industries, the address was on the box the gun came in, asking to buy a firing pin. It was not two weeks later when he received a reply, which shocked him. That was quicker than a return letter from Sydney, let alone crossing the Atlantic and back. The reply came in the form of a small box, which included a hand written note APOLOGISING for the weapon that failed.

Not one, but three firing pins were included, and there were also a few updates to the pistol included that he might like to apply. Not a cent was asked for, or charged. It was just sent, despite the fact he did not personally buy the pistol from Colt. They knew this as he had advised them he had purchased it off a local man.

"It was service and courtesy I never forgot. What is more, if anyone ever asked me about buying a Colt, I unreservedly recommended them and told the person of my experience. They could not do enough to make sure they had a happy customer."

Dad reflected, telling me the story for perhaps the twentieth time. "The world has forgotten that paying a fair price up-front for a quality product means that, when you need it, the service to help you is there. They haven't cut costs to the bone, so they can afford to employ people and be generous. Now it is all about the money.

"It's not all bad, I have a good TV that cost not very much. But if this breaks, as it will, I toss it out. I would not even think of writing to the people who made it asking for parts, nor would they respond if I did. We have all become disposable."

Sometime after this, he was pulling some bacon from the fridge to cook up his usual lunch. The ritual was always the same: Microwave the bacon, heat some frozen vegetables (Usually with a long dissertation on who sold the best ones) and canned corn, then put it all onto the oval melamine plates that he STILL had. Done, that was lunch.

He was just chatting when he showed me the fatty, crap meat on the inside of the packaged bacon. "It is deceit you know. They put the nice cuts to the outside, and the rubbish they fold into the middle. All the companies in the world practice telling lies. Two minute noodles take three minutes. Healthy and nutritious means they have added a lot of stuff to make them taste nice. If you have to ADVERTISE something is healthy and nutritious, it's a fair bet it isn't.

"The world is full of face-value promises that hide cost-cutting deceit. It makes you distrustful." Geoff sat down to have one of the prepared vegetable juices Nelida made for him in his last months. He was skin and bone by this time, but the mind was still sharp.

"People forget the importance of being well-thought of. Everyone is trying to get the best deal, cut the cost, and haggle over every last cent. It makes no friends, only enemies and resentment. I learned important lessons from the manufacturers of the Colt pistol, which is to always do a little more than people expect and be very generous with praise.

A Colt Pistol similar to the type that Geoff would have bought.

Geoff Quips: *Tempis Fugit. In fact, sometimes it fugits so fast, it is hard to keep up with it.*

Michael Notes: *One day at a shopping Centre, Geoff was with his Filipino ex-wife, Nell, when a mutual acquaintance came up. "How's your Bob?" Nell asked. The Filipino woman said "Ok," then they chatted for a bit before she walked on.*

"I didn't know her husband was called Bob." Geoff commented.

Nell was quiet. "Stands for Boring Old Bastard," she said.

Geoff paused and asked, "Was I your 'Bob'?"

"Of course not!" She exclaimed.

Later he confided in me, "I am sure she lied, so as not to hurt my feelings. But seeing things from their side, they marry old men, mostly to help their family. Can't blame them for calling us Bob's."

The Wheel Alignment Man

For some reason, Geoff's XC Ford needed an "on the hub" wheel balance. If you went to this special guy he spun up the wheel while it was still on the axle and, as a result, a nasty vibration at over sixty miles an hour was avoided. Let's not mention the fact that Geoff hated the highway and never did over fifty, but now, if he wanted to do sixty he could.

John, as we will call him, was a specialist. He was yet another one of the trades people Geoff stayed on good terms with, because here was a man who provided that necessary service he needed every year or two.

One day I was there with Geoff while he is getting the wheels balanced. We heard an awful noise coming from the shed beside us. Tools were being thrown, and a man was cursing and swearing, being extremely bad-tempered. "What is that?" I asked.

John laughed and said, "That is the sound of the car winning." He paused to explain. "I am a professional. I get paid to do the job, some jobs take more time, but they will get done. The amateur, like the guy next door, hires a shed to do the work, but he doesn't have the competence, the tools, or the patience. So what happens next is that the car wins."

It was the smallest off-hand comment, but it meant so much. If you are losing your cool, whatever the problem is, that problem is winning. There is no reason for getting angry at things like a car, but if you do, the only thing it says to a professional is that YOU are the one with the real problem.

In a world full of hurry, things like competence, honesty and patience are the most precious of commodities.

Homeless: *There was a time Geoff had absolutely no idea how he was going to get by. Rents were going up, he had no more assets, and he was very much living hand to mouth. Then from out the blue, he was offered a commission flat at Palm Beach. It saved him from penury, and shortly after he arrived there, another boost. He received a supplemental income from by way of a war service pension. At a Telegrapher, it was accepted this was the cause of his hearing loss, and so he got a small but necessary increase in monthly income, sufficient to ensure his last days were reasonably comfortable.*

The Beer Bible

wort - *noun*

suffix: **-wort**; noun: **wort**; plural noun: **worts**

- ○ used in names of plants and herbs, especially those used formerly as food or medicinally, e.g. *butterwort, lungwort, woundwort.*
- ○ *archaic* - a plant or herb used as food or medicinally.
- ○ *the sweet infusion of ground malt or other grain before fermentation, used to produce beer and distilled malt liquors.*

Geoff Wallace was a master brewer. Few realised this, but he really had an extraordinary ability to create beer and could do so from the core elements of hops, barley, malt, sugar, water and yeast. He used to joke that the ability for man to make beer was proof of the existence of God, because, unlike wine where you can toss grapes into a bucket and wake up with booze, you could not just stumble on the recipe for beer making. There are just too many things that go into the process.

The barley must be malted at a specific temperature for a specific period of time. The hops then have to be heated at a different temperature for another specific time period. If either one of these are out by a few degrees or a single minute, the whole thing can fail. So how did primitive man get the thermometer and clock needed for these very defined processes? The obvious answer: *God whispered how to do it to Adam, out of guilt for booting him from Eden.*

This is not a logic anyone can argue with. Of course, some may say this is because it is not logic, but they will probably be boring, sad teetotalers. Regardless of what anyone believes, beer and the ability to produce it is proof of man's earliest technology. It also shows the first combination of agriculture and science combined to make a commercial success.

And talk about turning water into wine, the mystery and magic involved in turning the wort into beer is man's earliest form of chemistry.

At one point in the 1980's Geoff recorded a very detailed book on every aspect of beer making. Geoff could taste a beer and, often on the first go, he could remake the same thing from scratch using variations of the above mentioned ingredients. He knew what he was talking about and I looked in vain for that book, but it had vanished. I asked where it was in his last months, but he just said, "It wasn't right."

To make the book complete, he decided that he needed to replicate commercial brewing. So he created a 'mini-brewery' using stainless steel tubs and brewing vats that he scrounged from somewhere, but sadly he never really got to make it work to his satisfaction. He wrote it up, but the disappointment of his failure to do a commercial style brewing meant he felt the whole book was not of publishable quality. The revised copy I have is a mere shadow of the original and is basically an informative book on how best to work with over-the-counter beer making kits.

Part of his motivation for all this came about when he had the chairman of Castlemaine-Perkins in his car, selling him some real estate. He asked the man, "What is the secret you people have? How do you not get bad batches?" The fellow was surprised and asked why Geoff was even asking this question.

"Every tenth batch that I brew goes off. I have been meticulous in measurements and temperatures. I have done exactly the same on all lots, but one in ten fails and I have to toss it out."

"That is fascinating," replied the man in charge of XXXX beer. "We have exactly the same issue."

"What do you do with all that failed beer?" Geoff asks.

"There is a very good reason why we have ten vats all brewing at the same time. Yes, one goes off, but all we do is mix everything together at the end and the result is the same overall, every time. It's a bit of a mystery and a miracle no one really understands," the man answered.

Now, some might rightly claim that this is proof that God has indeed blessed the production of Beer and that it is, most probably, Satan who gets a hold of every tenth batch. I will not seek to dissuade you from your belief, but this extraordinary conversation is what got Geoff interested in adding the commercial beer making aspect to his in-depth book.

And let no one be under any illusion, Geoff pumped out the beer. The flats at Milton Road would have from three hundred to eight hundred bottles of hand-crafted beer in storage underneath them on any given day. It reached a peak of some two thousand plus bottles. Keep in mind, this is not beer made from a pre-packaged kit you buy at the supermarket, this was beer made from scratch.

As a note, Geoff had done the sums and by buying everything in bulk he could drive the production cost down to less than three cents a bottle.

On rare occasions when the party ran out of fuel, I did a Jesus and turned petrol into Beer, by hopping in the car and going to collect the odd dozen. I can promise you, the party goers all said it was the best beer they had ever tasted. I don't think Geoff ever noticed the odd carton go missing, or if he did he must have accepted the Twenty Dollar note left behind and turned a blind eye. (At one point his 'beer empire' extended to two thousand, eight hundred bottles!)

As an addendum to this story, years ago I had the son of a well-known British brewer in the car, and he mentioned he had to get back to England to help his father prepare his yearly special brew, Hogshead Beer. "It's an ancient recipe only the family knows, and has been handed down from father to son for generations. No one else knows the secret!"

Well, some years earlier Geoff had discovered a cockroach in the wort (the prepared brew before it sits and converts to beer) but only after it had fermented into beer. Should he just toss it? He reasoned that the alcohol would have sterilised any germs, so he bottled it anyway. To his surprise, the beer was better than usual. He worked out the secret ingredient was protein, so he added a little gelatine to each batch after that.

Taking a stab in the dark, I said to the son of the British brewer, "Oh, I think I might have a good idea what the special ingredient might be."

He laughed and said, "Go on, solve the ancient mystery then!"

"You drop a hogshead into the wort."

To say he was shocked is an understatement. But really, Hogshead Beer? So obvious, the clue was right there in the name. Yet how often can we not see what is printed clearly right under our noses? We hear the message, but we do not understand, because we don't have the experience. Unless Geoff had experienced, then told me, about a cockroach in a wort, I would never have guessed in a million years that anyone in their right mind would put a hogshead into a beer-making vat.

Oddly enough, many years later, the Harry Potter series has as it's tipple, "Hog's Head Beer".

> **Seen on a T-shirt with a photo of a pub:**
> *Beer is God, and you know where I worship!*

The Ten Gods of Beer

Silenus
Dionysus
Ninkasi
Osiris
Aegir
Mbaba Mwana Waresa
Yasigi
Radegast
Raugupatis and Ragutiene

Retirement

In Geoff's notes I see he received final approval for the Department of Veteran Affairs (DVA) Pension on the 25th June 1981, but receiving this pension was conditional on him selling the Milton Road flats. The whole thing had been well organised, with the approval the pension coinciding with the sale of the flats. He had the contract for sale on Milton Road signed on 16 June 1981 and had already organised to buy the Urangan house just thirteen days earlier.

For Geoff, this meant starting his second marriage with the slate clean. When I asked him at the time about the sale of his one greatest asset he looked at me and said, "I want to be free of stress. This means I am free." He was moving to Harvey Bay with no debt and an assured income. Even at age twenty-three it seemed obvious to me that a real estate asset that paid money every week that was over and above the debt it owed was not something to sell. My brother Greg confirmed that he, too, thought it was very odd. But besides the pension, Geoff had long wanted to move to Harvey Bay. His brother, Bob, lived there with his wife, Helen, and I think Geoff had the notion that it was all going to be one big, happy family.

He bought a boat and he and Nelida had this lovely three bedroom brick house in a nice area. For the first few years the pair were extremely happy, but the reality was that Bob was not interested in playing older brother and the place was dead boring. The drinking increased and, according to Nell, Geoff started doing some pretty strange things.

Sleep walking had always been a bit of an issue, but now it became a major one. One classic incident was when Geoff decided to hop into the boat, whilst soundly asleep, and go 'out onto the water'. Only he was still in the garage, revving the boat happily. He subsequently destroyed it because he didn't connect a water hose to the water intake. Outboard motors tend to need water to keep cool. It needed a new motor.

Other things would happen, like he would get up to go to the bathroom, only the 'bathroom' might be the sock drawer, or any odd thing that would open which he might piss into. Maybe the release from the stress of money worries was part of it, but I suspect the sleep walking goes all the way back to childhood and bedwetting. Geoff suffered a good deal of ridicule from his brothers and father, getting called a 'sissy', because he would occasionally wet the bed.

I suspect it was fear driving it. Geoff was always highly intuitive and the strange energy around his oldest bother, Bob, and his father was quite similar. Both were domineering, controlling people. No one can truly know what happens inside a person that drives them to do the odd things they do, but Nelida started to fret about what Geoff was going to do next.

She didn't know if he would hop in the car and try to drive somewhere while sound asleep. He certainly started it up on occasions and she would run out to encourage him back to bed. Keep in mind, Nell was new to the country, new to marriage, and her grasp on the language was still fairly basic. She was genuinely concerned and mentioned these things a few times to me when I was visiting. Despite all the negative things that people might say about Filipino brides, she genuinely loved him.

But Urangan, while very beautiful, was a stagnant pond. After a few years Geoff could not stand it any longer, so he sold the house and bought the Joan Street property on the Gold Coast. Nell was annoyed, because while Geoff found Harvey Bay dull, she had found a large network of friends there. Geoff did not even ask if she wanted to move, he just sold the house and they were gone.

Nell had come from an upper middle class family that had fallen on hard times when her father passed away. She was the main support person for her mother, and by extension, the rest of the family.

She needed to make money, but any earnings over a fairly low amount affected Geoff's pension. She needed to work, but Geoff didn't want this. On top of this serious issue, Nell didn't like being cooped up at home, unable to look after herself. It was the real cause of tension, this and the fact she had no say in anything. "He never asked my advice or was interested in what I thought about anything." She said to me. It spelled the end of the marriage after a few years.

Nelida Wallace (nee Corbez)

Micheal Notes: *Prior to marrying Nell, Geoff had numerous girlfriends. He commented once to me, "There were some that were just lovely. They loved me, wanted to look after me, but I always ended up chasing the complicated one. It was pretty stupid of me, yet if they were difficult I found them interesting."*

Marriage Number Two

G eoff had gone to Manilla with brother Bob on 12 Feb 1980. He told me that, at the time, he had no intention of getting married. He was just there supporting his brother. Then Bob's future wife, Helen, said she knew the perfect person for him and sent him out into the wilds of Manilla to look up one Nelida Cortez. Apparently, the decision to marry happened inside a couple of weeks after this. Geoff returned to the Philippines on 12 March 1980 and confirmed that she wanted to marry him. Obviously, she did, and the one great question Geoff had was if she could cook all that wonderful Filipina food. She said "Of course!" He brought Nell back with him and they married on 24 May 1980.

I asked her about this and what she thought. "I knew I would marry Geoff as soon as I heard his name," she said to me after he passed on. "As a girl I was playing with a Ouiji board. I asked who it was that I would marry and the glass everyone had their hand on went to a series of letters. They spelled the name 'Geoff Wallace'. I was pretty shocked, because this was obviously a foreign name and I didn't even speak English at the time.

"When Geoffrey turned up, I was very surprised, because he was not like so many of the men that come there. I fell in love, so when he asked if I could cook, I lied. I am a terrible cook." She laughed as she told me.

"He was nice and I really did want to marry him. I was very sad that the marriage had to end, but I needed money, I needed to work. I could not sit around staring at the walls any longer. Plus, I had no say in anything. This was very frustrating."

The pair stayed on good terms, Nell would call in at least once a week to cut Geoff's hair. Geoff was very accepting of the changing circumstances, and the next man Nelida married was also welcome to call in. It was all very civilised, but being so accepting paid dividends. When Geoff was getting too old to care for himself, Nell kept her promise to him, that she would not let him go to a nursing home. (He had a morbid fear of hospitals and nursing homes)

Which is exactly what she did. She moved onto the couch in his tiny apartment and cared for him during his last eighteen months on the planet.

They had been divorced 26 Jan 1989 and twenty-eight years later she was still there for him. I think we can class this as real love: the selfless care of another, the honouring of a promise, and the simple fact that I never heard Nell say a single bad word about Geoff in my forty odd years of knowing her. Yes, a few complaints about his stubbornness, but never a bad word about the man she married.

We could learn a lot from the Filipino people about duty, family and respect.

I should also add, the block of flats Geoff sold in Milton Road came up for sale shortly before he passed away. In the blurb, it noted the selling price of the block beside it, which was smaller and lower down the hill. Thirteen Million Dollars it had gone for.

"It was a stupid thing, I know," said Geoff as I mentioned this. "But at the time I just wanted out. I was sick of responsibility, bills, everything. I just wanted a pension and to retire. The flats would have paid themselves off and I would be a rich man, but the reality is, I just never had the acquisition gene."

The Three Amigos

Geoff, Max and Frank were inseparable friends who met in World War Two. They remained on good terms and were firm friends till their passing. I was there the day Geoff got the news that his last friend, Frank, had moved on. It is hard to describe, not sadness, not despondency, it was more of a recognition that life will have it's way.

He didn't speak much of it, only that things are best let go before they are torn away. "The hardest part about a long life is seeing your friends pass on." He later commented. Then he added a few minutes later, "There is nothing good about getting old. You are not wiser, smarter, or better in any way. However, I should also add that it is still better than the alternative!"

Rich Dad, Poor Dad

Geoff often used to laugh about the title of "Rich Dad, Poor Dad", a book by Robert Kiyosaki. He would joke he has been both, which was completely true. However, in later years he used to comment how it was a metaphor for Reg and himself. He started out Rich, Reg was poor. By the end, he was poor and Reg was rich.

I think it is fair to say that Reg was his closest brother. They spent a good deal of time together over the years. After the war, they both travelled to New Zealand looking for work. Geoff was to comment that very little work was done in that particular quest, but to compensate for this a great deal of rum was consumed. "We lived on steak and rum, staying in pubs while we looked for jobs. There was not much going as far as jobs went and we ended up staying with Colin in Auckland. This soon brought an end to the trip." (Odd, because Reg wasn't a rum drinker)

Geoff never explained what happened, but we are to presume there was an argument of sorts and he and Reg came back to Sydney. Colin, of course, had suffered as a POW with the Germans and had life-long concerns as a result. Yet Reg was a prisoner of the Japanese and while he never spoke directly about it to myself, the extraordinary suffering those men went through is a matter of historical record.

He said, jokingly, "I got a free trip to Japan!" More than this, he saw the mushroom cloud and was in Japan at the time of surrender. I can but imagine the mental toughness needed to survive and even more impressive, the way he was able to rebuild his life afterward.

When Geoff came back from New Guinea, Reg was living in Red Hill, a very working class suburb, in the bottom of Kent Street. It was not a fashionable address like it is today, but though poor, he worked hard at Internal Revenue and rose up through the ranks. Geoff often took Reg on trips out West, as mentioned earlier, and I think it fair to say they got on well.

As the years rolled past, Geoff had a number of Tax Audits and, to both their credit, neither of the brothers sought to pull strings to avoid this. For some reason, someone in the tax office had it in for Geoff and, as a result, he was put through three gruelling tax audits in a period of under seven years. In the end, with nothing found, Reg simply commented. "You won't see them again. Not many realise it, but if you pass three audits, they are not allowed to do a fourth."

What I found interesting in recollecting this was how Geoff did not ask Reg to intervene, nor did he offer. Both were honest as the day was long, and neither men had anything to hide. Reg was taciturn, cynical, and could be sarcastic (a Wallace trait) but, like Geoff, he had a trademark humour. This was evidenced in the curious letters they would send back and forth, as you can see on Page 163.

I suspect the harsh upbringing by their father prepared them better than most for survival. Let us not forget, four brothers went to war, all four returned. Whatever their failings, all four of them knew how to survive and we can credit part of this ability to the extraordinary humour they all seemed to have,

Rattus Rattus

Geoff smelt a rat, literally. He realised a rodent had moved into his little apartment. He set traps, the rat would eat the cheese, but not set it off. So he invested in a 'deathless' trap, where a rat would walk in for food, and a door would shut, trapping him in situ. It ignored this completely.

Geoff got smarter, he left a trail or tasty morsels that led to the trap, but while the morsels would be eaten, the rat never went into the trap.

Nothing seemed to work. The rat was perfectly happy to live in Geoff's house, while being entirely unconcerned as to whether the feeling from Geoff was mutual. A battle of wits ensued for weeks, with the rat winning every round. Finally, Geoff gave up, and said, "You know, I think I am getting used to you now."

Later that day Geoff went out, but forgot to lock up the back door. When he returned, the rat was gone! "Imagine, I did everything to get rid of him other than open the door to let him out. The little bugger wanted out as much as I wanted him gone!"

Months afterwards, recalling Mr Rat's time, he commented, "It doesn't do a lot for your confidence to realise you were outsmarted by a rat."

Geoff Notes: *If you put two litre bottles of water in front of the average man, and demand he drink it all, he would not be able to get through it. But if you put two bottles of beer in front of him, no problem at all. Do you wonder why?*

Advising someone to do something because it is good for them is always a pain, but say "Do this and have fun" and it is never an effort. It is why I rarely offer advice, for one it is unwanted, and two, no one listens anyway.

Budgies

For some forty years Geoff always had a blue budgie with him. At one point he had three multi-colour ones, Hughie, Duey and Louis, but for the most part it was just Hughie. He was always the blue one. Geoff swore that it was the same soul, reincarnating in blue budgie body, coming back because it loved him.

Whatever the case, there was an extraordinary connection between the two, with Hughie always learning to imitate Geoff's voice. The last Hughie also imitated Nelida's voice and in its own way, mine. Though for me it was a sound like Skippy the Kangaroo, because this is the sound I made when I saw him.

One day, when the podiatrist was over, Geoff wasn't in the room and yet she heard his voice, saying "Hughie's a beautiful soul. Daddy loves Hughie." It was the Budgie. He really did love Geoff and whenever he went into the kitchen, Hughie would hop to a spot in his cage closest to where he stood and wait for attention.

He got lots. You were always asked to bring fresh seed from anything you found out in the world and at one point Geoff was handing out little bird seed packages for people to plant in their gardens, so Hughie would have a ready supply of fresh food.

His birds could be exceedingly long-lived for budgies, often going twelve years or more. When his second last one passed on, my then partner, who was a bird person, hunted about and got another blue budgie to replace it. Dad took one look, said he was not interested in another bird, and flatly rejected the offer. Well, we gave it away, yet two months later, he had another blue budgie.

We obviously had found the wrong one, but fate had intervened and when the 'right' one turned up, Geoff knew it. And honestly, it really did seem like the same bird returned. Same habits, same way of tilting the head, same way of not wanting to be touched and with no interest in living outside its cage.

After about eight years, this last one seemed destined for the grave, when Geoff talked to someone who said the problem might be constipation. Because they don't fly as much as they would normally, caged budgies can get constipated and they will die without a laxative. Well, they were right, and Hughie picked up immediately.

After Nell had moved in, Geoff wanted to secure the place for her after he passed away. I made trips with her into the housing commission and he specifically asked me to deliver a letter. In this, he stressed that his Budgie knew Nelida and would feel safe and secure if she were to carry on living there, in order to look after him.

One of the imperative things Geoff stressed in his letter was the well being of his bird. I am not sure if this got people laughing, or what, but it appeared to work. After he passed on, she was indeed permitted to stay on and look after Hughie.

The extraordinary thing, from the day Geoff passed away, Hughie never used his voice again.

Hughie, the blue budgie, is still living, and remains a real character.

He would speak in the voices of people around him, yet from the day Geoff passed on, Hughie never used his voice again.

Note from Michael: *Geoff was cooking some potatoes. He had peeled them, and popped them into water to boil, when he added quite a large amount of salt. He must have noticed the look on my face, because he stopped and said, "Do you know why you add salt to water when boiling vegetables? It is not to add flavour, as most people imagine, it is to preserve the natural salts in the food. Having a strong saline solution means the flavour of the food does not leach out into the water."*

The old ways had more common sense at work behind the scenes that we might have realised at first glance.

Chiropractors

Geoff largely got away from psychiatrists by the late 1960's. He looked for and found a better alternative for himself in what was then a 'quack' science called Chiropractic. Chidley was the 'go to' Chiropractor that Geoff used to see, as often as twice, sometimes three times a week. This 'bone-cracker' was the only person who seemed to be able to relieve the stress and tension he constantly felt. In retrospect, what Geoff really had were the symptoms of grain allergy, but there was no one talking about this sort of stuff in the 1960's. For Geoff, the visit to the 'chiro' represented his only relief.

He would often tell me how the effect was instantaneous. "The depression just lifts. All those years I had been taking pills from the psychiatrists and what I needed was my neck tweaked. It lasts for a few days, then I go back." He went back often and was Chidley's favourite client. Even when the man retired, Geoff kept making the long drive out to Thornlands to see him.

I often went along to keep him company and also because driving was difficult for him till the neck was adjusted. I was his backup in case of an emergency. One day after a visit Geoff returned to the car looking sombre. "Chidley's in real trouble. He and the wife went guarantor on a loan for his son, who wanted to start a business. The son defaulted and the bank is about to repossess his house. He doesn't know what he is going to do."

I was surprised, then Dad added. "Never ask me to guarantor a loan for you. I don't want to hurt your feelings by saying no." Driving back he was deep in thought and I know what he was thinking. *'Where will I find another chiropractor?'*

Well, he did try a few, but the real truth was, all the twisting and wrenching for so long had been breaking down the cartilage in the neck. I was the one doing a good deal of the muscle release now and I generally visited once a week to give him a treatment. Finally, he found a first class Palmer Graduate, Phil Barham at Burleigh.

This was a man who didn't wrench the neck, but used what they call an 'activator' ... effectively a small trigger-released 'punch' that tapped things back into place. So for the last 20 years or so of his life, the harsh treatment stopped and Geoff was able to get a bit of relief twice weekly. The really good news was that this was covered by his DVA Gold Card.

Between his Chiro, the nurse who came and did his feet every six weeks, and the Scottish Doctor he had trained to give him what he wanted, Geoff was doing OK. In truth, he was doing far better than he believed he was. Even so, Geoff was constantly checking his pulse, blood pressure and lungs for signs of degradation and infirmity, another side to the constant anxiety that gnawed away.

For a person who rarely suffered any form of ill health, he certainly acted like there could be something seriously wrong. Perhaps it was all just a precaution, but all in all, Geoff was a bit of a hypochondriac. Again, a side-effect of the anxiety.

The One-Eyed Goanna

Geoff had a term for the TV: "The One-Eyed Goanna, it stares you into oblivion every night. It removes all need for thought, and is the perfect accompaniment for beer."

I recall him talking about the 'idiot box' in terms like this quite often. It was not a complaint, but an admission of reality, and a comment on the solitude he lived in. "I am a monk, in many ways. I live on my own, do my contemplations, and let the world go past. I am not rushing towards the grave nor striving to attain perfection. I have no need to be out doing social things. I am happy being where I am, and grateful I can."

Dum-Dad's Comb-Over

Geoff started going bald in his early twenties. As a result, from the age of forty years he used to let one side of his hair grow long and did the classic 'comb over' to cover up the growing bald spot. Of course, over the years the comb-over thinned and the bald spot grew.

A favourite comment on his baldness came from Elijah, my oldest boy. As a child he stopped one day, aged maybe four, and took a long, hard look at 'Dum Dad'. (the name he had christened his grandfather with) After a time, he said "You sure have a long forehead, don't you Dum Dad?"

Geoff found it one of the funniest things, and spoke of that little quip often. Through it all the comb-over stayed in place, obviously in order to shorten the 'length' of the forehead. The hair was regularly died as well, to preserve the obvious image of youth that every eighty year old needs. I always found it funny to see the stained skin that took a few days to wear off after each application of hair dye.

The 'comb-over' by now was just a few strands of hair, a skinny bridge spanning a vast ocean of 'long forehead'. But this fact was invisible to Geoff, who still thought he had a thick thatch of hair up there. The reality: he had a horseshoe shaped band of hair that was natural, an utterly dreadful comb-over, and a forehead that extended back to behind his ears.

Then it all changed. One day Geoff was with Nell in a shopping centre and happened to look up. There were mirrors on the ceiling and he saw for the first time the truth of his comb-over. He was shocked, because he truly believed it was a thick swathe of hair, but when the obvious was shown, he conceded defeat. He went home and, at age eighty-six, he snipped off the last vestige of his youth, those scraggily few hairs of his comb-over.

"I finally saw myself as others would have seen me and I realised what an illusion I was under." He told me. From now on, it would just be a long forehead with no interruption.

This story came to mind when a friend came to visit. He was concerned about how he was being seen by others. He showed me letters he had written, expecting me to take his side and agree that HE was the reasonable one.

Well, what he had written to these people was essentially 'crazy talk'. I just looked at him and told him the truth. He got upset, saying it all made perfect sense to him. I replied, "Every crazy person believes what they believe is the absolute truth. It doesn't alter the fact that it is nuts."

I was thinking about Geoff and how he truly believed his comb-over was something it just wasn't. My job was simply to reflect the obvious to my friend. But the reality was that until he saw things clearly, no argument on the face of this earth would change his mind.

I explained it to him as follows, "Just because we believe that something is true does not mean it is. A hundred years ago, unless you had a jar of leeches, you were not a real doctor. But life is a river and the more we hold onto something, the more twists and turns we stir up in the waters around us as they flow past. I know you can't see it, but I ask you to trust me. What you wrote was crazy world bananas. When you let this go, when you go with the flow, you will look back and realise how nuts it all is."

Like Geoff's comb-over, many of the things we presently believe to be true are not. Mostly they are unimportant, meaningless, and foolish. But we can never see our own mistakes, or see through our own illusions. Life can, and does, and one day we will be shown the mirror. Then we a choice, Do we accept what is, or continue living in a dream?

The only question is: *When we finally see the truth, will we have the courage to change course and snip the stupid comb-over?*

"Whoa! Whoa! Whoa! ... You're in my favorite chair again, Carl."

Geoff loved his Jason Recliner-Rocker. He had one almost from the day they came out. It was a fixture as necessary and as important as a kitchen or a bathroom in his house, and was always situated in front of the TV.

Doctors and Hospitals

G eoff had always checked his blood pressure, with good reason as it tended to be high. Yet it became somewhat overdone in his later years. He was checking things twelve times a day, while making notes and details in order to chart the course of events.

I was always asked, when I called by, to put the stethoscope to his back, to see how his lungs were doing. He really was a bit of a worrier about health, which was odd considering he rarely if ever got sick. He got the odd flu, maybe twice in thirty years. He almost never caught a cold, which he attributed to regular and large does of Vitamin 'C'.

He had a 'well trained' doctor. Geoff would figure out what pills he needed and use Doctor Google to find out what had to be happening for these to be offered to you. As long as what you asked for fitted the symptoms, his doctor was very obliging. "You have to train doctors up to do what you need them to," he would say to me on odd occasions. "But you have to also let them believe they came to the notion of what to prescribe. It's a tricky thing, but essentially, you go in asking about specific symptoms you are suffering. He rummages through his book, then you suggest, *'Apparently, a friend of mine who had similar problems was prescribed xxx?'* So he looks that up, it fits, and after that is very happy to write you the script.

"You have to be well-researched and never ask for any specific drug. That's a guarantee you won't get it. You must only ever suggest options and usually my doctor gets the hint. That's why I keep going to him, despite his opinions that everything but a pill is useless"

Geoff had a Basel Cell carcinoma on his cheek. The Doc said they had to get him to hospital immediately and get it cut out. Geoff deferred, then went home to put on Bloodroot paste. As it had done so often in the past, it dissolved the cancer. A month later, Geoff was back to see the doctor, and the Doctor said, "I am very glad you got that cut out!"

Breaking with the tradition of never saying anything the Doc didn't want to hear, Geoff told the fellow that he didn't have surgery. Instead, he just used a cheap, over the counter remedy and it dissolved the cancer without surgery. Of course, the Doc would have none of 'that' sort of poppycock. Apparently Geoff just got lucky and it went into remission. As Geoff would say, "Another rule you must follow when dealing with people who are firmly convinced their way is the only way: Do not try to contradict them, it only proves you are wrong."

I am paraphrasing a fairly common discussion Geoff would have on the subject of people holding fixed views. "You are dealing with belief. A Doctor believes in 'this' way of doing things. A Spiritual follower believes in 'that' way of solving problems, with prayer, etc. If you suggest a different way, they will ignore you. I used to have long talks with religious believers and I would spend hours discussing the pros and cons. I would use logic to come to an inescapable conclusion. But if this conclusion differs from what they believe, they would simply say, after everything, *'Yes, but WE believe...'*. Telling people the facts, the truth, the reality, whatever, it will make absolutely no difference at all to what they believe.

"Just like my Doctor could not accept that there was a simple cure that killed skin cancer, even when the facts and evidence presented to him were incontrovertible. Why? There are none so blind as they that will not see. The whole point is there is no REASON for blind belief, or adherence to a dogma, or choosing to have faith in an all-knowing God. Use reason to defeat belief and reason becomes a sin. Reason is Satan because it contradicts belief.

"God loves you, but not enough to save you from hell. It is a logical loop of impossibility, yet so many believe it and find rationales to justify the absurd. The argument is 'free will'. We choose our path! Yet God knows everything, he knows what you will choose, therefore he created you knowing you were going to live forever in hell.

"Not much of anything makes any sense to anyone, which is why people dig down and just believe in what they were taught to be true. And the objection to a reasoned contradiction in their faith is never 'I' believe, it is always 'WE' believe. The Doctor doesn't say 'I don't believe you', he says *'There is no evidence to back up your claim'.* Another form of 'We'.

'You' are not right if you hold a contradictory view, but good science will prove it. Just show the proof! Of course, when shown proof, that is never sufficient. It has to be funded by a University and paid for in triple blind studies. Dogma and tradition choke common sense.

"A good case in point is Max (Turner). My best friend is trustworthy, honest as the day is long and good hearted. But he had a blind belief in doctors. I tried to suggest to him for years that some vitamin supplements, even just a little vitamin 'C' every day, would help his health conditions. He laughed, saying his doctor gave him all the advice he ever needed. Well, those little pills from the doctor are what caused the bad circulation, the amputations, and they are what eventually killed him.

"It did not matter a whit that I was healthy, and still able to do things. That was just the luck of good genes, nothing to do with the vitamins or exercise, or having a diet with a good range of foods in it. Max would not even read Diane Cilento's book on Vitamin 'C'. Why? Because he had a religion called "The Doctor". He believed in the Doctor, despite the overwhelming evidence that the Doctors were failing badly in his case."

Geoff had nothing against Doctors. He had nothing against anyone. When he needed a knee replacement, he went (not so happily) to the hospital. He hated being confined, and hospitals were the definition of confinement in his view, but he had to get the knee fixed. When he needed his teeth fixed, he went to the dentist. He used every facility open to improve his way of life, but he didn't 'believe' in any of them. Just as he did the very best job he could do when presenting and selling a house when he worked in Real Estate, he expected that a good person will do the best they can in any endeavour, be it taxi driver or brain surgeon.

He did believe in people, he did not believe in their beliefs. "Now, I don't argue with people's beliefs anymore," said Geoff. "If someone tells me the moon is made of blue cheese, I just smile and say how interesting. If Jesus is going to come down on a cloud to save the world, or change daylight saving, it's all good. If someone wants to believe anything, I don't want to disagree with them, or contradict them. That only buys me an argument that consumes hours of my life."

And again he would quote that favourite line, "Robbie Burns said *'Oh wat gift the givee give us, to see ourselves as others see us.'* This is what people need to believe in." Geoff did have a firm belief in giving people the room for discovering their own truth. It was not for him to tell anyone what to think or believe, but I know he did hope they would come to see themselves and their actions as others might see them.

It is really saying we need to be detached from our beliefs to see things clearly. This is what changes people, not words or arguments, but seeing themselves more clearly.

Note from Sue: *Dad used to send me cuttings from the newspaper in the mail with some poignant phrase hand written on it, like the cutting of a pie eating competition featuring the photo of a very fat man. Written on this were "Fat, flour and sugar" and a drawing of the skull and crossbones.*

His quest for information on nutrition started a long time ago. In the early 1970's, when I was about 16, he was researching the use of hair analysis for diagnosing a person's unique health needs. He cut a small locket of my hair and sent it off for analysis. A wad of typed information came back with what was in balance or not with my mineral intake. This was accompanied with the types of food that you were to avoid or to take. For example, dried apricots were good for me. Apparently, I was lacking potassium.

Astrology

FOOLPROOF WORDS FOR DEALING WITH MYSTERIES, UNCERTAINTIES OR THINGS WE CANNOT CONTROL.

Hogwash   Poppycock   Balderdash   Crap   Bunkum

It would be remiss of me not to mention that Geoff was a very good astrologer. He used to joke in later years, when asked about details of some Aspect, "I have already forgotten more than I ever learned." There are some that doubt the veracity of Astrology, and this in understandable. After all, there are three different systems of Western Astrology just on its own. There is also Chinese Astrology, Indian Astrology, etc.

Geoff himself was doubtful, and studied out of curiosity. He was as interested in seeing if it was right as he was in proving it was wrong. Time and again, when he went through a chart things worked out to be accurate. Not just the Sun Sign, or the Rising sign, which are very general. It was the combination of all the aspects that invariably seemed to add up to a fairly accurate picture of the person.

One day, Geoff noted in his own chart that a very specific aspect was present and that the meaning for this was extremely specific: It meant marriage. When he tracked back the dates when this Aspect arose in his own life, it occurred only twice. The first time was on the day he married Joy, the second was on the day he married Nelida.

If you calculate the odds of this, it approaches impossibility. For Geoff this was a confirmation as to the validity of the study. For others, they will say it was coincidence, but to say this defies mathematics and odds. When ONE Aspect, in the thousands of Aspects in Astrology, can only mean one thing, marriage, and when this one Aspect occurs ONLY on the days a person got married in this lifetime, with the person getting married being entirely unaware of it, it's a clear sign for any who with to see it.

Geoff always kept Astrology to a curiosity factor in his life. He would do charts for people and he bought professional software that allowed all this to happen much more easily, but I noticed something interesting about human nature. When Geoff GAVE a chart to someone, they never read it. If they paid him to do one, they did.

It's absolutely true! Geoff would quip, "There are some things in life you just can't give away. Wisdom is one of them. Honesty is another. Oddly enough, you can't even give away Respect, unless you are giving away your own self-respect."

Ah, Sugar Sugar!

I am visiting, as usual, on the weekend when Geoff looks up. He has 'that' look in his eye, and there is no need to guess who is the guinea pig for his latest notion. He tries out a line on me that he would have been working on all week. "Have you noticed that no one ever calls their loved ones 'nutrisweet', ' aspartame' or 'saccharin' ?"

I laugh with the simple truth of seeing the obvious.

"We always say, 'honey' or 'sweetie' or 'sugar' so why don't we think of loved ones in terms of artificial sweeteners?" He asks, "Can you imagine writing to a loved one, 'Dear Aspartame!'?"

I had no answer, because there really isn't one. Our terms of affection are what they are, but it really did strike me: No-one in their right mind would call their loved one Aspartame. Why is this, do you think? It sounds unnatural, for one. And I mean, it really does sound unnatural because it is a synthetic product.

It seemed to me that something in our core nature recognises that for affection to be real, it has to be based on what is a natural thing. You can 'pretend' affection for someone, but that is usually just to manipulate them, or to get their money, or whatever.

Then I started to get the picture of what was really driving the thought. Geoff was looking despondent. I asked what was wrong, and he said, "Why do my children have no affection for me? They never really call in, or say hello. If I had money, I would have gotten a lot more attention."

Now I see it. He always thought of his children with deep affection, and consideration. He understood them in ways they often did not understand themselves and he would occasionally try and say something. But there was no bridge of affection, no natural flow of love coming back that allowed a deeper connection.

Many times Geoff was half at fault for this. If someone wanted to call, he would always be going out, or have some excuse to avoid them. He was not an easy person to reach and I guess, partly because of his upbringing, he was inherently protective of his privacy. Yet there were some people who were always welcome to drop in.

Geoff had a small cadre of people who were his 'regulars'. They were people he trusted, and he could trust them because there was a bridge of affection in place between their hearts. The things he never got in childhood were what he craved: affection, kindness, understanding. He grew up with parents that apparently didn't like him.

Then it goes 'click'. He grew up starving. He wanted sweet things so much, even aspirin as like a candy to him. This is where the 'sugar' thing came from.

I got it, and responded, "Dad, you perhaps need to see this from a different angle. Have you ever considered that THEY are the ones missing out? I come here, and have a great time. You are full of funny and interesting thoughts, observations and wit. I get so much from you. (He looks at me with a 'are you telling the truth' sort of stare) Yes, you can be a pain, but I still get so much from our time together. You are not the one missing out, they are."

He looked at me for some time, and I know, he was looking to see if I was just buttering his bread, or if I meant it. You didn't often see this sort of frank stare from Geoff, and the only thing I can compare it to is the look a Lord of some castle might give a subject, a testing look to see if they were telling the truth. In the end, he just nodded. It was true, he had SO much to give people, they only had to ask.

The problem was, they never asked. It is the real reason I am writing this book, so others in the family can share a little of what I was given.

But then a bombshell. Just before I published this book, I discovered a secret he had kept. His father had not just taken him, his own mother had given him up, in order to get Duncan out of her life. She did a deal and Geoff was the cost she paid to be free of her dreadful husband. Finally, I began to really understand WHY he found trusting another so very hard.

Judo and Tai Chi

G eoff was highly skilled at Judo and Tai Chi. He was never a fighter, but he learned how to defend himself. Plus, it gave him a party trick at the pub. When he was fairly well sloshed, he used to play this game where people would try and get him in a hold, any sort of hold, and he would walk free of it. The big men would come up, try some sort of strangle hold, or whatever, and Geoff would slip sideways and be out of it before they knew what had happened.

He had studied with Geoff Gertz at Coorparoo in Brisbane. I occasionally went along to watch proceedings. The day was essentially people tossing another and being tossed about, as this was 'full contact' judo. It was not a gentle experience and no one left the mat who was not in a heavy sweat. Of note, the Gibb Brothers studied there, later to be known as the BeeGees (Brothers Gibb). I saw them there on occasions and by recollection they were very good at it.

Later in life, Geoff took up Tai Chi and achieved a high level of understanding and practice of the art. This, in particular, would have been helping to reduce stress levels and keep him fit. He took it up for those reasons. Plus the regular lessons were at the Cascades, a long-time favourite park of his on the Gold Coast.

Max Turner was the highest rated Westerner in the real full-contact Ju-Jitsu (not the grappling form they use now) and once when the two of them were drunk, Geoff decided to try and put a hold of Max. The next thing he knew he was 'arse over kettle' across the room, with Max saying, "Don't EVER do that again Geoff, I might have hurt you." They were so well trained in martial arts that there was no thought involved.

Max also offered me very sound advice in what to do if I was attacked or someone wanted to get into a fight. He tapped his legs and said, "These are always your best defence. Do you know why?"

I said, "Because you can kick people with them."

"Because you can use them to run away." Then he added, "People don't get it, because they watch TV and think that is how fights go. They don't. If you go more than three hits in a serious bare knuckle fight, even if you win, you have lost. Something will be broken and you will be in pain. It is better to avoid it."

Geoff had the shed at Rochedale farm fitted out with Judo mats. It was there for Max and he to practice, but also for the kids to have fun on. They were rolled up, but could be brought out onto the floor. They would have cost a small fortune and had very little use, but it is another example of Geoff's 'money is no object' attitude when it came to his personal interests.

This small section highlights a warning. When researching some of the background, I Googled 'Geoff Gertz, Coorparoo Judo' but nothing came up relating to it, other than Judo classes that were not connected to him.

This is a side-bar, but something few consider. There are thousand and millions of small details that are not in any search engine for one simple reason: They were gone from the scene before Google or Alta Vista existed and since then no one has bothered to post those details to the web. The truth is that Google is a very poor recorder of history.

Geoff made an askance note of this, and the general state of the world, "In thousands of years, what will remain? Iron will rust, concrete will crumble, the plants will take over the cities. I find it difficult to imagine that this is all there is, this sad world. Most are taught an invisible mantra: *We die, and are no more!* What a pessimism our science is leading us to."

Geoff Quips: *I notice in catalogues that Pulsar watches are being advertised as being water resistant to 50 metres. A dearer model is advertised as water resistant to 100 metres. I wonder how many 100 metre ones get returned under warranty for leaking water at 90 metres, and how would the owner prove it?*

GUNS

Geoff's Hunting Jacket

G eoff loved his rifles and guns. He was a champion skeet and clay shooter, and the single greatest regret in his career was the mistake he made when approaching the legendary one hundred and fifty clays. He had the one hundred badge, and was already up to 127 clays in a row. This is a phenomenal achievement, and there was no need for him to push on immediately.

"My hands were sweaty and slippery, my shoulder ached, and I was getting double vision. I should have stopped, taken a twenty minute break, and picked up the gun when I was in better shape, but I just wanted to get to the one-fifty, I wanted it. So stupid, in retrospect, falling a few short." Geoff said to me some years before he passed.

We were discussing the gun laws in Australia, and looking at his old hunting jacket with all the pins proudly displayed. There was his 100 badge, but you could tell by the way Geoff looked at it, it COULD have been a 150. There are only a handful of shooters in the country, in the world, who had a single session 150 badge for clay/trap shooting.

On the farm, Geoff had a wall of guns and rifles. I was trained how to use them, very carefully and methodically trained. There were going to be no accidents in Geoff's house due to mishandling of weapons. He deeply regretted having to hand them in when the tighter gun controls came into force. He knew that HE was never the problem, but the blanket laws meant so many of the truly beautiful weapons he had were not just going to be handed in, they were going to be destroyed.

To him, this was the criminal act. I remember the 22/250 with particular fondness. Devastatingly accurate, with a German scope, it would punch a bullet hundreds of meters yet had so little recoil you could keep shooting all day. Essentially, it was a glorified 303, with a similar calibre, but far more accurate. Reliable, and lightweight, it was one of the guns of choice for real hunters.

I was effectively given the Mauser .22 rifle, again, with a German scope. A toy rifle in one sense, but I was still a boy. To me it was heaven on a stick and a huge improvement on my original 'slug gun' which was an air rifle. Geoff kept that rifle along with his beloved Remington shotgun, despite what the law said. Only right towards the end did he send them in, with deep regret.

We never went hunting again after the restriction of gun controls were introduced. Geoff detested them and pointed out often that, in spite of all the emotional arguments that were put forward as to how the new laws were about 'saving lives', the reality was that there were very few issues regarding weapons in Australia. The entire basis for the action, the Martin Bryant attack at Port Arthur, came about because the POLICE put the gun he used in a public auction. Plus, the fellow was criminally insane. I personally knew the detective that was trying to get Bryant charged for what he believed to be the murder of the woman who effectively raised him. He wanted her money, so he killed her.

"Not enough evidence", he was told and in truth THIS is what led to the massacre. A good and reasonable detective being blocked by paperwork and having to let someone out onto the streets who he knew was a danger to the community.

But guns laws are a small part of the overall picture. Geoff often commented on how our natural freedoms were being eroded. "They deny common sense and create a nanny state," he would say. The excuse of protecting the public against terrorists, saving lives on roads, or whatever: It all adds up to the loss of choice and is like a tide that never turns. It just creeps in, taking one more freedom, one more right, until we have a passive population drowning in fear.

Guns and Rifles owned by Geoff. He was extremely proud of these weapons and very sad over the buy back scheme that would destroy them

Computers

When the gun laws changed, it affected Geoff quite badly. This was in 1996 and he was loathe to hand in his weapons. They were beautiful things and handing them over meant they would be destroyed. He saw no sense in it. It was not that he used them, but the option was always there to head to the Belmont range and fire off a few. Now it was gone. (It should be noted: In 2007 Geoff wrote a letter to Reg detailing the current cost of a visit to Belmont, saying it was now too high for him to consider)

It may have been the gun laws that triggered him into looking for a new interest but when I suggested he might enjoy computers, he was interested. He had absolutely no idea what they were about, but I took him shopping and found a store where he bought a 'latest model' 486 PC with the new-fangled Windows 95 on it. It cost $3000 in 1996

There were a few related ventures afterwards, looking for a printer and other bits and pieces, but the one thing he never imagined he would need was a modem. I bought him one, so he could connect with people all over the world. Geoff was puzzled about this 'internet' thing and initially failed to see any point to it, but then he logged on and started discovering people in every country. He loved it.

Of course, he was already an excellent typist, so the keyboard was no threat, but I received a a lot of calls about the computer that would not do as he asked it to. I gave him the advice I was initially given, "Wait three months and then your computer will start to behave." It was true!, After a few months the computer stopped arguing with him.

One day, when out buying a printer, we went to a store in Ipswich. Once there, the man in charge stated a very odd thing, "I have complete control over my staff, even their thoughts!" It was a most curious claim and when asked how, the fellow explained. "I have my staff hypnotised." One of the proofs, he claimed, was that one of the girls only needed to IMAGINE a thing, such as a piece of fruit, and another girl there would be able to 'pick it up'.

He then set up a demonstration, putting the girls 'into a trance' and asking one of them to write down the name of a fruit. The girl wrote down "banana'. He then asked the other girl what her friend written and she said, almost with confidence, "Strawberry".

"Not quite. Please try again."

After a few more tries she eventually got around to naming the most common fruit in Australia and said "Banana!". The fellow was triumphant, and overjoyed that he was able to prove the power and control he had over the staff.

We didn't buy a printer from him, Geoff was concerned the only thing it would print would be bananas.

"He certainly was bananas," I said as we left.

"Everyone is a little fruity," answered Geoff. "However, we should be grateful that he didn't ask the girls to nominate a dishonest politician, because then they would have been guessing all day. At least fruit narrowed it down!"

This was another example of how Geoff embraced new technology. He was in his Seventies when he undertook a complete change of life and set about learning new skills. And it paid dividends, because as he got older he could place bets on-line, talk with people, and generally feel connected to the world rather than just be trapped in a flat with only a TV for company.

Geoff paid $3030 for his first 486 Pentium chip computer, complete with Windows 95. It was to become a central theme that kept interest and focus in his life, especially in old age. He adapted well to this new technology, as he had always done, and went to TAFE to learn about how to operate them.

Horse Racing

Anyone who visited Geoff of a Saturday would be engaged in polite conversation, right up to the point when a race was on that he had put money on. He would have the radio on in the background, but when he race was about to start, the volume went up and you were expected to be silent.

He took his ponies very seriously, studied their form, kept track of the jockey's and trainers, and made what he considered to be astute and careful bets as a result. I can't say how often he won or lost, but it was a real passion for him. "I don't bet on the big race days, or the city races much, because you know they are rigged. The country races, where there is less at stake, is where you get the honest racing."

Having a computer and that 'internet' thing meant that, after a while, he got himself a TAB account. I would occasionally be asked to drop $400 into it and be told not to tell anyone. I have no idea why no one else should know, but those were the instructions.

Shortly before he passed on, I was sent on such a mission, but the rules had changed. I presume because of drug money laundering, you had to present ID that matched the acct before you could put money into it. I told Geoff when I got back, and he looked at me as if I was lying. "I had someone drop in money only six weeks ago," he snorted.

I am fairly sure he felt I was purposely restricting his favourite hobby, for reasons that cannot be explained. On the day of his passing, he asked me to log on to his email, and see what the racing form guide was saying! He was quite dedicated to that particular pursuit.

"I like to put money on any horse that has 'spirit' in the name. I find they seem to do better, I don't know why." He made this observation only months before he left us. "I used to be very focused on the jockey and the form of the horse, and I guess it matters, but now I just go by simple things. Is the horse 'on the up', is it out of town, and does it have spirit in the name in some way."

If Geoff was driving about in the Chev of a Saturday, the radio was always tuned to the racing broadcast. I will never forget the extraordinary drawl and humour of some of the commentators. The slow chatter about this horse, or that jockey, and then: "They are OFF!" This is when the real 'rattle gun' verbal assault started.

Vince Curry was the main one Geoff would listen to. The man had an extraordinary ability to detail every little moment of the race, the horses and the jockey's and to do so with a speed that was, literally, breathless.

But you heard every word. It is an art, the race-calling tradition, and I suspect half the charm and addiction of horse racing was the excitement those voices managed to generate over the radio.

And so many of the comment were funny, "Going slower than a nudist through a barbed wire fence." and "he's gone so wide on the turn he'll be eating the pies out of the punters hands". I can't remember them all, because there were so many. Each little gem was shot off like a machine gun, but I remember laughing and I had absolutely no interest in horse racing.

"Move it, man. MOVE it!" DHW would say
this to anyone slacking or being left behind

The Lone Ranger, long since retired,
makes an unpleasant discovery.

PILLS

Geoff would take a regular line of Vitamin Pills every morning. He had read a lot of books on health and was one of the few people coming into the 1960's that had a clue as to the value of nutrition in maintaining health. The proof was in the pudding, he rarely suffered so much as a cold, which he attributed to regular and large amounts of Vit C.

One day at the Milton Road flats, I had stayed overnight and watched Geoff's morning routine. There were thirty six pills all line up and he popped them all down, explaining what each was for. "This is Vitamin "A", good for the eyes. This is Vitamin "E", good for the skin, and so on. But when he came to the last two pills, he said nothing.

"What are those last ones for," I asked.

"Anti-depressants," Geoff replied. "I need them when I work out how much all the preceding ones have cost me." Geoff rarely hid anything, but 'some things' you had to ask specific questions about. As an example: He did not HIDE his anxiety, but he didn't want to advertise it either.

Geoff always encouraged learning and if I showed interest in any subject, he lent me a book about it. One example was Louis Kervran's "Transmutation of the Elements". An insightful book that still has an impact on me today. There was also the famous book by Jervis on Apple Cider Vinegar and its usefulness in healing. I have to say, the work done in the 1950's was remarkable and of tremendous value because this was at the time before 'big pharma' got its hands on the medical profession.

Simple books, by authors such as Jervis and Kervran, had a profound effect on me. I came to understand that healing was not found in a doctors surgery, but in the every day maintenance of our being. Dad had everything that was current: Iridology, astrology, palm reading were alongside books on health and well being. When asked his religion, he said he was eclectic and I used this standing joke of his to great effect on more than a few occasions when passing through customs.

"What religion are you?" This is a question posed on many entry documents for a good number of countries. I always fill in this query with the word, 'Eclectic'. No one has ever questioned it!

Geoff was an eclectic. He would as happily take the doctors pills as the naturopaths, but he always did his research into the effect of either. After all, one of those pills almost killed him and was the reason he booked into the lunatic asylum for a day. To this end, he had a volume that all doctors had in the drawer. A book the described what each medical drug did, what it was used for, and what the side effects might be. In the pre-internet days, this was an incredibly valuable tool.

It was one of the specific things that he needed to help get himself out of the grips of psychiatrists and their medications. "I piss out more vitamins that I take, I reckon," he said to me one day, half joking. "But I can't complain, I have had a pretty trouble-free run and I credit this in part to all those vitamin pills."

Geoff Quips: *The new term for failure is 'deferred success'.*

Michael Notes: *One of the curious things about the Rochedale farm was Geoff's 'tanning lamp'. He used to sit there, naked, to get an all over tan. Even as a kid, I wondered why, on 50 acres, he didn't just go out in the sun! He also had one of those vibrating belt machines, designed to help you lose weight. It was great fun, and Geoff clearly did not buy it for any weight problem, he was quite slim. I suspect he bought it because he enjoyed the sensation of being shaken about by it.*

Based on what he had read in health and nutrition books from the 1950's and 60's, Geoff started on a regime of vitamin taking that he kept up for his entire life. He would also keep up to date with Doctor Mercola, and regularly sent out sections of his web page that he felt would interest me.

Anxiety

Anxiety and depression, the 'black dogs' as Winston Churchill called them, were constant companions for Geoff. He never gave me a specific time when it started and from this I presumed he did not remember a time without this sense of being haunted by unknown fears. I admit to being somewhat blasé about this affliction of his. It did control him and I thought this was somewhat of a weakness on his behalf. And yes, it was, but it was not until after he passed on that I got given the message more clearly.

For about six weeks I woke up every morning with severe, crippling anxiety. The smallest sound would set off batwings in my stomach, and getting up to face the world was a real challenge. I know I went through an extraordinary depression when Mum passed on, for six months I had no desire to do anything. But this was different, I felt anxious, worried, but there was absolutely nothing that appeared to be the cause of it.

Then it went 'click'. THIS is what Geoff suffered every day of his life. Every sharp sound, every new event, it all set off an extreme stress reaction. At that point in time I had no control over it at all, and was helpless before the onslaught of what I knew to be utterly senseless yet equally uncontrollable panic attacks.

NOW I understand the look Geoff gave me when I told him about the weird reaction I had in a sleep centre, when they put a mask over my face to test for sleep apnoea. I panicked. I could not lie there and have this thing controlling my breathing. I could not rationalise it away, nor could I mentally control it like I could virtually everything else. It was a base level reaction, from the cortex of the brain.

"It's good that you understand how it feels," was all he said at the time.

I realised, though father had passed on, he was sending me a message. And it wasn't even about the anxiety, it was about compassion. Accepting another as they are, allowing them their difficulties, offering help where you can. Walking a mile in their moccasins, so to speak.

Once when my sister was up, we were sitting in his flat, chatting about stuff and Geoff mentioned how hard it was dealing with the incredible stresses of living. I looked at my sister, she looked at me, and I asked, "And what exactly might these incredible stresses be, dearest Father?"

He looked straight ahead, went silent, then changed the subject. My sister and I both laughed and so did Dad, barely. He knew the stresses and fears were imagined, he knew he had absolutely no real concerns at all. A little while later he told me about how he made a joke about the invisible stresses, when someone asked how he was.

"Not good, not good at all."

"Gosh Geoff, what's the problem?"

"Well, you see, there is the problem. I don't have any problems at all."

"Why would this be a bad thing?" the poor woman asked, not realising she had been set up for a joke.

"Well, if I don't have problems, then obviously I must not be growing spiritually. Don't you see?"

The penny dropped and the poor dear laughed. It is a perfect example of Geoff's two-way humour: He KNEW he had no problems, yet he was still haunted with anxiety. "The incredible stresses of living" was the same sort of thing as the joke he told, but in a not-funny way. Dad had 'kind of' accepted his condition as a form of spiritual impost, put in place so he could understand whatever it was he needed to learn. But it still controlled him, and made stretches of his life very difficult. This is probably why he liked to control all the small details of his life.

He would write down all the tiny minutiae of existence: The mileage when he filled the car up. The date he bought a battery. Every little detail was recorded in some way. I believe it was an attempt to bring order into his life and, in doing so, pour oil over the tempestuous waters of his internal demons.

But what a drama if anything occurred out of the usual pattern! At the last family gathering, Geoff had to go to a different unit to the one my sister generally rented when she was up. This became another cause for extreme stress. Nelida was with him, and said she almost could not get him out of the house, he was so bad. This was a huge concern, just going to meet the family at a different unit that he normally went to. And yet, as always, when he got there he was fine.

There was a point I had been making with my brothers and sisters, and at this last gathering it was fully recognised. Geoff almost never hit his kids. Peter and Greg occasionally got a smack, but at some point even that ceased. Growing up, no one thought anything of it but I realised that, at some point, Geoff had stopped the chain of violence that was rife throughout the entire Wallace family. All Geoff's brothers could be quite acerbic, a couple of them were physically harsh, but I cannot recall Geoff ever letting an angry word go past his lips with his own family. He could be sarcastic, but even that faded with the ongoing years.

We all thanked him for stopping the violence and not passing on those patterns he had suffered, as was so often the norm. He didn't really say a lot. I suspect he was adding up the level of sincerity and wondering how long it would last, but I believe he was grateful something had been said.

Alcohol

There would be few people who would argue that any of the Wallace brothers suffered an overdose of sobriety. They all liked a drink, and preferably a second, and a third. One day Geoff looked at me over his glasses as he poured himself some cheap red from a cask, "I am not an alcoholic, you know. But I would hate to live without it."

One day, when cousin Geoff was visiting Stewarts Road, Geoff turned up in the 1961 mushroom coloured Chevrolet and proceeded to open the boot. In there he had a brown luggage case, the type school kids used to take to school and inside it was his 'emergency kit'. Out of this he took a bottle of Sherry and took a few swigs, saying to young Geoff, "Emergency top-up". Then he put it back into place and headed into the house.

When he got too old to brew his own beer, Geoff used to buy these cheap and nasty casks of cheap, sweet red, which we would decant into plastic bottles, usually old soda water ones. It was a two-person operation, with myself holding the bottle and turning on the tap, while Geoff steadied the cask and supervised.

It was not dissimilar to the way we would decant the five litre bottles of GTX oil, spreading it to five, litre-sized plastic bottles, one of which would go into the 'emergency kit' that he still had in the boot of his car. And yes, he still had a bottle of booze in there, for emergencies.

Otherwise, his standard drink was Carlton Mid and I was often to get him a carton when they came up on special. "You can have two or more cans and feel quite normal," Geoff explained.

In the last months of his life, Geoff lost all desire for alcohol. "It does nothing for me." he said. "I used to quite enjoy a drink, but now it just does nothing." Then, after a small pause, he looked at me, and said, "Can you imagine how much money I would have saved if I had lost the taste for booze at some earlier time?"

Humour Between the Brothers

*R*eg and Geoff wrote letters on a regular basis all their lives. There were full of humour and wit, as well as commonplace events detailing the day-today. These examples (above and over) are very faded, but it gives you a clear idea of the sort of antics they used to get up to. Snipping pictures from local papers and adding their own slogans to them was a common game.

Included in the letters would be comments about general affairs, "I bought two tyres for the Ford, 185/16 Goodyears, cost $65" but the real treat was the quips and snips of general things the brothers found curious and interesting.

One specific thing I discovered right at the end of this book was something Geoff never spoke about. In a letter to Reg, he details how his mother felt guilty for "selling him up" to the old man, in order to get him out of her life. I finally understood his odd mistrust of everything, because his own mother willingly handed him to "that psychopathic bastard", as he described his father.

The Forgettory

G eoff was sitting quietly one day, then looked up and said, "Sometimes a forgettory is far more important than a memory."

He didn't add to the comment. There was no story tagged to it, there was not even a smile as he said it. It was something he needed to say to me and as the years go by I begin to understand what it might be. He was talking about letting the past go, that nothing can be changed by either regret or hope.

At the time, I believed he was talking about his own past, but later on, I suspected he was directing the statement to me. I had lost millions in property with the financial crisis and that was it. It was done. Let it go, stop gnawing on how you could have done things differently. The more I thought about his comment, the more I wondered. There was no story that went with it, no funny bit attached. There was no question asked to elicit a response and then, at last, I started to get the message. It was a simple statement of truth. *Let it all go.*

Was he talking about his fears, or his mother abandoning him? Was it his hatred of the father? Who can say: I am passing it along, in case it has some meaning for you.

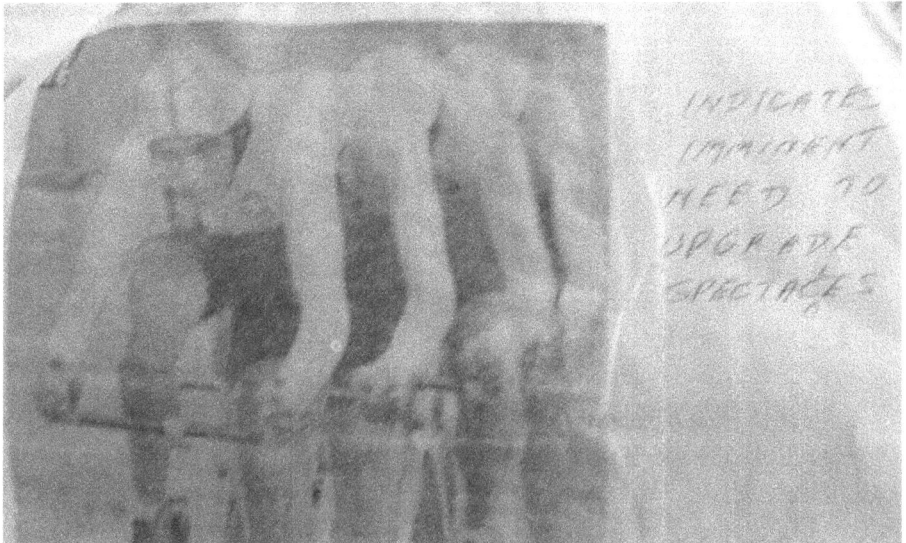

Snippet of Letter from Reg: Bike riders lined up one behind the other, looking as if they are staring at each other's butts. The quip: **"Indicates imminent need to upgrade spectacles"**

A Close Shave

One of the things about visiting Geoff was the surprise that often awaited you. He really prepared and had a worked-out routine, like a stage artist preparing for an audience. He learned specific lines and had very clear agendas about where he wanted a specific visit to go to. Yet there were times when he just flew off and improvised the day.

Of note is the case of the close shave: He rarely remembered these improvised events and one such one was when he decided to give his forty six year-old son advice on shaving. I included this discussion in one of the early chapters of my book, *Ratology II (Who Gives a Rats)*.

As a summary, one day when I turned up Geoff decided I needed shaving advice. "Use hot water to soften the whiskers first," was all he said. But it set me off wondering, what father in their right mind wants to give their forty-six year old son advice on shaving? I decided to have a little fun and pointed out that I shaved in the shower, thus warm water was not a real concern.

To this he was puzzled, how could I make sure I could get all the whiskers without a mirror? And so it went with a general conversation. The point of this was that this little quip of his was the start point for myself kicking off a follow-up to *Ratology, Way of the Un-Dammed*. It formed-up some of the early thinking that went into the second book.

Yet some years later, when proof reading this book, Geoff asked me, "Why did you include that made-up story about the shaving?"

Which is curious, because that little incident was the core motivation for starting the book What happened with Geoff, I suspect, is that a good deal of the time he was guided by an unseen hand. He did and said things purely as a vehicle for a higher power, often not recalling what he said, or even why he would have said it.

And other times, he just did dumb things. Like the time he was at Hervey Bay, and could not figure out how to open one of the tear-off plastic bags you used for putting the fruit and vegetables in. "How do I know what end is the end that opens up?" he asked the shop keeper.

The man takes the bag, rubs one of the ends between his fingers, revealing the opening into which things could go. "It's the bit that opens up, unlike the other side that stays shut." he said acerbically.

Michael Notes: *Geoff always parked his big Chev well away from other cars in a car park. He didn't want it scratched. Yet when we came back to the car, there was a collection of other cars parked around it. There never was any reason or explanation for this, but it happened every time.*

Passing On

Geoffrey John Wallace breathed his last the early afternoon of the Fourteenth of August 2016. He was surrounded by family, with his hand held by his former wife, Nelida. She was singing to him. He was still complaining about too many people being about in his last hours!

Nell had become a permanent fixture in Geoff's life in the last stretch. When she had left him some thirty years earlier, she had made the promise that she would make sure he never had to go to a nursing home. Most would think, "Oh that was then, said in haste. No one expects her to honour it." But Nell kept her word.

For the last eighteen months of his life, she slept on the couch in the very small one bedroom apartment he had moved to and cared for him everyday. Not that he appeared to be very grateful, despite all he said about gratitude. It was more that Geoff really didn't like people around in his space all that much, but he was very happy she was there, all the same.

Saturday was the usual day I called by, but Nell was worried, so I made sure to call in early and check on him. It didn't look good and from what she had said he had most likely suffered a mild stroke the day before. I called my sons, suggesting they would want to get here ASAP. I had already called my sister, Sue, the night before. She immediately flew up from Sydney to see him.

Yet when I got there, the first thing he asked about was his email and could I check it for him? Dad then asked for me to go over the tips for that weekends racing. He was still wanting to place bets on horses!

When going over his messages I saw that a family friend, a palliative care nurse, said she was dropping in this coming Wednesday. I sent her a note, suggesting if she wanted to see Geoff that she needed to call in right away. Kathy must have known something was up, because minutes after I sent that, she called he phone, saying she was on her way. She proved to be an extraordinary boon in those last hours.

My sister Sue, when providing proof reading this book, asked me to add the following .

"We (Sue and Geoff) had been talking every day in the week before and I knew that he wouldn't be alive much longer. It was so great to have Kathy there. She was generous and understanding with Dad about his oxygen level. She suggested that it be increased and Dad was concerned about this. Instead of just doing what she thought best, she honoured his wishes and just increased the oxygen level a little. I massaged his legs and

feet, which he appreciated. Although dying he was mentally acute. I noticed that he had had a hair cut.

"As I kissed him goodbye (I was booked on a flight back to Sydney) I said to him that it was OK to go. He died an hour later. It was truly a gift to have been with him in those last hours."

He needed moving so that a new padded mattress could be installed. I picked him up and realised he was just skin and bone. You have seen the photos of the refugees from the death camps? He looked a lot like those. He weighed less than 40 kilos, and did not seem at all happy I could lift him like a feather.

Geoff's chiropractor had now called in to see his patient, despite it being Saturday, as I had let him know the news. He took one look and said to me, "He will not be here Monday."

Soon after my sons arrived, said hello, and were just hanging about, chatting. Sue was in the room when he complained about there being too many people around! She had to leave to catch a flight for Sydney, but we all laughed about Geoff's little peculiarities, such as always wanting to be loved, but when everyone showed up, it was a bit much!

I was in checking on him, seeing what he needed when he made an odd comment about him not being sure anyone loved him. I replied, "No one does, because you're old and sick and we are all just hanging about for the money." He looked at me, somewhat askance, knowing it was a joke. Yet at the same time ... Maybe it wasn't? I just laughed and said, "You look fine, father."

"Then why is everyone here?"

"Are you worried about moving on?" I responded. "I know I would be a little concerned right at this point."

"I didn't think you were at all worried about dying," he answered.

"I was just being nice. But it isn't long now."

Soon after this, I was chatting with Kathy in the lounge room, my sons were chatting outside on the veranda. It was extraordinarily peaceful and calm. Nell was singing to Geoff in his bedroom, just holding his hand and singing. This was when he slipped away, peacefully, without a sound.

Geoffrey John Wallace
Born: 10 Dec 1925
Passed: (Sat) 14 Aug 2016

Geoff Quip: *"Speak the truth, and the truth shall set you free"*
(This is most especially true when speaking your truth to the boss)

Funeral Service

Geoff often talked about the greed of this world. It became self-evident as I started to organise his funeral. The funeral homes charge an awful lot of money for people to come and pay last respects and none of them seemed truly appropriate. I had already loosely organised one through the funeral director, but when Dad passed and I called to book this, I was told that man who had organised things had been fired and the $400 funeral home fee had shot up to $1800.

I didn't have that cash spare, and anyway, I figured Dad would have objected to this last bit of theft. So I organised a simple memorial, an ECK Service, to be run at a hall at Burleigh, a place he loved. I ordered some plates of food, set up a time and place, then sent out invitations. After this you just had to battle through the myriad of details that such things present.

Prior to the service, we had Yum-Cha at Geoff's favourite Chinese restaurant. So, all in all, a very relaxed and easy going way to say our farewells. Well over fifty people attended, along with my brothers and sisters. They spoke of their memories of Geoff, with my cousin Geoff. Then any who wished to speak a little about how Geoff had impacted their lives were invited to speak.

The local main man for Eckankar, Phil Finkelstien, was running the event. There were a lot of people coming up to chat and eventually he laughed, suggesting we close the ceremony and speak with each other afterwards over coffee.

The thing that surprised many people was just how atrocious an upbringing Geoff had. No-one other than the kids knew how abused he had been as a child. And the point was made, Geoff CHOSE to stop this violence. He made a decision early on, not just to 'not' be cruel or unkind, but to seek to be generous and forgiving towards others.

I am not sure there could be a better epitaph for a man.

Here lies Geoffrey John Wallace:
He chose love over hate.
He preferred laughter over tears
He enjoyed freedom more than tradition

Geoff's ashes were buried with his first wife, Joy, and his oldest son, Peter, in a grave at the Pinaroo Crematorium and Cemetary. The costs were covered by his son Gregory.

Do Mirrors Lie?

As has been made very clear many times through this book, Geoff had always suffered severe depression, the black dog. It trailed him all his life and, along with the associated anxiety, this pretty much controlled everything he did. It cost him a fortune, not to mention relationships, and worst of all, it cost him his confidence. In many ways he was helpless before the weight of the internal pressure that held him down.

I admit, I just accepted it for what it was and pretty much ignored the moods. As I saw things, depression and anxiety are like a hole you can fall into, but like everything it's a choice. Stand on the edge if you must, but choose a different path. My motto could be found written on the wall of a coffee shop in Subiaco, Perth, Australia, where I saw a piece of graffiti. *"When your back is against the wall, turn around, and WRITE on it."*

Take charge of your emotions, be a man, stand up and walk proud despite how you feel. This was what ran under my thinking, but as we have mentioned earlier, in the months after his passing my Father kept sending me a message. (I presume to make sure I understood him) Every night, I could barely sleep. Every morning, I woke with a shock to some small noise. Every day my stomach was churning with stress, stress I simply did not have, but could not shake.

It took six weeks before I got the message: "Do not judge another until you have walked a mile in their moccasins." And after I hear this, the familiar voice of my father says "Because once you are a mile away, then you can judge them freely and they can't catch you because you have their shoes!"

His sharp perception, married to his often sardonic humour, was the way he escaped from the black pit. Thus the blackness, the hurt, became the source of the many curious and funny things he said. One of my favourites, and the one that I only really understood when organising his funeral, was his little quip made some years earlier, when I came to visit.

"Did you know Mirrors Lie?" He said, straight faced, when I turned up one weekend. He looked at me, and I knew there was more. I know a setup when I walk into it.

"Do they now?" I asked back.

"Yes," says father, "They lie."

"How so?"

"Well, here 'I' am, a handsome, virile twenty year-old looking into it, but this ugly eighty-six year-old bastard is looking back. I tell you, it LIES!"

A few months later, my Mum was visiting. This was her first visit to see Dad in maybe thirty years. It will also prove to be the last visit she will make to her former husband before she passes on in a few years. She is standing there, and Dad quips, "I know how you feel, looking into a mirror," he says. "There you are, a twenty-four year old, but there is this strange, old person looking back."

"Exactly!" Mum exclaims, happy that at last someone understood.

I laughed so much, though on the inside. Dad glanced over with a twinkle in his eye. He had set the joke up for me, but not really to make fun of Mum. He was telling me, *"See? Everyone sees themselves like this."*

But I STILL did not really get it. Only now, when the curtain of his life is pulled away, do I discover behind his simple jest there lies a deeper truth. It was something he had often tried to show me over the years. It was his variation to the old quote he repeated again and again: *"Oh what gift the givee give us, to see ourselves as others see us."* What he was saying was that it really does not matter how we see ourselves. If we are to get on with others, if we are to have an easier way in the world, we need to understand how others see US.

It was his curious way of saying, "Be humble."

One step further along, he was saying "Just trying listening for a bit."

And if we go just one step past this, he was saying, "Accept yourself as you are."

I am generally not one to be overly guilty of any of these particular crimes, (humility, listening, or accepting myself) but I find in his quiet way, he was getting me to address this. Rarely did I find myself prepared to accept things as they stood. Stand on the edge of doom and shout at the devil, I say. Take the experience of life, wrestle its wisdom from the moments, and then write it down!

For a writer, this is a good policy, but as for getting on with others? The constant quest is not a good thing when it comes to relationships. And so, as this message soaks in to my Soul during the months after Father has passed, I find myself starting to listen more. I am starting to step back from my thoughts, and to earnestly try to hear what another is saying. And as I listen, a remarkable thing begins to happen.

Things just work better. Being a little humble and listening. Accepting myself and others 'as they are', all this seemed to make getting along with life and other people a little bit easier.

Dad was right. Who would have ever thought it?

I am guessing he might have when he said to me at age seventeen, *"You will be amazed at what your father learns between now and twenty-one."*

How did he know?

We can all look in the mirror of our Soul and see what we want to see. The criminal sees a person hard done by, the priest who molested young boys sees God's forgiveness waiting for him, the middle-aged woman who has lost her looks still sees the bright young thing she used to be. What WE see as ourselves is not necessarily how the rest of the world sees us, yet anyone who looks honestly into the mirror of Self can see the truth. Geoff was trying to encourage me to find the middle ground, between a necessary self-belief and the essential ability to connect with others. Inside there is the dream, outside, the reality. He suggested that humility was the bridge between the two. Humble listening and observation improves everything in our lives.

We all need a little one-eyed self-conviction to make progress in this world. We need to believe in ourselves. But we also need to be able to 'fit in' with others and our society. The question is: *Where is the balance between our dreams and our reality?* And if we keep getting the message that we are not doing things right, are we really going to insist that everyone else is wrong, that the mirror is lying?

Close

Geoff asked me what I intended to do with the notes I was taking. "I will knock it all up into a book when you are gone," I answered

"Would anyone want to read it?" he asked. Geoff was genuinely humble, it was not an act. He was well aware that there were larger and better stories out there grabbing at people's attention, so why would anyone be interested in his small and insignificant life?

"Maybe," I answered, "but the record will be there for whoever wants to take the time. Possibly the grandkids will have an interest, or the great grandkids."

Geoff just nodded. That made sense. "You heard about the monk who got an award for humility from the Pope?" he asked. I just watched, knowing that twinkle in the eye. "Well, he put it up on the wall. Big mistake, the Vatican police bashed in his door and took it back ."

I didn't tell him I would publish his story on Amazon and make it available to a world-wide audience, because that sort of thing would have just embarrassed him. He did not see his life as a significant event. He did not really understand that because he stopped the hurt he suffered, which caused him tremendous anxiety, this created the space for his son to write a book about his father.

We all have the hurt in our hearts, and whether it is real or imaginary is not the point. The child suffering because the cookie jar is just out of reach is dealing with the same suffering that a child experiences from beatings or starvation. We may not believe this, but it is true. The individual has no perspective on the world at that age, everything is as it is. It is just easier for the child without a cookie to get that treat when he grows up, and so find a solution to their pain. For the abused child, how do you find a lack of abuse to solve the problem?

However, because ONE lonely, deprived child chose to not pass on the hurt they suffered, he helped raised a family not imbued with the pain of his parents. It may not seem like much, but as a child who went to a Catholic boarding school, where I was caned every day for what was really nothing, I got to see both sides of the coin. A family where violence virtually did not exist, to a world where violence was the norm.

And the choice for me came early, at age fourteen. A friend was picking on a weak boy at Marist Brothers, just punching him, and the kid was defenceless. He handed the helpless child over to me, saying "your turn' and I said "Why would I want to beat up helpless little George?"

Of course, after this that bully hated me, but it was the right decision. Because of my father's choice for kindness instead of cruelty, when it came down to it I was able to choose a better way. I choose Love over hurt, freedom over the tyranny of emotions, and appreciation over regret.

Yet I am still not certain I can trust what I see in that mirror.

This book is my final farewell to my father. I have learned more about him writing it than I ever did visiting and talking with him throughout my whole life. My deepest wish is that you will feel the same.

Geoff Quips: *If you walk a mile in someone else's moccasins, how well will you understand them if the shoe doesn't fit? You might end up with blisters, cursing them, not understanding them better at all. Surely it should be, walk a mile in moccasins vaguely close to your foot size.*

God at His computer

On the occasion of Geoff's Eighty-Fifth Birthday his son, Greg, created a 'mini-book' for him called, in reference to the long-running TV show, "This is Your Life"

The mini-book details many events, as recalled by Geoff, that are worthy of inclusion in this story of his life

I have recreated the book here using the original Word file for reference.

Please note that a PDF of "Parables of Geoff" is available for download. Contact the author at grcaustralia@gmail.com for details.

Michael Notes: *Not to say that the Svenson family were unemotional, but many years ago Cousin Geoff made a pilgrimage to North QLD to find "Swanty" Svenson. He tracked him down, way out in the bush, in the middle of nowhere. Young Geoff introduced himself to his relative, and Swanty just said "OK." ... And then shut the door on him*!

THIS IS YOUR LIFE

GEOFFREY WALLACE

BORN: 10 DEC 1925

PREPARED FOR GEOFF'S 85TH BIRTHDAY
BY HIS SON GREGORY MAXWELL WALLACE

The Early Years

You were born on the 10th December 1925 at Chermside, Brisbane and named Geoffrey John Wallace by your father Duncan Harry Wallace and mother Annette Wallace. (nee Svennsen) You are the youngest member of the family.

From the eldest to the youngest the other children in your family are
Bob (Dec'd)
Colin (Dec'd)
Reg (Dec'd).

Here is Reg powering along and enjoying the blue water and sunshine.

You and Reg were to enjoy many years of fishing and camping and generally being together.

Geoff: "All of my family served in WW2, Reg in the Army, moi in the Navy, and Bob and Colin in the Air Force. All did Morse code in one form or another (Bob full-time and fast as was I), as did my father. I was astonishingly proficient at Morse". He said with a modest smile.

Here you are at age nineteen-ish.

Right:

Editor's comment: "There is a resemblance to young Geoff Wallace but perhaps more so to myself (Greg Wallace) although better looking."

Below:

On the left is Max Turner, your very best mate, with you in the Navy. The bell-bottom trousers make you almost look like nuns in habits.

A rare solo photo of you in the Navy.

Your family moved from Broken Hill to live in the bush at the Black River, Townsville, around 1934 when you were about 9. At age around 10, you were unwillingly handed over to the sole care of your father. At this time, you were attending the Christian Brothers School in Townsville and boarding in that city. You then moved with your father to Sydney. At some stage, all your brothers were living at the Black River.

Before we look at Black River, Townsville, Queensland, let's take a peek at the more distant past. You have a photo and on the back of which your father, Duncan, has written some names and details.

Now it is hard to read but one can see "Grandma on left. Her place at Lovedale, Nilgiri Hills, South India" and it actually exists today as a huge school complex. The rest of the writing is unclear except two years are given 1916 and (1724 or 1924) so perhaps the photo is taken in 1916.

Nīlgiri Hills, Tamil Nadu, India is in a National Park. The town of Ooty is the nearest major town and Lovedale is a little south of it.

Geoff Notes: *When the parents separated, I was sent to Townsville to board with private people, and attend the Christian Brothers school. They were a pretty brutal lot, belting kids for any little excuse. I could spell anything in those days (even can today). We were given a spelling test of 10 words, with the promise of the cane for every one we got wrong. I didn't have a pencil, so couldn't write anything, and was adjudged by their strange reasoning to have got 10 wrong, even though I was a top speller. That got me a sixer with their thick, and much-used strap which was about 20 inches long, half an inch thick, an inch or more wide, with a hacksaw blade sewn in the middle.*

Here is the front side of the photo and so Duncan's Grandma is on the left. She was principal of the Girl's School.

The photo called DHW Grandmother I don't know anything about, whether it was in India or where (but I think it says on the back) in the Nilgiri Hills in India. The other one is Duncan's handwriting on the reverse of this photo describing it, which is very hard to read.

Here is a modern photo of part of the school.

The Lawrence School, Lovedale, (Tamil Nadu, India) was founded on September 6th, 1858, and is named after Maj Gen Sir Henry Lawrence, who first projected the idea of founding a school in the Nilgiris for children of serving soldiers and ex-soldiers of the British Army in India so that they could have the benefit of a sound education in a bracing and healthy climate.

For more information about the school see Appendix A.

Here is a family photo taken at Black River near Townsville.

Geoff Notes: *In the photo called "Photos Black River". the chap on the left is not known to me. The other four are my mother's brothers and sisters (my uncles and aunts). My mother's name was Annette and they called her Nettie. The big woman is Ida, the girl in the chair is Violet, the tall male is Swanty, and the short one is Carl. It must be a pretty old photo, because when I met them at age 9 or 10, little Carl was a mature adult, and little Violet in the chair would have had a daughter my age whom I later came to know well, first when I was about 7 and later as an adult in Port Moresby.*

Geoff Notes: *On the southern side of the river, there were NO habitations, except for about a mile or less from the Black River mouth, my Aunt Ida (my mother's sister, the large one in the photo) and husband Johnny Brabon had a very large holding where they ran cattle. My mother used to cross the river not far from the mouth on horseback with me walking at her side hanging on to the horse with water up to my armpits at low tide (the river was at low tide, not my armpits - I like to be explicit).*

The river used to regularly flood around January or so in the wet season. Sometimes I wonder how I came out of it all unscathed. My Uncle Swanty there used to cut firewood and take it in his truck to Townsville where he sold it. Mum used to accompany him on these trips. Duncan didn't like Mum's relatives. He used to call them the Black River Bastards, or some similar epithet. The feeling was mutual.

Here is some more of the story in your own words.

My Father's name was Duncan Harry Wallace and was called Duncan or DHW, not Harry. He was born at Bangalore on 7 March 1878. so couldn't have figured in the operations you mention. He was 12 years older than my mother whose birthday was 31 July 1890 at Townsville. My Nowshera could have been Nashera if there is such a place.

He was born in Bangalore on his birthday! His father was involved in building dams across the country, either as an engineer (or concrete mixer, or something else   ). I have a picture of his female relatives somewhere. I'll see if I can find it. He served in the British army and did a march from Now-sheera to Ferozapor (phonetic spelling). He taught me some Tamil, wherever he learnt it from.

He had a unique, quick and successful way of teaching. If you got it wrong, you received a swift fist to the head.

Memories

My mother was born at the Black River, about 15 miles north of Townsville of Swedish and Danish immigrant parents. The father was Per Svennsen who disappeared in the sea off the beach when attending to fish traps. A crocodile no doubt, as when I was an 9 or 10-year-old kid there, it was still rugged, virgin bush full of lantana, big snakes, dingoes, crocs etc. I used to wander barefoot through the bush with a single-shot air gun that was harmless to everything, even if you managed to hit it. Many times I was followed on my bike by dingoes, padding along behind me.

I used to play with my cousins, kids of one of Mum's sisters, Ida. We used to get .22 rifle cartridges, extract the lead bullets, and chew them (the lead bullets, not the brass cartridge cases or the gun powder). We used to have the odd smoke with tobacco we had stolen from adult relatives, then chew eucalypt leaves so others wouldn't smell it on us. Ever chewed gum leaves? I fail to see what enjoyment koalas get out of them. It's a wonder we didn't get lead poisoning!

I used to ride a bike 8 miles, much of it on a stony main road, to a little country school at Bohlevale, about 7 miles north of Townsville, a one-room wooden building on high stumps. Mr Smith, the sole teacher was a very benign and kindly bloke, who commuted from Townsville. There would have been about 18 or so kids in various grades. We wrote on slates - no paper or pencils in that particular education facility. Incidentally, many years before, Duncan was the first teacher at that school. (Editors Note: This possibly is where he met Annette)

When the parents separated, I was sent to Townsville to board with private people, and attend the Christian Brothers school. They were a pretty brutal lot, belting kids for any little excuse. I could spell anything in those days (even can today). We were given a spelling test of 10 words, with the promise of the cane for every one we got wrong. I didn't have a pencil, so couldn't write anything, and was adjudged by their strange reasoning to have got 10 wrong, even though I was a top speller. That got me a sixer with their thick, and much-used strap which was about 20 inches long, half an inch thick, an inch or more wide, with a hacksaw blade sewn in the middle.

I must have been about 11 or so when we left there for Sydney by coastal steamer which were common in those days. They were about 10,000 tons and had names such as Manunda, Manoora, Kanimbla. I remember the trip well, the Whitsundays, and spouting whales.

And more of your memories...

I don't know the name of Duncan's (my father's) father. There is no Harry that I know of, except Harry Belafonte.

Incidentally, the gun that Geoff referred to in the pig episode was my Remington semi-auto, not the Browning. I had disposed of my Browning at that time. The Remington was as accurate as a rifle when used with the solid lead slugs instead of pellets. With the Browning, years earlier, at the Brisbane Gun Club, I had shot about 147 clay targets without a miss - a rare feat unlikely to be seen at Olympic Games.

As to the Black River address, there were none in those days. I can give you a rough idea of where we lived. If you go north from Townsville towards Ingham (it would be the main northern highway), cross the Black River bridge and immediately turn right. We could immediately (or nearly immediately) cross the railway line there. Between here and the coast, there were NO dwellings or habitation, except our little house. Go along the Black River perhaps a mile, and then go north about another mile or two. That would be where we lived in the bush. We used to go to a creek called Alex Creek where there were oysters in the mud, plus crocodiles.

On the southern side of the river, there were NO habitations, except for about a mile or less from the Black River mouth. My Aunt Ida (my mother's sister, the large one in the photo) and husband Johnny Brabon had a very large holding where they ran cattle. My mother used to cross the river not far from the mouth on horseback with me walking at her side hanging on to the horse with water up to my armpits at low tide (the river was at low tide, not my armpits - I like to be explicit).

As to the location of the pig incident, it was on the north side of the Dumaresq River (we camped on the river bank) about 10-15 miles or so west of Texas on the road to Goondiwindi.

I joined the Navy at age 17 about in April 1943 and was demobilised in mid 1946 as Telegraphist. My first posting was Townsville to the naval wireless station, part way up Castle Hill, then a month or so at the Port War Signal Station on the highest hill at Magnetic Island. Then I flew to New Guinea by American DC3 to Milne Bay, after a while to Lae for some time, and to Madang where the Navy had a whole small island solely as a communication centre with about 100 wireless operators (morse of course). I had some time on HMAS Kanimbla, but not nearly as long as the year shown on my Record of Service. I was in the very top echelon of wireless operators, and in fact absolutely loved it. I just had natural aptitude, and the challenge was to send perfect morse which I could do with my special morse key. I was later a telegraphist in the PMG

Department after undergoing a 9-month full time course in touch typing, teleprinter operating, Murray MULTIPLEX perforated tapes that we had to read the holes, and of course morse, but the sounder type, in telegrams not what is called the buzzer in radio morse. I didn't have any love for the PMG sounder (clicking) type.

Kamaliki is the correct spelling (no R- the other spelling is correct) was on the Asaro River about 4 miles in a straight line from the bottom end of the air strip which had a distinct downward slope. In bad weather with little visibility, pilots used to fly up the Asaro River until they found our house, and then turn immediately right to land at Goroka (countless lives saved here?) It was sold to the Divine Word Mission through Bishop Arkfeldt at Wewak, a tall, austere, humorless figure, with endless, endless negotiating. They installed to run it all a Brother who was an ex-bootmaker (not bookmaker) and not exactly executive material.

I had four years in the Civil Administration, initially as a native labour supervisor at Port Moresby, then got married, then to Manus Island at Lorengau as acting District Labour Officer running the government native labour compound (hundreds of natives) as well as administring the Native Labour Ordinance which stated all the conditions under which natives were to be employed by private enterprise. I had to provide native labour to the RAAF at Momote and go over there to pay them. I have a news-paper photo of me paying the natives there

Incidentally, the War Crimes Trials were being held there at Lombrum. High ranking Japs were tried and some of them were hung as a result. I used to go in and watch the trials at times. Manus was mainly coral islands, and was a HUGE American Base on Seeadler Harbour during the war. You could just go and get yourself a jeep or other vehicle. Out of the bush, I got a big Studebaker truck with 2 lots of double wheels at the back, and 4-wheel drive. Hardly any miles on the clock and drove like a car. I had an American 30.06 service rifle and found a cache of ammo the size of a bedroom in sealed tin cans. I used this rifle to stand on a low bridge and shoot into schools of fish, which stunned them. Natives would dive in and harvest them and they soon recovered (the fish, not the natives).

My final time in the Administration, following a posting to Kokopo near Rabaul, was at Goroka which had not long been opened up to the first white men. This involved running the Highlands Labour Scheme whereby native highlanders could go to work on the coast under certain conditions. Had charge of up to about 1,500 of them at various times awaiting processing as well as the local native labourers in a compound. So my whole 12 years in post-war (from 1948) New Guinea involved close association with natives, and I deeply realise now what a really decent lot *they were, albeit often frustrating. Kembu, the house boy at Kamaliki, I admire more than anyone I have ever met as a superior human being. Also the boss boy Nomi (pron. Normie) and another named Seni.*

All this may be of interest to your descendants many years since. What are you doing at the moment? A "This Is Your Life" sort of thing?

You never evinced any interest whatever in going bush. Mick liked it, but was not interested in guns (except shooting air rifle slugs into my commercial papaws). Geoff lapped it up and was really congenial company (otherwise I would have let the pig get him).

Let me know if you want any more. Nudding but qvestions, qvestions!

I must have a look at Google one day and see just how far it was (and still would be) from the Black River bridge eastward to the beach. The river used to regularly flood around January or so in the wet season. Sometimes I wonder how I came out of it all unscathed. My Uncle Swanty there used to cut firewood and take it in his truck to Townsville where he sold it. Mum used to accompany him on these trips. Duncan didn't like Mum's relatives. He used to call them the Black River Bastards, or some similar epithet. The feeling was mutual.

Duncan was an avid gun buff. He got me a shotgun at about age 12 and I had a natural aptitude for shooting. I shot about 6 flying quail straight at my first attempt. I remember his surprise. He looked like the judges at Susan Boyle's first public appearance. Then, as a kid, I used to win at trapshooting against the adults.

If only DHW had used his talents for good instead of evil, as Maxwell Smart would say. He had a talent for investigating subjects and thoroughly mastering them. Reg has inherited this. Reg had DHW's notebooks (may still have them) when he was studying to be a health inspector. DHW used to be a functionary in the Fiji police force. There existed a photo (Reg may have it) of DHW in uniform standing alongside a Fijian native policeman in sulu and sandals. He may have been the Chief. He was also a prize fighter at one stage somewhere (that's where he developed his talents for hitting me). I was a quiet kid. He just needed someone to take out his frustrations on, and I was there. He used to fly into an uncontrollable rage.

(See main book stories, "The Bridge" and "The Haircut")

Here is Black River seen in relation to Townsville.

You recalled living near Alick Creek and this has been found on the map so that will be it for sure. You recalled is phonetically as Alex Creek and Alicks Creek sounds the same. See the map below. I think your property may be at the end of Bowden Road which is very close to Alick Creek and about 3 miles from the Bruce Hwy so see how that fits your memory. *"There were no roads then, only winding bush tracks."*

I'm glad you remembered Grandma Annette's surname because there is a Svennson road evidently named after them. How come Bowdon Rd is not Wallace Road?

Maybe someone called Bowden bought it later. The house at the end of the road often gets the road name – as in it's the road to Svenson's. There is Low Creek near their house and probably named after Mount Low which is closer to the highway. It is a low hill rather than a mountain. If your parent's house is where I think, it does not look like anyone wants to live there as it seems undeveloped even today.

Over the page is a somewhat guessed location but it looks like you lived where is says Wallace's here. There is no obvious house there now. Your Mother Annette's family lived where is says Svenson's here.

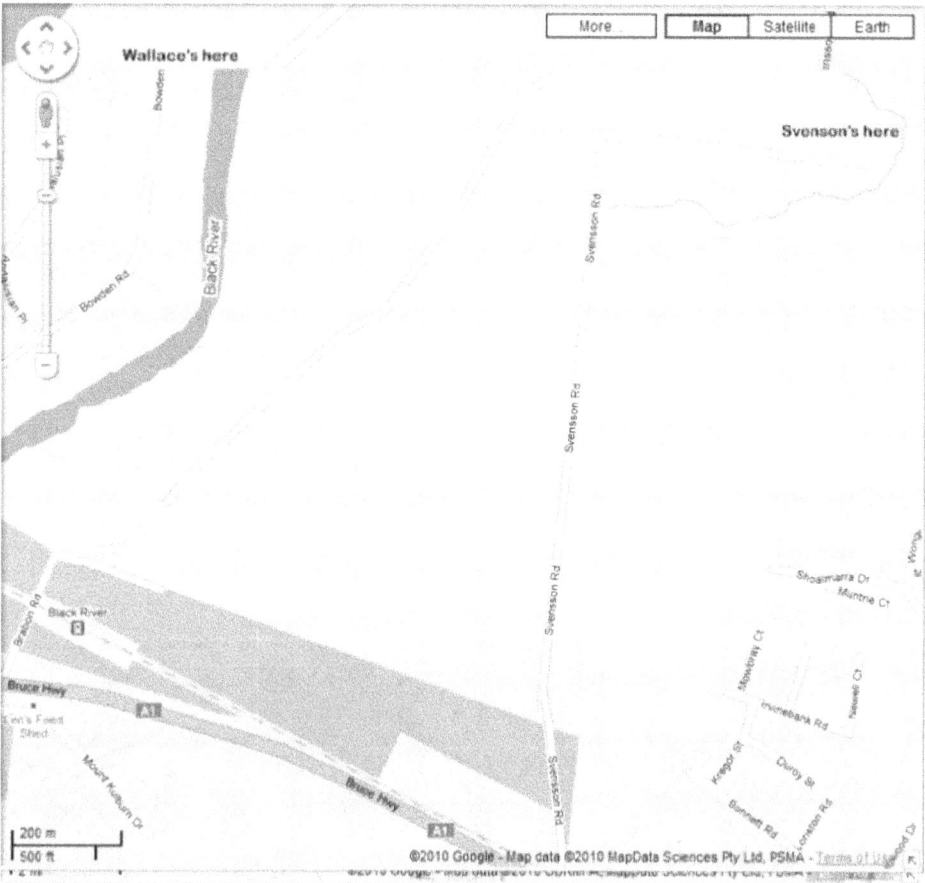

Here is a close up of the end of Bowden Road in Satelite view. Crossing Black River up to your armpits would have been very hazardous, especially with so many crocs around.

This shows Bowden Road with Alick Creek nearby so we must have found the approximate location of your house. My guess is a clearing among the trees where it's a little higher. You would have crossed Black River on the right to get to Svenson's place.

You became quite good at shooting. I'm not sure when it became an Olympic Sport but if development for young people was around then. you probably would have got a Gold Medal.

Duncan's famous encounter

Now let's revisit the story about Duncan Wallace and the McIntyre River boardwalk.

At Inverell where he was health inspector, he wanted to cross the McIntyre River over a narrow boardwalk. A dark person was in his way (not an Aboriginal). He hit the bloke and there was a subsequent court case. The plaintiff was asked, "What happened?" and the dark chap said: "Mr Wallace he say 'Out of the way black bastard. White man first.' Then he hitta me."
"And then what did you do?"
"What I do? What I DO? I go kettle over arse. What else I can do!"
This quip became fairly famous. I don't recall the outcome of the case.

Here is the approximate location where this infamous event took place.

The War Years

During World War II you joined the Navy as a Wireless Telegraphist.

*My first posting was Townsville to the naval wireless station, part way up
Castle Hill, then a month or so at the Port War Signal Station on the
highest hill at Magnetic Island. Then I flew to New Guinea by American
DC3 to Milne Bay, after a while to Lae for some time, and to Madang
where the Navy had a whole small island solely as a communication
centre with about 100 wireless operators (morse of course). I had some
time on HMAS Kanimbla.*

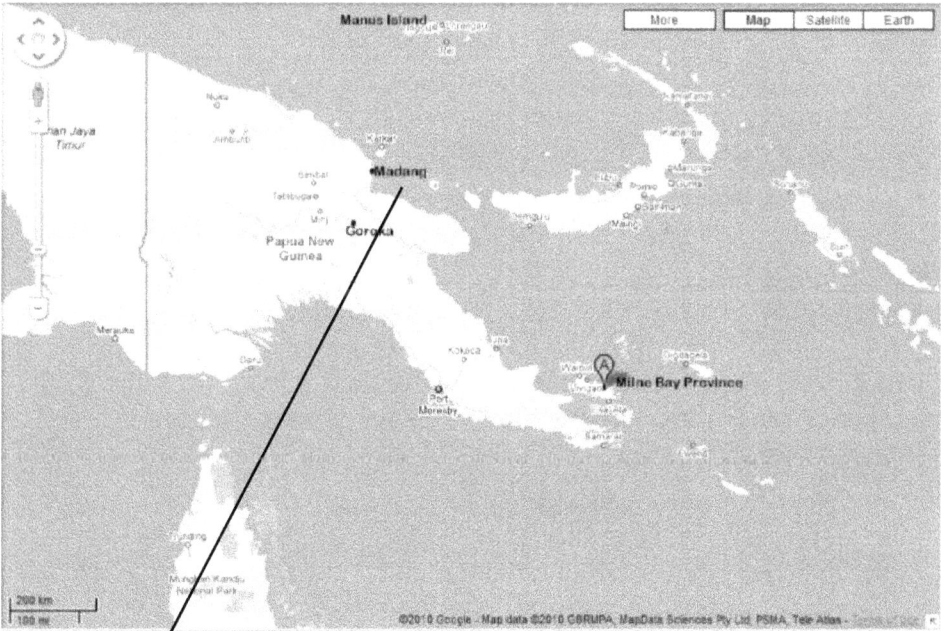

*Bil Bill was where Geoff was posted as a Telegrapher. A tiny speck of
an island off the coast, near Madang, it had only communications and
primitive air defences It is likely they were stationed there so as to not
be a target for other military installations, as radio was traceable.*

A New Guinea Pioneer

During the war you met Joy Wintle. You had two best ex-navy mates Frank Wintle and Max Turner. Frank was to subsequently introduce you to his cousin Joy.

After marrying Joy, you both moved to New Guinea and eventually had a coffee plantation at Kamaliki. First moved to Manus Island and you had a job in Administration with the Government and looked after Native Labour. You were well liked. From there you moved to Kokapo near Rabaul then then Goroka and eventually nearby Kamaliki.

(See Appendix B for more information on the property called Kamaliki.)

You added some trivia to the foundation of the word Kamaliki.

My land was owned by the immediately adjoining village called Kamarigi. I found it easier to substitute the soft L for the R, but still naming my land after the previous village owners. They pronounced it Ka' MAR' i ge. It was so much easier to say KAR' ma licky.

I thought it strange to hear from you that there are currently things at Goroka named Kamaliki. They may have no relation whatever to my land there. I don't know.

Anyway, we were all descended from Four Bears.

The Leahy brothers were the first white men into the highlands of New Guinea in the 1930's. They were looking for gold. There was some gold but later coffee was found to be more lucrative. Perhaps that's why they called it New Guinea Gold.

Here is an aerial picture of later Goroka about the time we left. This picture when blown up on the screen has a red dot which pinpoints the government house we used to live in (not clearly - just the position). The open patch of land there is the native labour compound where I used to work.

This one of Kamaliki shows some of the coffee in the foreground (much was planted later). The house is at about 2 o'clock at what appears to be the foot of the mountains (but they are in the distance). There is a big, swift-flowing river below the house. What a pity we didn't take more photos! I have some colour slides but haven't got around to viewing them.

It was while here that you bought the Peugeot 403 1956 manual. You brought it to Australia and it later became Joy's main car and then later she gave it to me (Greg). You also had a green Willy's Jeep.

From New Guinea to Australia

This is a photo of you standing by a car around 1981. It happens to be a Valiant Charger which was a classic icon of the era. Wherever it went people would give the V for victory sign. It was not yours but the Valiant you bought was one of the first family Valiants. It was an Auto and had the image of a car tyre bulging from the boot.

This photo to the right is you in a wig that frfrightened Joy and Mrs Raetz. (See Main Book, The Orange Haired Hippie)

Joker Geoff

Talking about frightening people, young Geoff vividly recalls the night you called at their place at Red Hill. You were dressed in a trench coat and hat and had a toy pistol. You knocked at the door and frightened Judy who slammed the door and went to get Reg. Reg came out with a loaded gun with young Geoff behind. They saw you go under the house and Reg threatened to shoot you. You had to meekly identify yourself before he might shoot.

Now the story moves to the adventures of pig hunting.

Stories change with the telling but there is a legend swelling around a pig hunting trip involving your nephew and namesake, Geoff Wallace, whose life you saved by killing a charging pig. He is herein called 'young' Geoff to save confusion.

This is a true story of you now dubbed 'Paladin Wally'. He is fast shootin' and slow talkin' (laconic). He peacefully roams the West in his white Ford V8 Ute hunting mean pigs that threaten the livelihood of the country folk. With him goes his faithful nephew 'young' Geoff. Whenever he drives onto a property they welcome him with relief that finally something will happen to stop the pig gang attacks. He usually leaves a one-ounce lead slug behind to show where he's been. He always dressed in black, and had a penchant for chewing on brownies. His mission in life was to roam the west (of the east) on hire saving the lives of people by shooting charging pigs. They called him "Paladin Wally".

Here is a Remington Autoloading Model 1100 Classic Trap. It is identical to the gun that saved nephew Geoff. You used a 1oz slug rather than pellets and such a bullet could bring down an elephant.

Around this time you had a Ford V8 Ute Customline similar to the one shown here. (Single Spinner Ute had a 'saucer' round disk at the radiator that gave it is's name)

Here is the Dumaresq River out from Texas. The location of the life-saving pig shoot. 'Young' Geoff might be remembered as a white cross here if it was not for some good shooting.

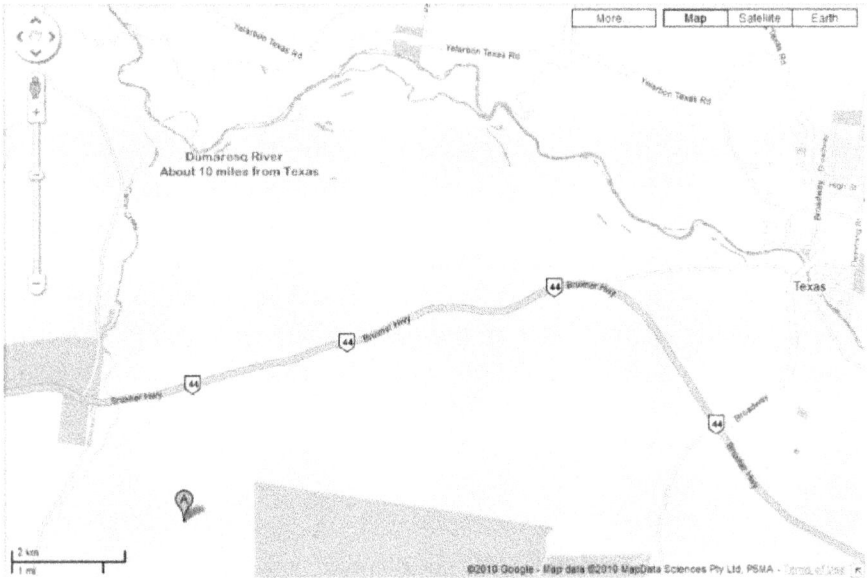

We can envision 'Paladin Wally' with his pock-marked face and black outfit, and hear the song:

Have gun will travel reads the card of a man
A knight without armor in a savage land
His fast gun for hire heeds the calling wind
A soldier of fortune is a man called Paladin
Paladin Paladin where do you roam
Paladin Paladin far far from home.

Here are some links to youtube video about the series "Have Gun Will Travel" starring the original Paladin 'Richard Boone' with the theme song "Have Gun will Travel" to which the above words are part of the theme song. It's called 'Stand by me – The Ballad of Paladin'

http://www.youtube.com/watch?v=To-wfwkmXds&feature=fvst

Black and white TV came to Australia in 1956. Shows like 'Have Gun Will Travel' were benchmarks of the era.

The More Recent Years

In about 1959, you settled the family at 17 Stewart Road, Ashgrove, Brisbane. The cousins lived not far away at Red Hill. You and brother Reg were good mates. Drinking, shooting at the range, hunting and camping were favourite pastimes. There were occasional outings with Reg's family. Reg drove a Zephyr while you changed cars more often but the pink and white Chev was dominant in those years.

Before that, in around 1963, you bought a Valiant 'S' series like the one shown here. It had 3sp Auto with 3697cc 6 cylinder engine.

I (Greg) recall being driven to school in it. As we passed by the lower sports fields of Marist Bros Ashgrove, we would ask you to accelerate. You would slow down and in second gear would plant the foot and the acceleration would push us back into the seats. We loved the sense of exhilaration. Pedestrians would turn their heads as the car was a real looker. It had a 'hemi' engine which became a marketing sales pitch. I was later to learn that the older Peugeot 403 also had a 'hemi' engine with a cross flow head and independant rear suspension.

Here is two pictures of the 1961 Chev at Rochedale.

The Chev was pink and white and automatic. It had huge bench seats front and back. You could carry two adults and six children. Seat belts were not compulsory then.

At Rochedale you had a farm. The land had to be cleared first. Your house was a section of the large shed. It was amazing how a living area could be nice and comfortable within a shed. You had a Judo/Jujitsu mat and your mate Max Turner would visit and teach you self defence. He was in the Police force. I recall him breaking your ribs at one stage. With friends like that who needs enemies!

You became one of the earliest Hills Hoist private business ventures in Brisbane and recall one of your first installations with the lady of the house watching. You were trying to look like you knew what you were doing and felt you bumbled along but she was so impressed she thought you were a genius. This was new technology. A clothes line that could be wound up as well as spun around.

We had one at Stewart Road. As children, we found that one could hang from an outer bar and make it spin around. Unfortunately, it bent with this weight and yours truly would hope that with six children it would be hard to know which one did it.

Camping and shooting at Texas was a favourite past-time. The Chev is featured here. The white and green canvas tent was a classic basic tent and had no floor.

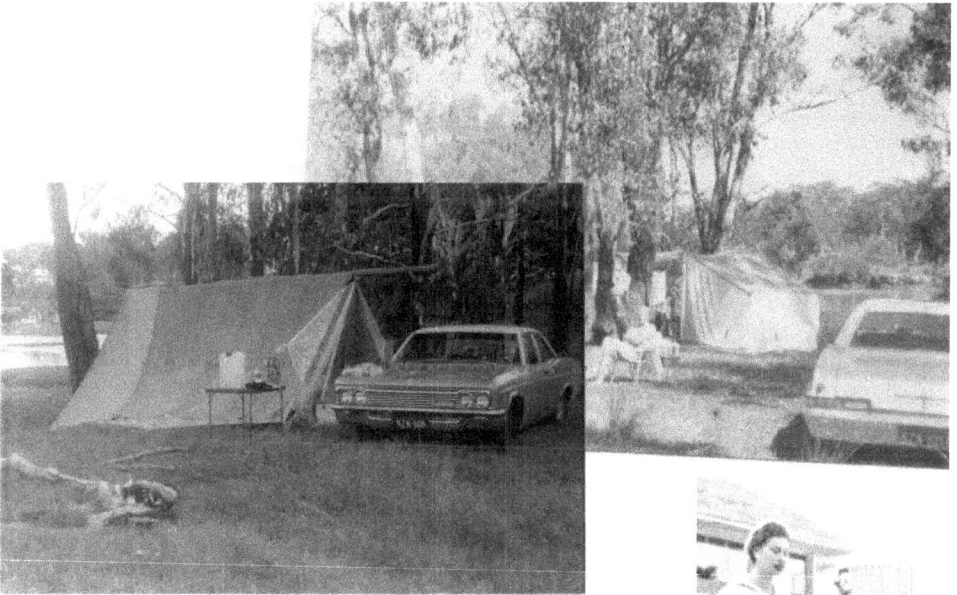

You also owned another Australian icon known as the Victa Utility Mower. This was one of the first mowers. It was a two stroke. It even earned itself a Victa Ward in the local hospital. It lacked a safety apron or sheath coming down lower than the blades. Rocks could spin out and a foot or toe could easily be put to the blades. This also made it less likely to choke from cut grass getting stuck underneath and probably made it more famous as the 'good old' Victa.

You bought flats at 502 Milton Road, Toowong and ran a Social Club for some time. Sadly, around 1963, a marriage separation occurred and you developed a farm at Rochedale. Another even sadder occasion was the death of your oldest son, Peter, at Eighteen, after a motor car accident. He was also in a Zephyr, by coincidence.

Taxi drivers, used car salesman and real estate agents were not your favourite types. Nevertheless, you later became a Real Estate Agent in your own right, and later with Conias Apollo, Paddington.

At that time you bought an incredibly luxurious, but astonishingly unreliable Chrysler with a 360 Hemi V8. It had the noteworthy ability to break it's own engine mounts if you 'floored it'. It got sold and you bought the reliable XC Ford (pictured) which you drove for many years, until it was replaced with a Mercedes 190e

You moved to the Gold Coast and married Nelida (Nelly) with whom, though divorced , you remained good friends.

Today, you live at Palm Beach in a unit. You still enjoy your own home brew stout. At 85, you are in good health but driving around is a problem, though you still retain a 5 year driving license.

The family is a little spread out. Joy is in a self-managed, aged complex in Brisbane. Greg is at Bray Park, Brisbane. Julie is living in Mt Isa. Trish in Sinnamon Park, Brisbane. Sue in Sydney. Mick at Wynnum, Brisbane.

We all wish you a Happy Birthday at 85

Appendix A. Lawrence School, Lovedale, India.

The Lawrence School, Lovedale, has a sprawling campus of 750 acres (3 km²). Lovedale, six kilometres (3.7 miles) from Ootacamund, is located at a height of 7200 feet over sea level, slightly lower than the Dodabetta peak (altitude: 8000 feet), the highest peak of the mountain ranges of the Nilgiris. The school campus is divided into prep school, junior school and senior school based on the classes. Prep school - Class 4 to Class 6 Junior School - Class 7 & Class 8 Senior School - Class 9 to Class 12 The classrooms and dormitories of the different schools are housed in the respective buildings. All the girls are housed in the girl's school and are required to go to the respective schools for classes. Though the campus is huge, the built up area is only 45 acres (0.2 km²). It's at Lovedale, Ooty, Tamil Nadu, India. The school fulfilled the objects of its founder until May 1949, when it was taken over by the Ministry of Education, Government of India, to be run as a public school, open to all, with 40 percent places reserved for the children of defence personnel.

There is a girl's school within the complex. I wonder if anyone will ever travel there and look for Great-Grandmother's name. This could be the school that presented her with a Gold Watch.

From the map scale, Google puts the Nilgiri Hills 10 kilometres to the West of Lovedale.

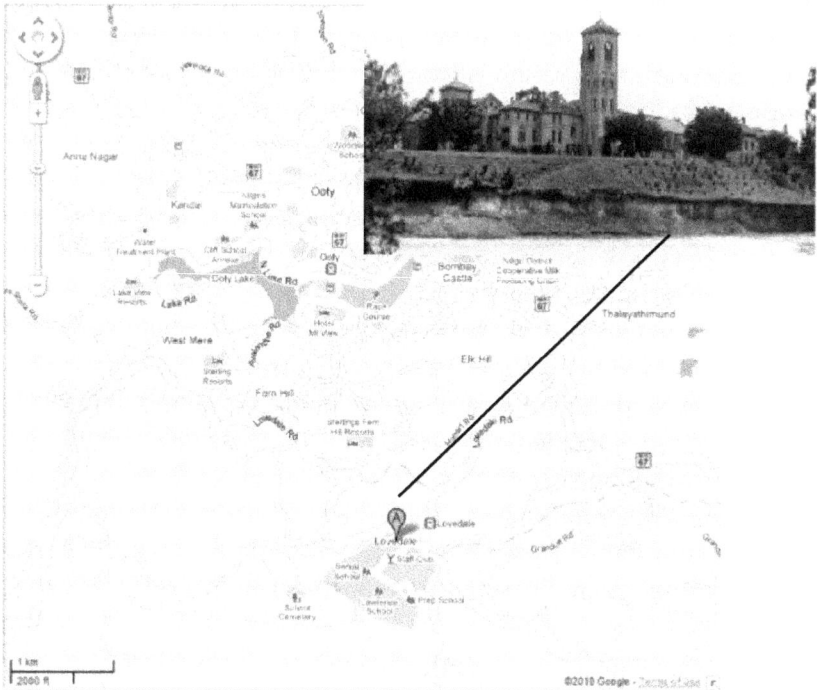

Life

Appendix B. Kamaliki.

Geoff *"I can't vouch for the following. It may be a similarity of name."*

A Google search on Kamaliki revealed the following information.

Kamaliki no longer seems to be run by the Missionaries and it's now a skills training centre. The coffee only gets a mention as part of a coffee festival so they must still grow coffee there. Here is some info from Google.

Kamaliki Vocational Training Centre outside Goroka, Eastern Highlands, has over the years won a reputation for the kind of courses that it teaches and the students that it produces.

The products included baby carriers, cookie trays, fruit bowls, laundry baskets, place mats, round baskets, round trays with handles, shopping baskets and trays.

Kamaliki is known for teaching students about downstream processing skills, appropriate technology and arts and crafts.

These skills are very relevant for rural areas as well as to help the students be self-employed or run their own small businesses.

Downstream processing includes honey, jam, marmalade, peanut butter. Its appropriate technology students are taught how to make such items as drum ovens, mechanised coconut and tapioca scrapers, as well as many other useful items.

Kamaliki's craft shop - which is open tithe public seven days a week - sells canecraft which it buys from local weavers as well as other items produced by trainees of the centre.

The villagers, many of whom are illiterate, find it hard to get find a market for their quality products so they sell them to the Kamaliki Vocational Centre near Goroka. The centre's stall at the 2006 PNG Coffee Festival in Goroka on May 4, 5 and 6 was a major crowd-puller.

Kamaliki, in fact, won a consolation prize from the Small Business Development Corporation for being one of the outstanding small businesses at the festival. According to instructor, Mrs. Maria Nom, Kamaliki was giving a lot of hope to young school leavers.

The school is located about 10km out-side Goroka on the Lae/Madang side ofthe Highlands Highway. Kamaliki has been actively involved in providing skills training for students from Eastern Highlands as well as other parts of Papua New Guinea. The school provides eight courses, and every year, more applications are received but only 210 students are selected.

The students who are not selected are encouraged to take up short

200

courses which the school offers.Kamaliki enrolls students with Grade 8,Grade 10 and Grade 12 qualifications with good passes in core subjects.

It runs two-year courses in motor vehicle mechanic, carpentry and joinery, plumbing, auto electrical, computing and business studies, metal fabricating, metal beating and spray painting, and advanced studies in agriculture.

Short courses are run in various skills trade areas to assist people enhance their skills. The short courses are in motor mechanics, computing and business studies, home economics, carpentry and joinery, sewing machine and repair/maintenance, block laying, advanced skills in agriculture, animal husbandry, cash crops, technical skills, honey production, and farm management.

Further information can be obtained from the address as follows: Kamaliki Vocational Centre, P.O. Box107, Goroka, Eastern Highlands Province, Papua New Guinea.

Tel: (675) 7322336Fax: (675) 7322336.

http://malumnalu.blogspot.com/2008/08/kamaliki-vocational-training-centre.html

This is also called a school, Goroka educational institution, and Rural Development Centre. They had a stand at the Goraka show - The Kamaliki Rural Development Centre stand was a big success, with many items sold and many orders taken.

Here is a bit about Goroka and Kamaliki gets a mention - http://harrygreenwell.wordpress.com/2010/01/23/png-road-trip-goroka-and-eastern-highlands/

This guy has a taken a landscape photo from Kamaliki - http://www.flickr.com/photos/tway76/3939409329/

Here is a stack of New Guinea photos - http://www.pngbd.com/photos/

Here is a Coffee Business with Kamaliki mentioned.
Nowek Coffee Ltd - Kamaliki
P.O Box 332
GOROKA, Eastern Highlands Province
Papua New Guinea
And
Kamaliki Kommodities Ltd
Company Products/Service: Quality VOP jute coffee bags

Company Brief Description: Kamaliki Kommodities is an import an export company which exports quality arabica green bean coffee from Papua New Guinea and imports jute coffee bags. The company is in the process of expanding its operations to import and distribute other items.

Also a Kamaliki Abbatoir :-

Rumen contents: approximately 30 t of fresh rumen contents are available per year in Goroka (Kamaliki Abattoir, 1 123 cattle, 493 pigs, 9 buffaloes and 3 horses were slaughtered in 1985) and at no cost.

From the above one may deduce that Kamaliki has been subdivided into a skills school, a coffee plantation and an abattoir.

Here is a sad story of a Kamaliki Village girl with AIDS.
http://www.pnggossip.com/news/stigma.html

"The Highlands Trilogy"

The ABC has a documentary of 3 DVD's called "The Highlands Trilogy" which tells the story of the Leahy's who were the first white men into the highlands of New Guinea. They settled in Mt Hagen which is not far from Goroka. The series shows coffee growing and gives some insight into the native culture.

From Left: Geoff, Bob and Reginald Wallace

Geoff Quips: *Did you know the world record for base jumping by a husband and wife is held by 'Mr Singleman' ?*

Let lovers all distraught and frenzied be,
And flown with wine, and reprobates, like me;
When sober, I find everything amiss,
But in my cups cry, "Let what will be, be."

This book was created in the loving memory
of my father, Geoffrey John Wallace
Born 10 Dec 2025 - Deceased 14 Aug 2016

Geoff in his Jason Recliner at the Palm Beach flat, a few
months before he passed. Note the writing pad on his
lap, which was always present in order to help him
remember what it was he wanted to say to you

The Last Family Gathering (Geoff aged Ninety)

From Left: Greg, his wife Marg, Michael (the author),
Steve (Sue's man) Sue, Trish, Geoff and Julie.

Circa 1965 at Ashgrove. From Left: Michael (the author),
Julie, Peter (deceased), Sue, Greg (co-author) and Trish.

Other Books by the author:

Michael has written a number of books, from non-fiction study books on Numerology and the art of Dice Divination, to franchising workbooks, to children's stories and science fiction, all the way through to short stories and a genre known as Modern Myth.

Psychic Nazi Hunter. *Very popular on Amazon. This is a remarkable biography about Alan Wood-Thomas, a well respected artist, friend of Kerouac and Ginsberg, and a man the Attorney General of the US would call in to have coffee with.*

Yet out of hours, Alan would have lucid dreams, visions of where Nazi's were hiding after the war. He would sketch their faces, write down the address he saw, and send this to friends in the French Underground. They would check and verify if the person was indeed a Nazi that went unpunished, and they would execute the individual.

Hello Planet Earth: *This will be one of the most delightful books you will ever read. In a series of short stories, the author gives an insight into just about everyone you have ever known.*

It is written as a 'Modern Myth' in that it is set in the present time, yet it is also written like an old time fairy story, or myth.

Written in 1988, when the author was in serious ill health, and not likely to survive, it has only just been edited and published. It cannot be recommended more highly.

All books available through Amazon or at www.laddertothemoon.com.au

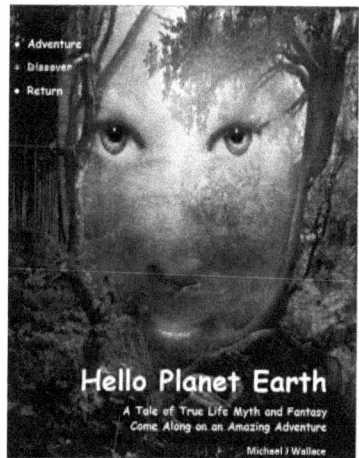

Credits: The author would like to thank Luenig and Gary Larson for the use of the cartoons scattered throughout the book. Geoff had a particular liking for their bent sense of humour.

*Geoff Wallace, outside his favourite Yum Cha
restaurant at Broadbeach in 2012*

Parables of Geoff
COPYRIGHT 2018 Michael Wallace

ISBN: 978-0-9941798-9-0
Copyright 2018 Michael Wallace
Publisher: Ladder to the Moon Productions
Email: info.numberharmonics@gmail.com
Web: laddertothemoon.com.au

Addendum

As I was preparing to send this book of to the printer, I found some overlooked files which changed my understanding of things in a fundamental way. I realised something Geoff had never spoken of, that his mother bargained him off to be rid of Duncan from her life. The actual paragraphs are cut and pasted below:

14 June 2004 - Letter to Reg

I got to know Mum very well over the five years she was in Hopetoun (no one could see her living that long–you and I thought about three months at the most). She confided to me that she had lived a life of wretched guilt for all those long years since she handed me over to DHW at age about ten or whatever, and had given me some extra money by way of compensation.

She finally learned how to give and receive affection. And yet I had never, ever, held anything against her. My firm belief back then, and now, had always been that anyone who had an opportunity to get away from that psychopathic bastard, for whatever reason or at whose expense, should cut and run. Once at the Black River, he hid me behind the sofa on the front verandah, then called Colin and they both sat on the sofa while recounting Mum's doings with Teddy Wolfenden, (her lover) Colin denouncing and reviling her in no uncertain terms.

But all that is now history and I have expiated most of my karma, particularly that which gave rise to my enforced sojourn with DHW. I wonder where he is now? He won't be the bully-boy this time. Yes, reincarnation is fact (the evidence against is nil and the evidence for is voluminous).

We are here to learn, and we keep reincarnating until we clearly realise that there is nothing but love. God is Love and we are all going through the process of fulfilling our destiny, which is to return to our Source. At the time of your travail at Marie's funeral, you uttered a profound truth. You said to me: "We all gotta love one another." Nobody says it is easy, but when we really realise it, and can DO it, we can relinquish the physical plane forever. I can't love everyone, or very many for that matter, so I'm not talking about myself. But one can stop karmic reincarnations if he is sufficiently interested.

As a note: We will never know the exact circumstances of WHY Annette let Geoff go, but given my understanding of Duncan, there may have been little real choice in the matter. She may well have feared for her life and the lives of her children. It is something we will never know.

Other Recollections: (Snippets from Letters to Reg)

In Inverell at one time we lived right on the outskirts away from everyone alongside hundreds of acres of grassy land. Somehow, I managed to start a fire alongside the house where we had a cow and a calf in a railed area. My fire brought out the fire brigade and burnt out about 100 acres. In retrospect, I really think I was a bit of a dog. Or is it a case of give a dog a bad name? I recall that it didn't bring any praise from DHW, particularly as he had to rescue the calf which dragged him for many yards through the ashes. He was not pleased at all. I wondered if I really did deserve the dog title.

I can remember the neighbours at Chetwynd Road, Merrylands. On the side nearest the paddock were the Tarantos. Then us. The ones next to us had a kid I shot in the leg with the air gun. Next to them were the mob of Kennedys who were catholics (cattle ticks we called them). Across the road with a farm were the Flewitts. Dave Flewitt taught me to ride a bike. Behind their place was a muddy little watercourse where I used to fish for yabbies. But ask me to remember something useful....

Looking back, life has gone in a flash. I remember as a small child that six weeks school holiday at the end of the year was an eternity that would never come to an end. Childhood memories linger. One of mine is that about at the age of five, my burning ambition was to have a whole pound note. I would run away from home and live on Zuzu biscuits forever.

At the Brisbane club back in those days, I was in a shootoff with a chap named Bob Golden. We got up to about 125 or 127 and I had to walk off the field to the car to get ammo. When I got back to the traps, I missed the very next one, making Golden the winner. At least I got a 100 break badge out of it. Not long after that, at the Southport Gun Club, I was involved with a similar long shootoff with Bob Golden and had the satisfaction of beating him. All that with the Browning auto.

We take modern conveniences for granted. In my early days at Goroka, the house I built had a grass roof, walls of plaited cane grass and a floor of woven bamboo. The bath tub was a 44 gallon drum cut in half lengthwise, and the washbasin was a 4 gallon kerosene tin cut similarly. Water for drinking and washing was carried from a nearby swift-flowing creek (after heavy rain, you could hear boulders crashing together in the rushing water). Light was from kerosene lamps. No fridge. But we didn't feel hard done by. When working for yourself, you can put up with anything.

There is so much more that there is no room for. Obviously, I cannot compress a man's life into 212 pages, but I trust I have given you an insight into one Geoffrey John Wallace. I miss him dearly.

A Brief Note on Depression - a Potential Cure

In the 1950's and early 60's depression was generally believed to be a response known as "Learned Helplessness". When Geoff was seeing Psychiatrists, they would have been seeking to deal with what they believed was a learned response from repeated stress in childhood.

When humans or animals are put into a situation they cannot control, they go into "helpless' mode. This is where the person or creature effectively freezes, they lie 'doggo' and hope the situation passes. It was noted that, when a person is trapped and under stress, they exhibit eight of the nine characteristics of depression, with the exception of suicide. As a result depression was treated as a learned behaviour from a difficult childhood, or similar.

In 2000 research proved that a section of the brain responsible for this passivity as a reaction to stress was common to all mammals. Prof. Martin Seligman presented a discussion on this topic on Radio National . The link is included, should you wish to know more.

http://www.abc.net.au/radionational/programs/allinthemind/martin-seligman-1/9886008#transcript

What was discovered is that depression is not learned behaviour, it is an *automatic reaction*, triggered in the dorsal raphe nucleus. Depression is a normal reaction to stress. Further, what was also discovered was there is a specific switching mechanism that goes from the ventral medial prefrontal cortex down to the dorsal raphe and turn off the dorsal raphe which can switch depression OFF. Optimism and hope trigger it.

Geoff suffered terribly with anxiety all his life. As of this moment there are no treatments to deal with this potential breakthrough, other than HOPE. It's not a joke, a sense of hope triggers the release mechanism for the part of the brain that is locked in depression.

However, now a specific circuit of the brain has been discovered that can assist in the treatment of depression, it is believed that in the coming decade there will finally be a clinical treatment for this debilitating illness.

Our home at Kamaliki before the curtains were put up, & garden made.

Max Turned Referral: *Max was not just Geoff's best friend, he was a Detective in the Commonwealth Police. The letter is self explanatory.*

17 St. Leonard's Street,
COORPAROO. QLD.
7th April, 1968.

TO WHOM IT MAY CONCERN.

This is to advise that I have known Geoffrey John Wallace for the past twenty-five years. In close association during that time, I have come to know him particularly well and can recommend him without reservation whatsoever on a personal basis, in any business capacity, or to any prospective employer.

I know him to be a man of unimpeachable integrity and utmost reliability, whose word or promise can be considered as better than a written agreement and a person who would never sacrifice principle for monetary gain or personal advantage. He is modest and unassuming, can always be relied upon to excercise tact and has a very considerable interest in and knowledge of human nature and practical psychology. I know him to have been very successful in his own business affairs.

I recommend him with complete confidence and will be pleased at any time to verify the above facts or provide additional information if required. My telephone number is Brisbane 97 8332.

Maxwell G. Turner
RETIRED DETECTIVE-INSPECTOR
COMMONWEALTH POLICE.

Published by Ladder to the Moon
www.laddertothemoon.com.au

This book is available on Amazon
(US) goo.gl/7Z7nzJ and (AU) goo.gl/3kV5RG

Special thanks go to Sue Wallace for proofing and the anecdotes she contributed. We have moved a little closer to Geoff's goal of literary perfection as a result, though I am sure he would look and still find errors.

Greg Wallace contributed not just the funds to produce this book, but a great deal of sage advice and consideration. His "This if Your Life" section is but a small part of his overall help with the project.

Finally, thank you to Gary Larson and Leunig for the funny cartoons that made Geoff laugh so much. I have sprinkled the book with their work as a tribute.

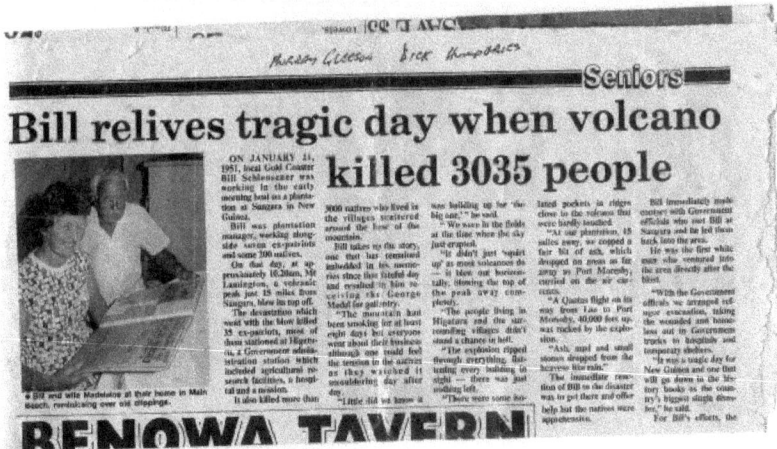

Bill relives tragic day when volcano killed 3035 people

The last place Geoff wanted to go for his nest posting in New Guinea was Goroka. He pushed for, and got, Higatua. The day the family were to fly there, he got seriously ill, and the next day, the day they would have arrived, the volcano exploded, and all the white people in the town were killed. "You think you know best, but life knows better. Imagine if I had gotten my way?"

www.ingramcontent.com/pod-product-compliance
Lightning Source LLC
Chambersburg PA
CBHW071216090426

42736CB00014B/2850